Stop!

You may be reading the wrong way.

In keeping with the original Japanese comic format, this book reads from right to left—so action, sound effects, and word balloons are completely reversed to preserve the orientation of the original artwork. Check out the diagram shown here to get the hang of things, and then turn to the other side of the book to get started!

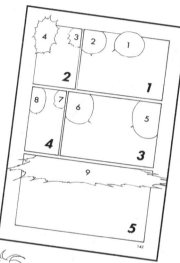

My Love Mix-Up!

7

Art by **Aruko**
Story by **Wataru Hinekure**

Contents

Aoki borrows an eraser from his unrequited crush, Hashimoto. He finds the name "IDA♡" written on the eraser, and his hopes are dashed. Then Ida sees him holding that very eraser, and thinks Aoki is in love with him. While attempting to resolve the misunderstanding, Aoki ends up falling for Ida. Aoki is still reeling from his own emotions when he musters up the courage to confess to Ida. He's ready for rejection...only to find the feelings are mutual?! The two hesitantly start dating and begin to think of their futures once they become third-years in high school. Then Ida abruptly says he's thinking of going to a college in Kyoto... Meanwhile, now that he's going out with the ever-studious Hashimoto, Akkun starts meeting her at the library for dates, but...

Chapter 26

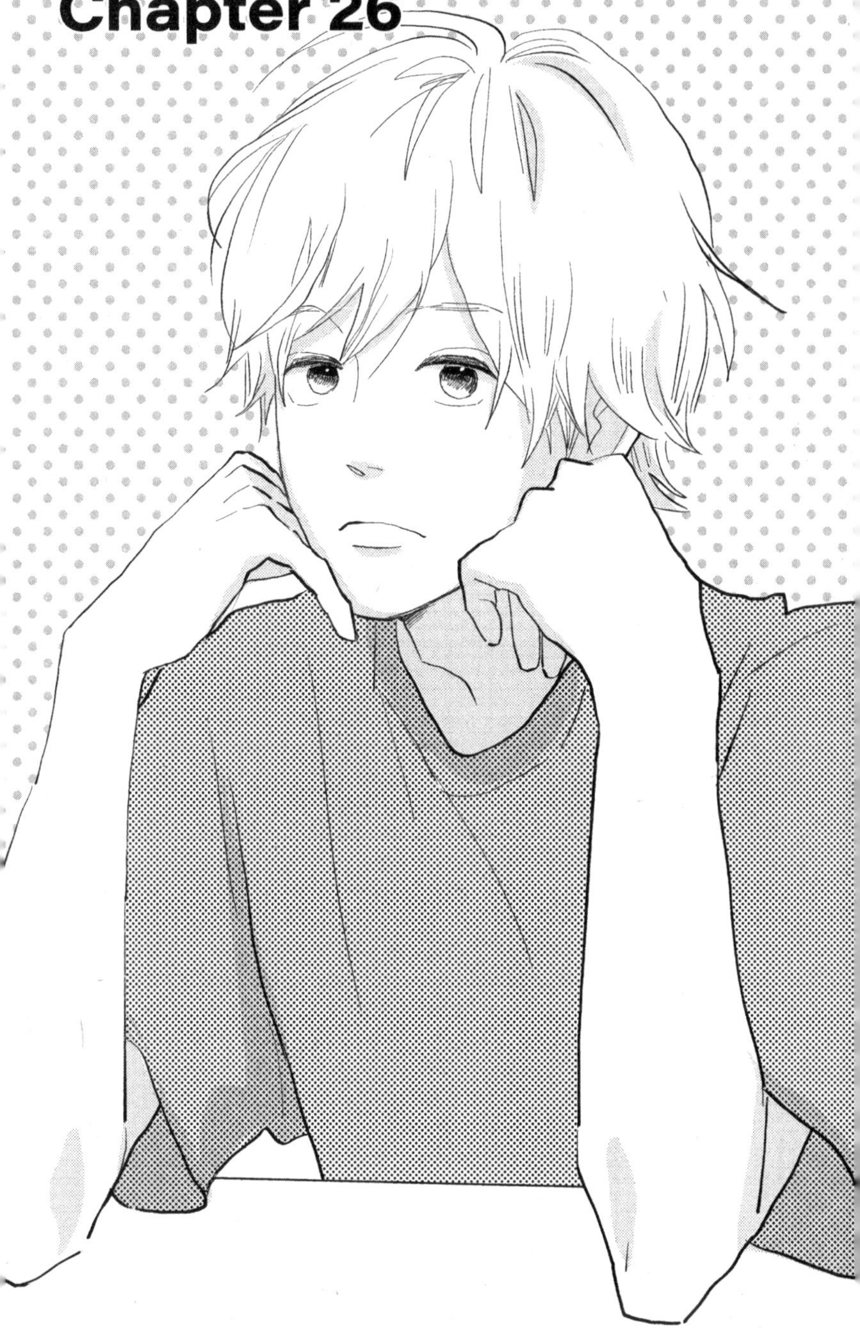

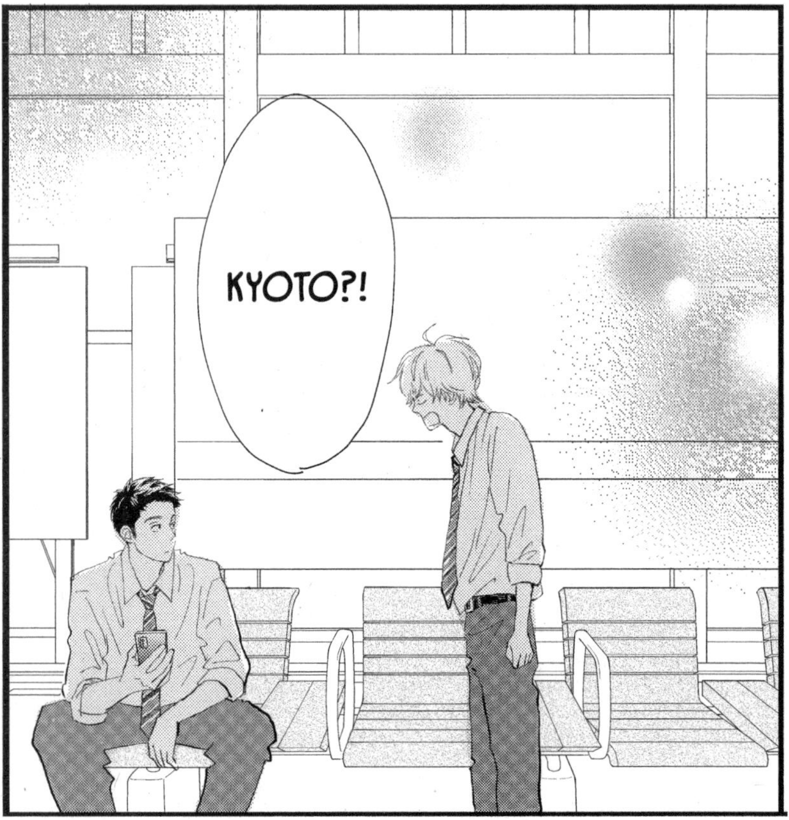
KYOTO?!

My Love Mix-Up!

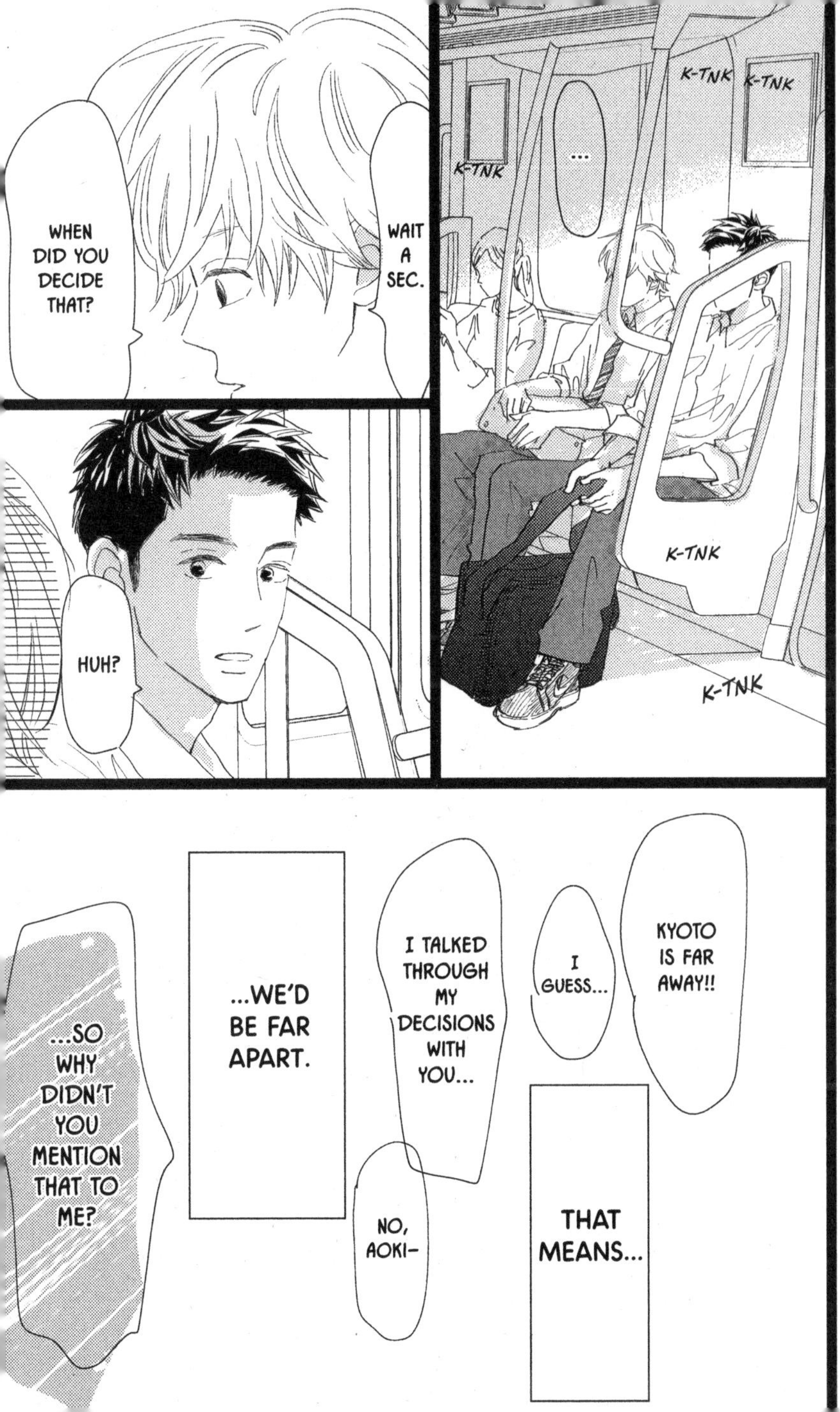
K-TNK K-TNK
...
K-TNK
K-TNK
K-TNK
WAIT A SEC.
WHEN DID YOU DECIDE THAT?
HUH?
KYOTO IS FAR AWAY!!
I GUESS...
I TALKED THROUGH MY DECISIONS WITH YOU...
THAT MEANS...
NO, AOKI-
...WE'D BE FAR APART.
...SO WHY DIDN'T YOU MENTION THAT TO ME?

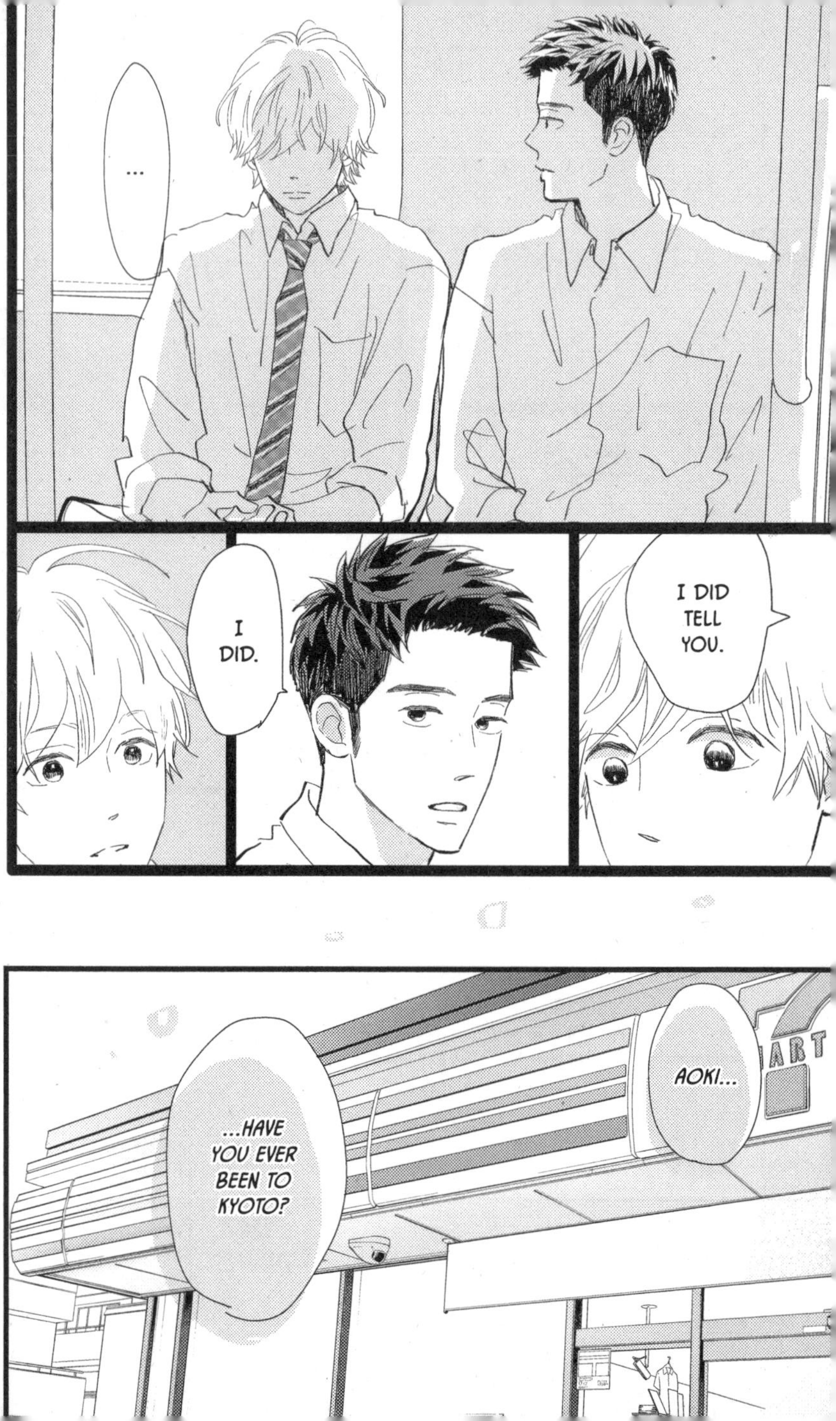
...
I DID TELL YOU.
I DID.
AOKI...
...HAVE YOU EVER BEEN TO KYOTO?

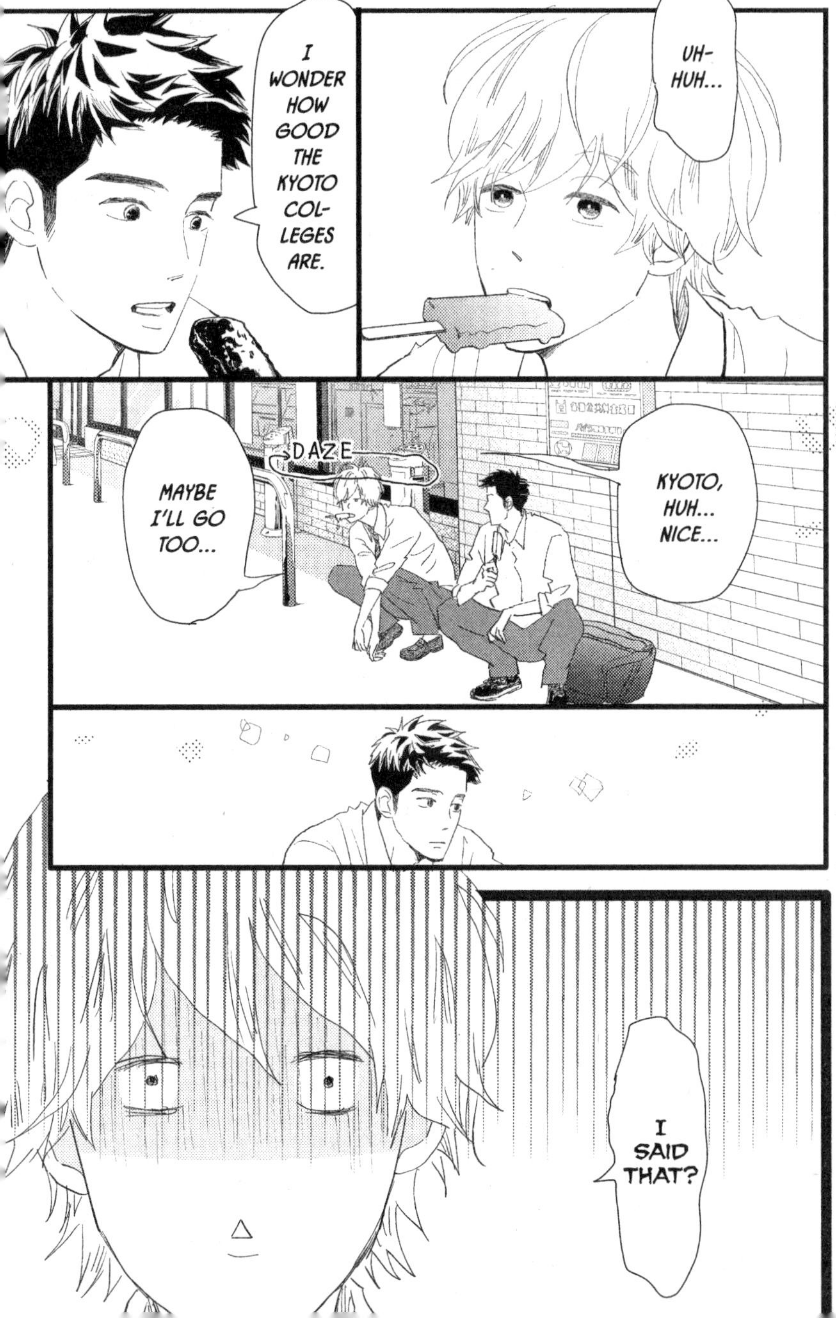
UH-HUH...
I WONDER HOW GOOD THE KYOTO COL-LEGES ARE.
KYOTO, HUH... NICE...
DAZE
MAYBE I'LL GO TOO...
I SAID THAT?

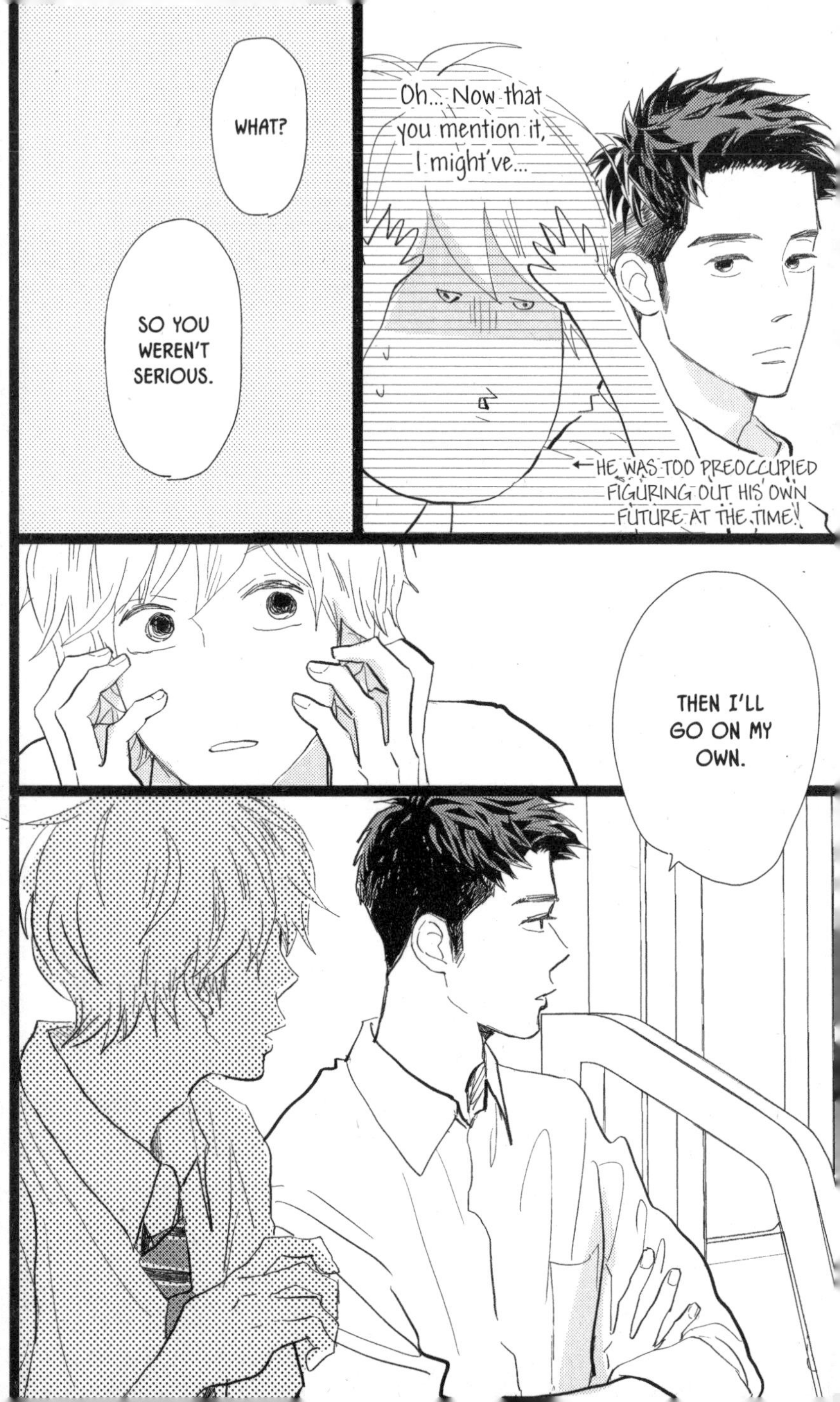
Oh... Now that you mention it, I might've...
← HE WAS TOO PREOCCUPIED FIGURING OUT HIS OWN FUTURE AT THE TIME!
WHAT?
SO YOU WEREN'T SERIOUS.
THEN I'LL GO ON MY OWN.

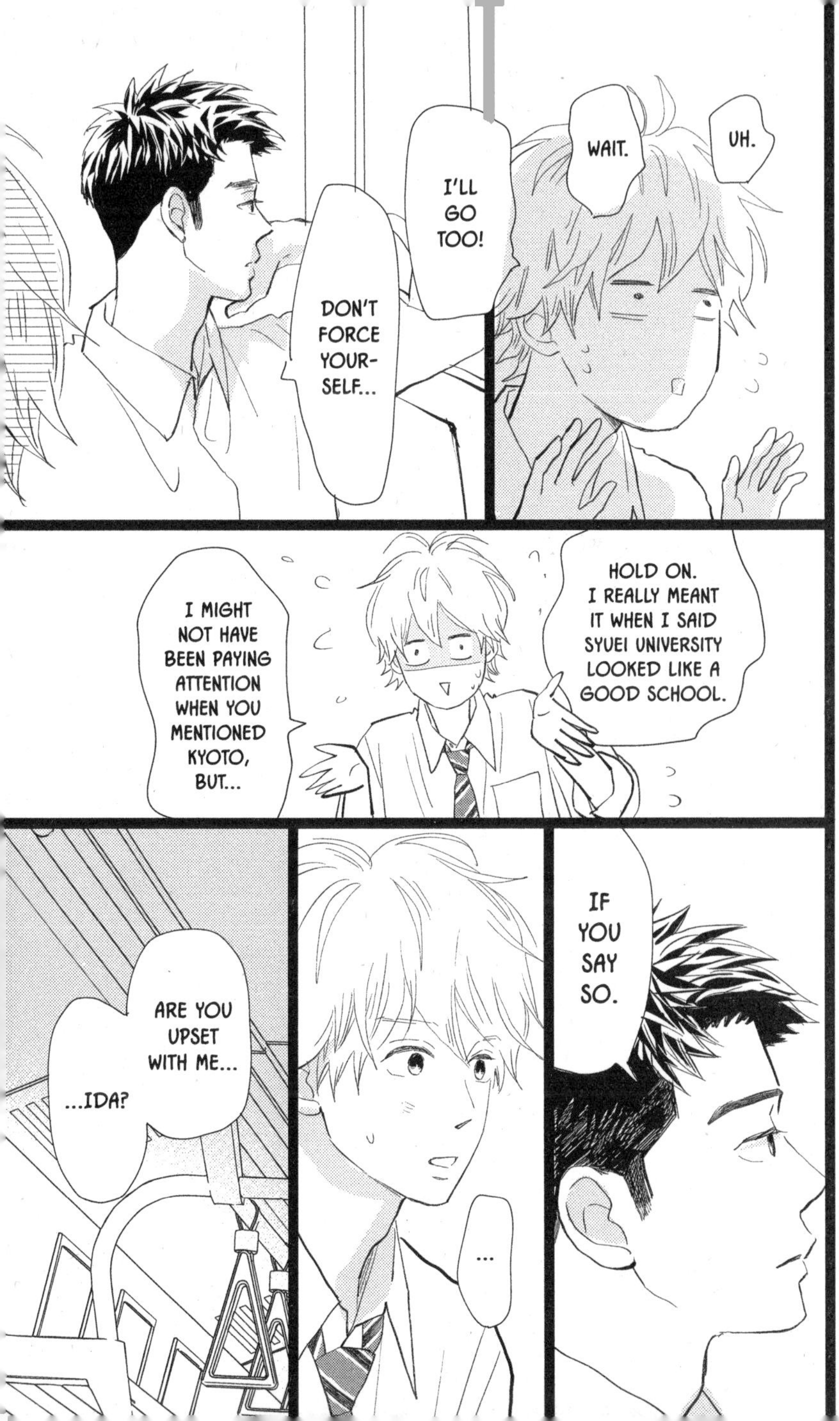
UH.
WAIT.
I'LL GO TOO!
DON'T FORCE YOUR-SELF...
HOLD ON. I REALLY MEANT IT WHEN I SAID SYUEI UNIVERSITY LOOKED LIKE A GOOD SCHOOL.
I MIGHT NOT HAVE BEEN PAYING ATTENTION WHEN YOU MENTIONED KYOTO, BUT...
IF YOU SAY SO.
...
ARE YOU UPSET WITH ME...
...IDA?

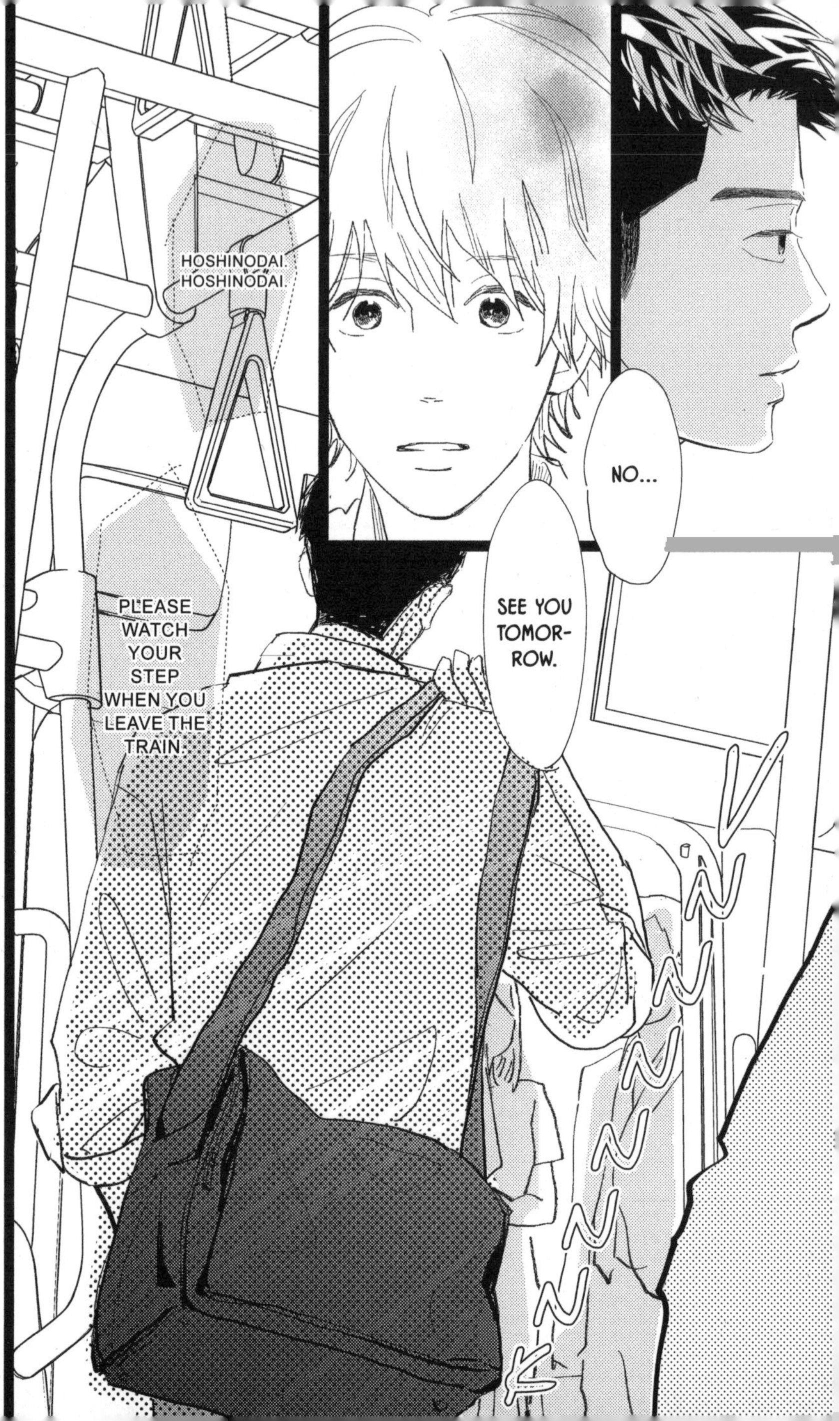
NO...
SEE YOU TOMORROW.
HOSHINODAI. HOSHINODAI.
PLEASE WATCH YOUR STEP WHEN YOU LEAVE THE TRAIN.

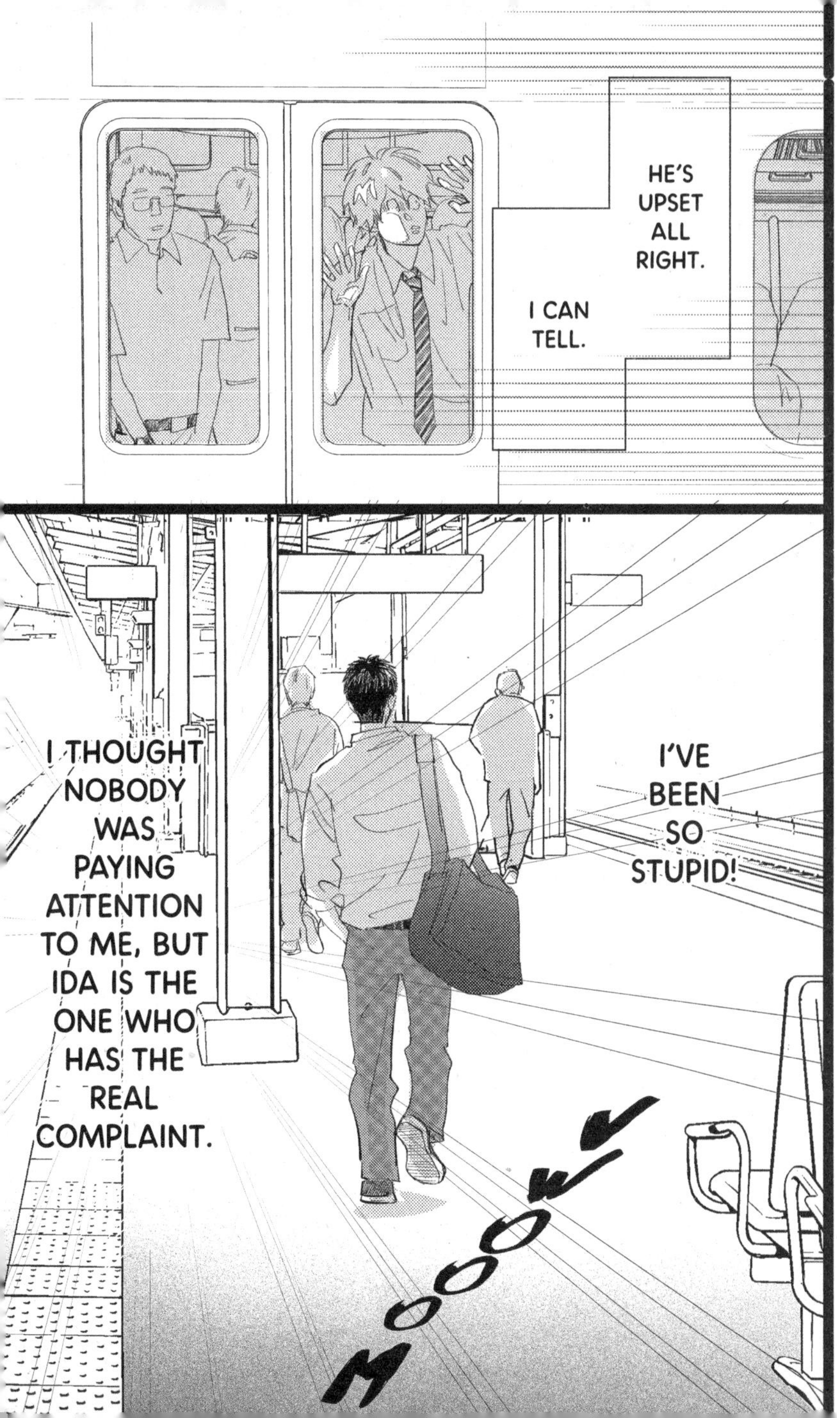

HE'S UPSET ALL RIGHT.
I CAN TELL.
I'VE BEEN SO STUPID!
I THOUGHT NOBODY WAS PAYING ATTENTION TO ME, BUT IDA IS THE ONE WHO HAS THE REAL COMPLAINT.
VWOOOOM

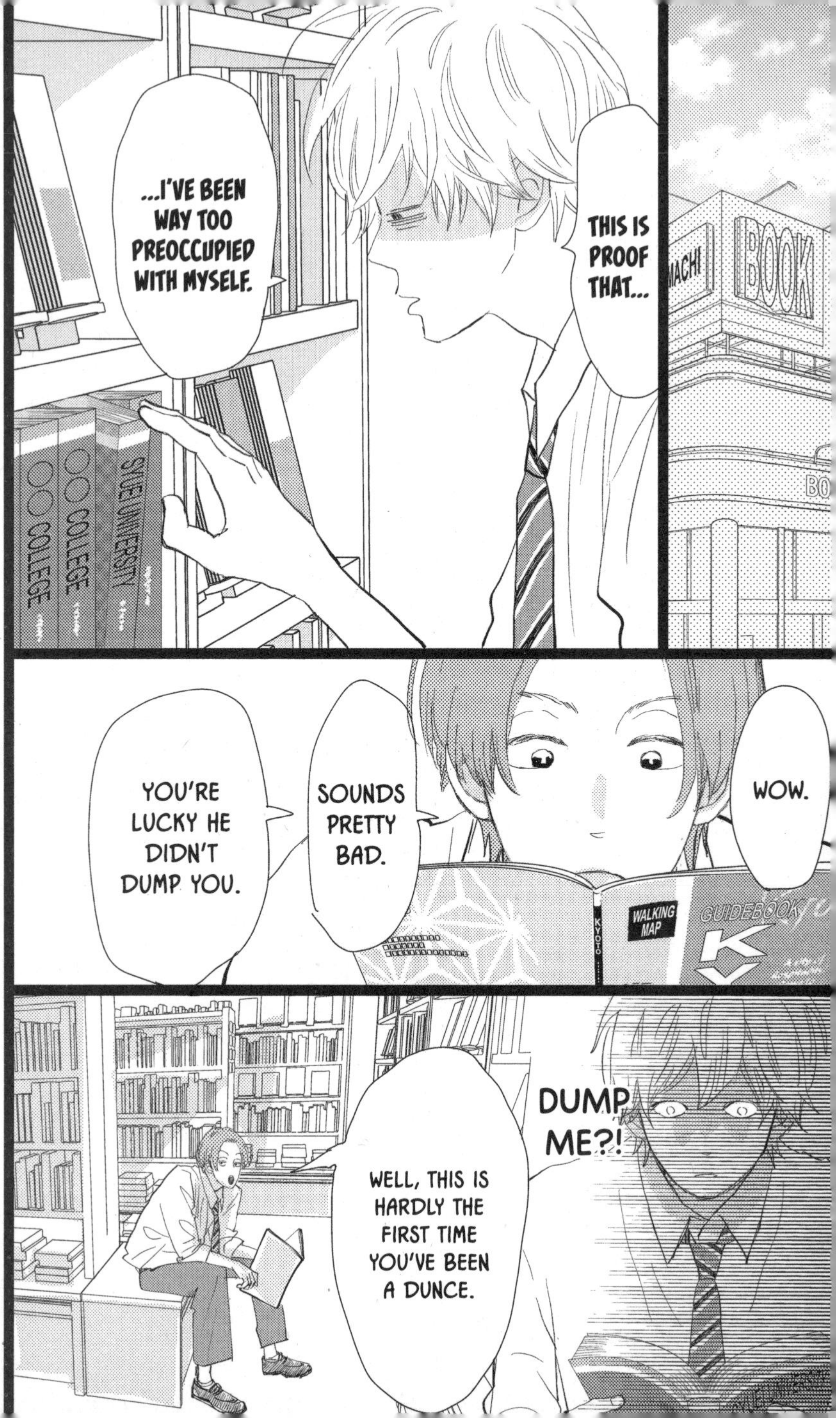
MACHI
BOOK
THIS IS PROOF THAT...
...I'VE BEEN WAY TOO PREOCCUPIED WITH MYSELF.
SYUEI UNIVERSITY
○○ COLLEGE
○○ COLLEGE
WOW.
SOUNDS PRETTY BAD.
YOU'RE LUCKY HE DIDN'T DUMP YOU.
KYOTO
WALKING MAP
GUIDEBOOK
DUMP ME?!
WELL, THIS IS HARDLY THE FIRST TIME YOU'VE BEEN A DUNCE.

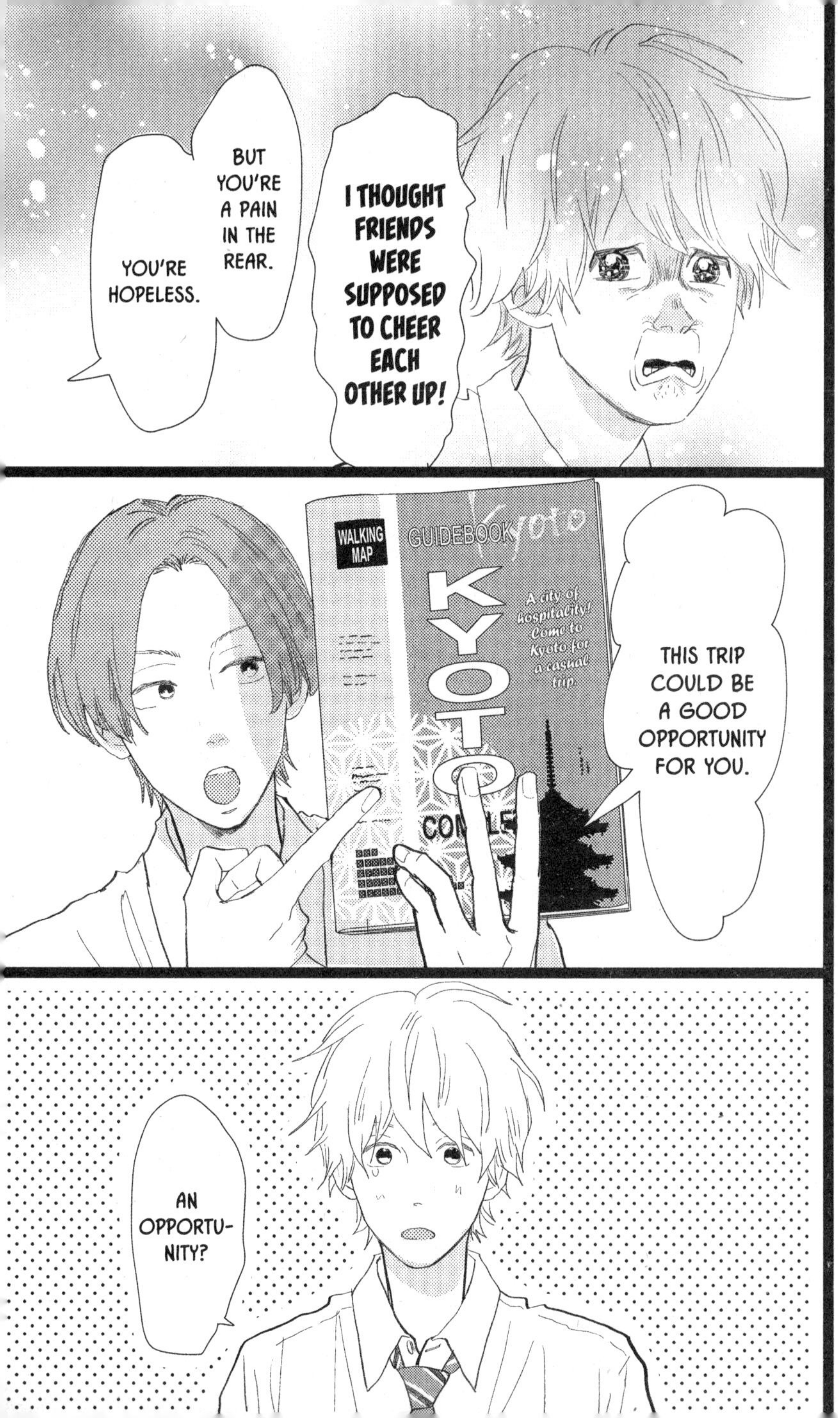
I THOUGHT FRIENDS WERE SUPPOSED TO CHEER EACH OTHER UP!
BUT YOU'RE A PAIN IN THE REAR.
YOU'RE HOPELESS.
THIS TRIP COULD BE A GOOD OPPORTUNITY FOR YOU.
GUIDEBOOK Kyoto
KYOTO
A city of hospitality! Come to Kyoto for a casual trip.
WALKING MAP
AN OPPORTU-NITY?

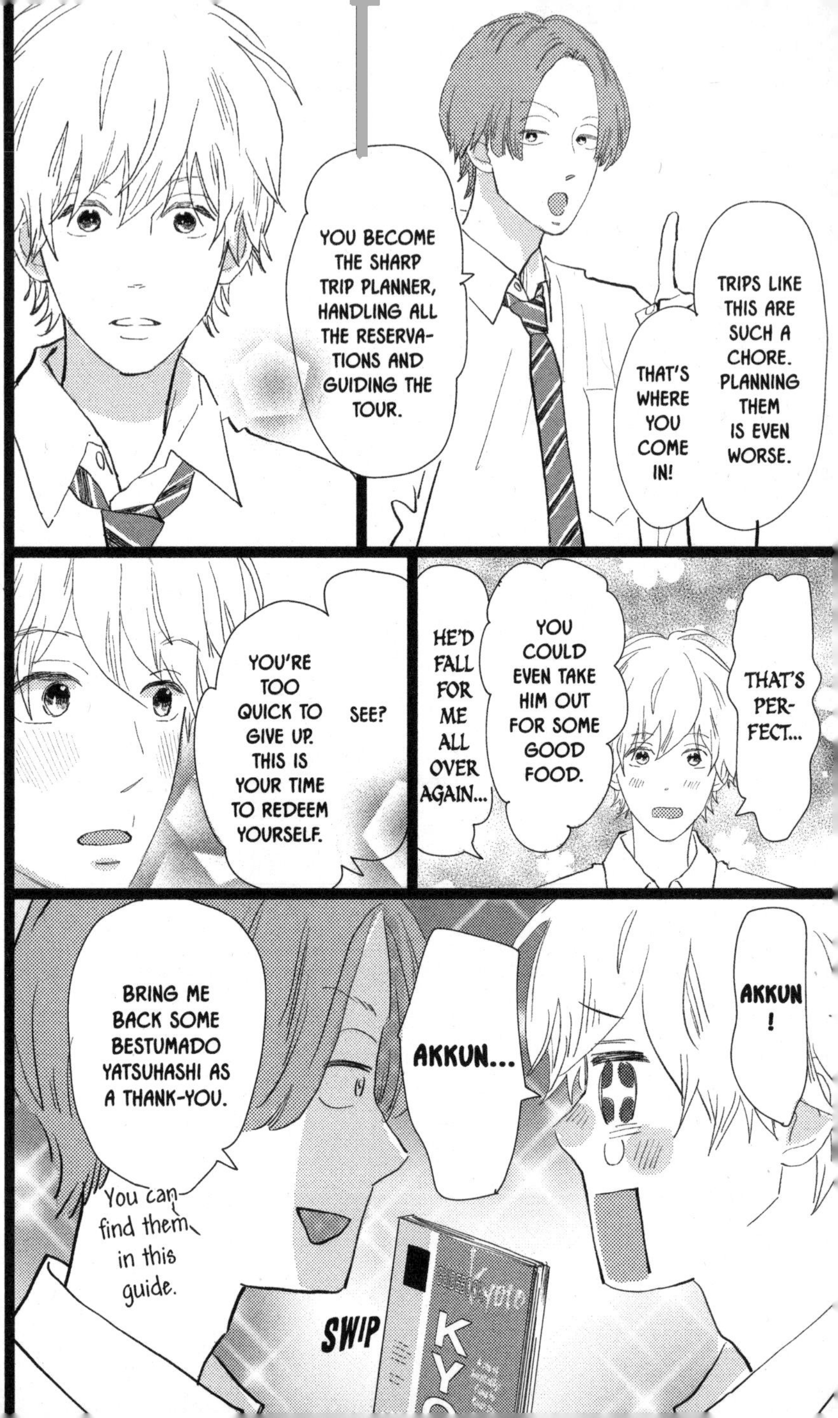
TRIPS LIKE THIS ARE SUCH A CHORE. PLANNING THEM IS EVEN WORSE.
THAT'S WHERE YOU COME IN!
YOU BECOME THE SHARP TRIP PLANNER, HANDLING ALL THE RESERVATIONS AND GUIDING THE TOUR.
THAT'S PERFECT...
YOU COULD EVEN TAKE HIM OUT FOR SOME GOOD FOOD.
HE'D FALL FOR ME ALL OVER AGAIN...
SEE?
YOU'RE TOO QUICK TO GIVE UP. THIS IS YOUR TIME TO REDEEM YOURSELF.
AKKUN!
AKKUN...
BRING ME BACK SOME BESTUMADO YATSUHASHI AS A THANK-YOU.
You can find them in this guide.
SWIP

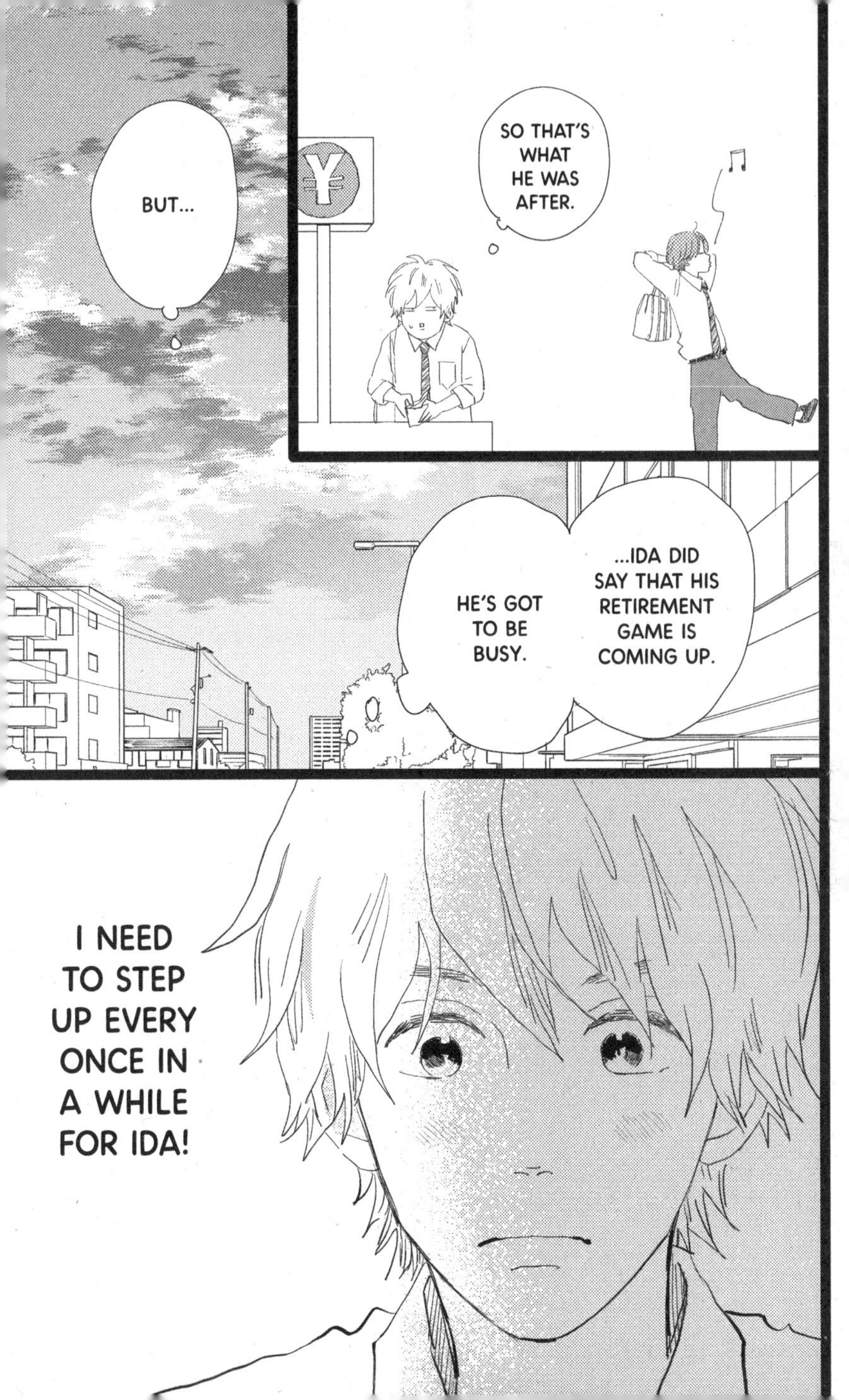
SO THAT'S WHAT HE WAS AFTER.
BUT...
...IDA DID SAY THAT HIS RETIREMENT GAME IS COMING UP.
HE'S GOT TO BE BUSY.
I NEED TO STEP UP EVERY ONCE IN A WHILE FOR IDA!

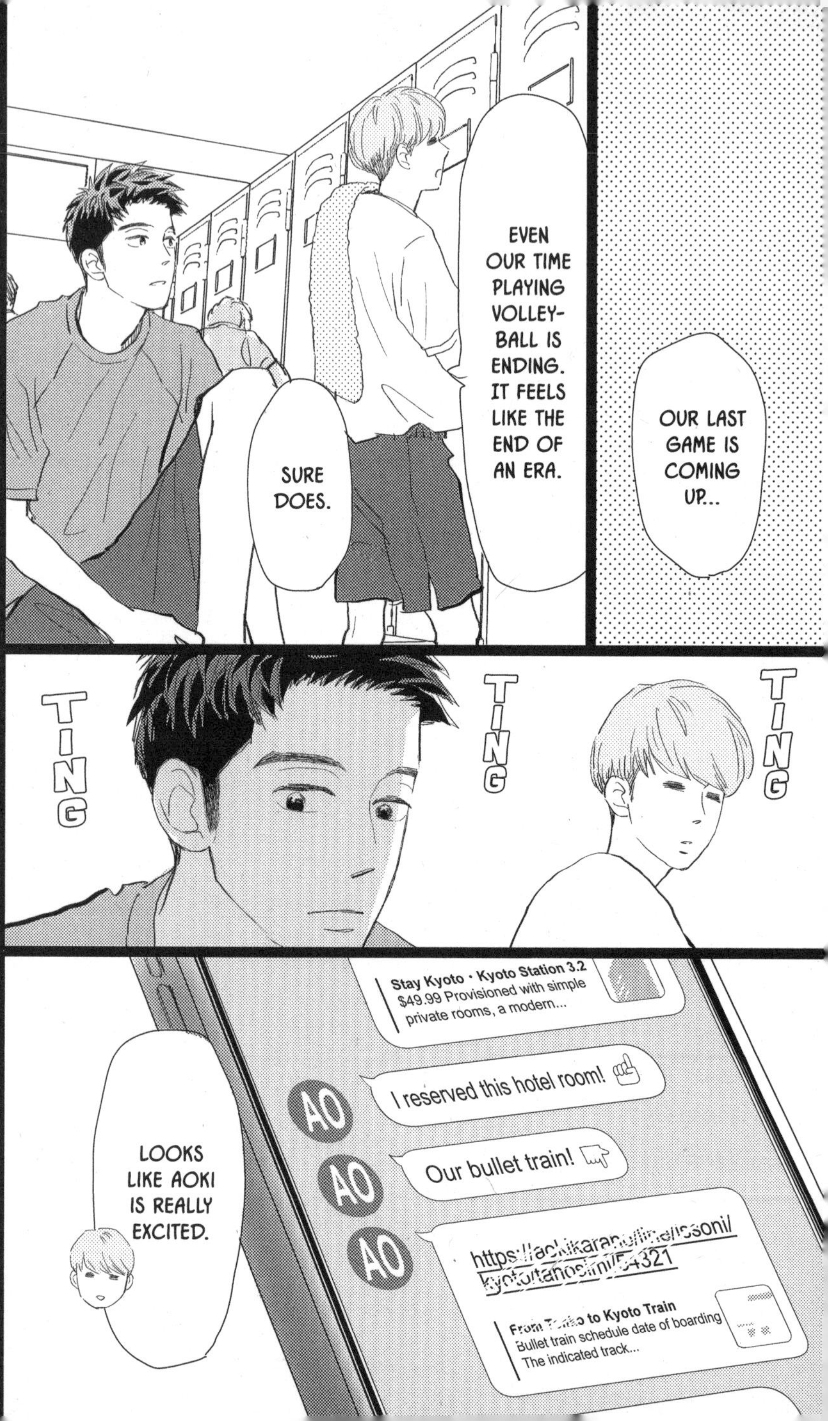
OUR LAST GAME IS COMING UP...
EVEN OUR TIME PLAYING VOLLEY-BALL IS ENDING. IT FEELS LIKE THE END OF AN ERA.
SURE DOES.
TING
TING
TING
Stay Kyoto · Kyoto Station 3.2
$49.99 Provisioned with simple private rooms, a modern...
AO
I reserved this hotel room!
AO
Our bullet train!
AO
Bullet train schedule date of boarding
The indicated track...
LOOKS LIKE AOKI IS REALLY EXCITED.

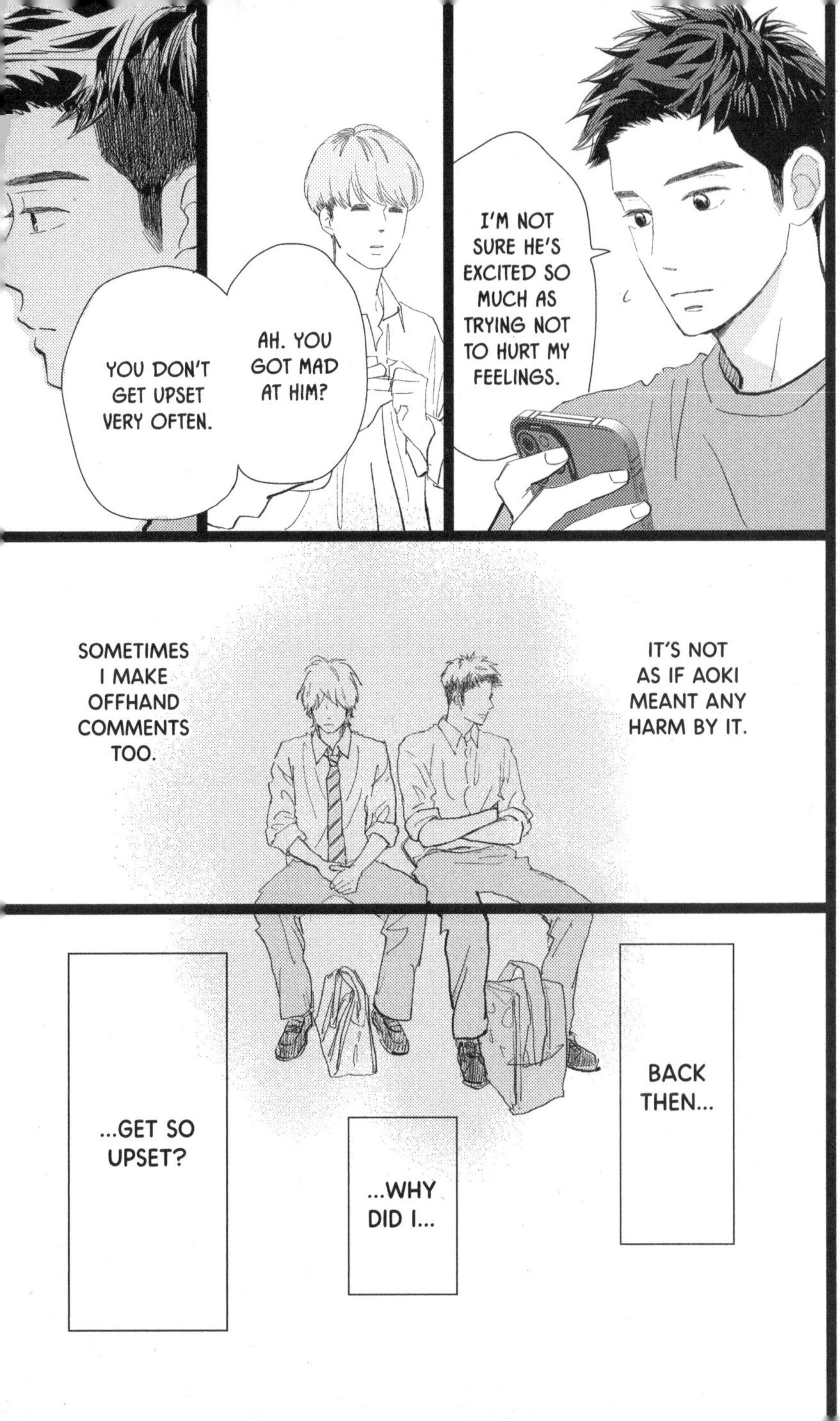
I'M NOT SURE HE'S EXCITED SO MUCH AS TRYING NOT TO HURT MY FEELINGS.
AH. YOU GOT MAD AT HIM?
YOU DON'T GET UPSET VERY OFTEN.
IT'S NOT AS IF AOKI MEANT ANY HARM BY IT.
SOMETIMES I MAKE OFFHAND COMMENTS TOO.
BACK THEN...
...WHY DID I...
...GET SO UPSET?

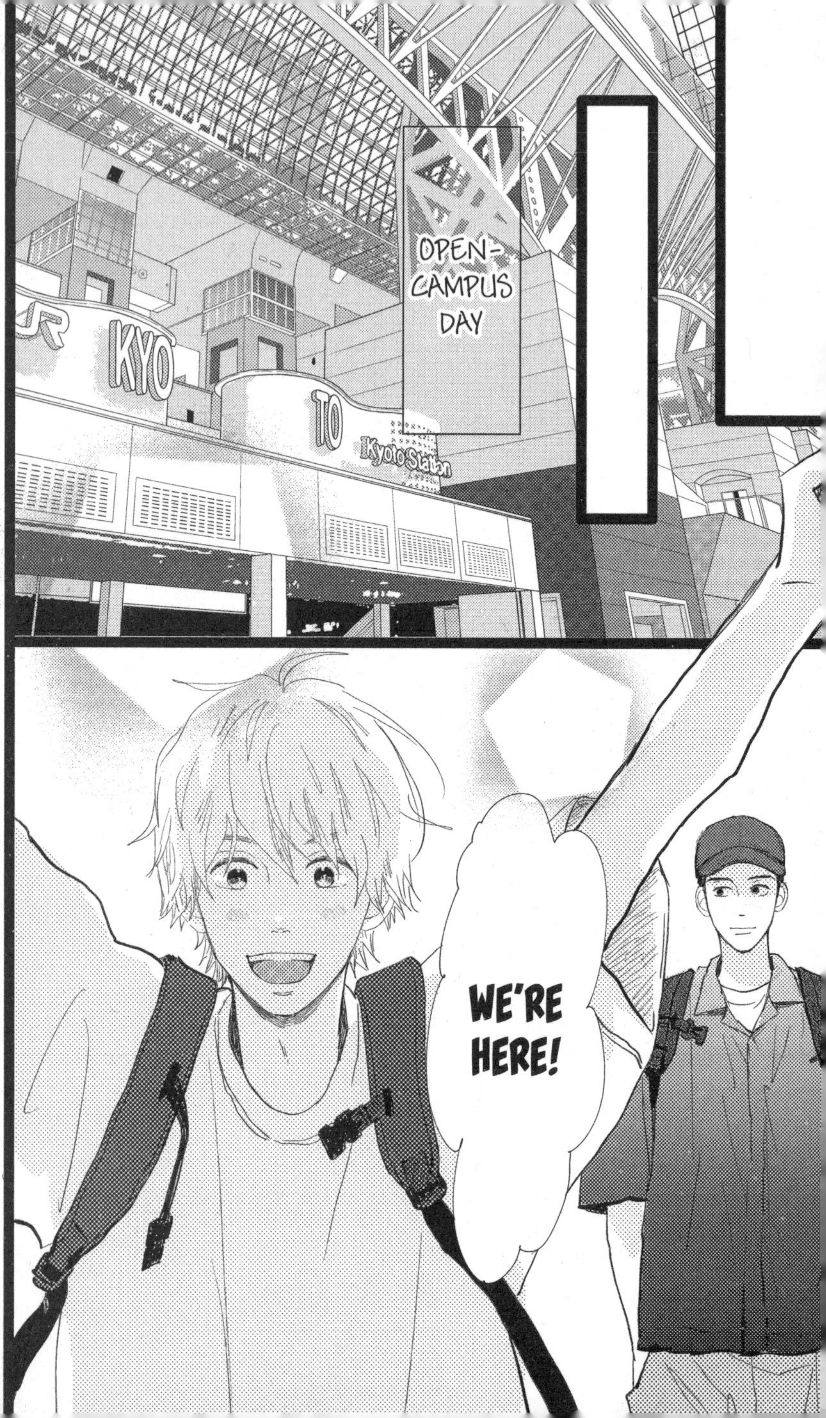
OPEN-CAMPUS DAY
JR KYOTO
Kyoto Station
WE'RE HERE!

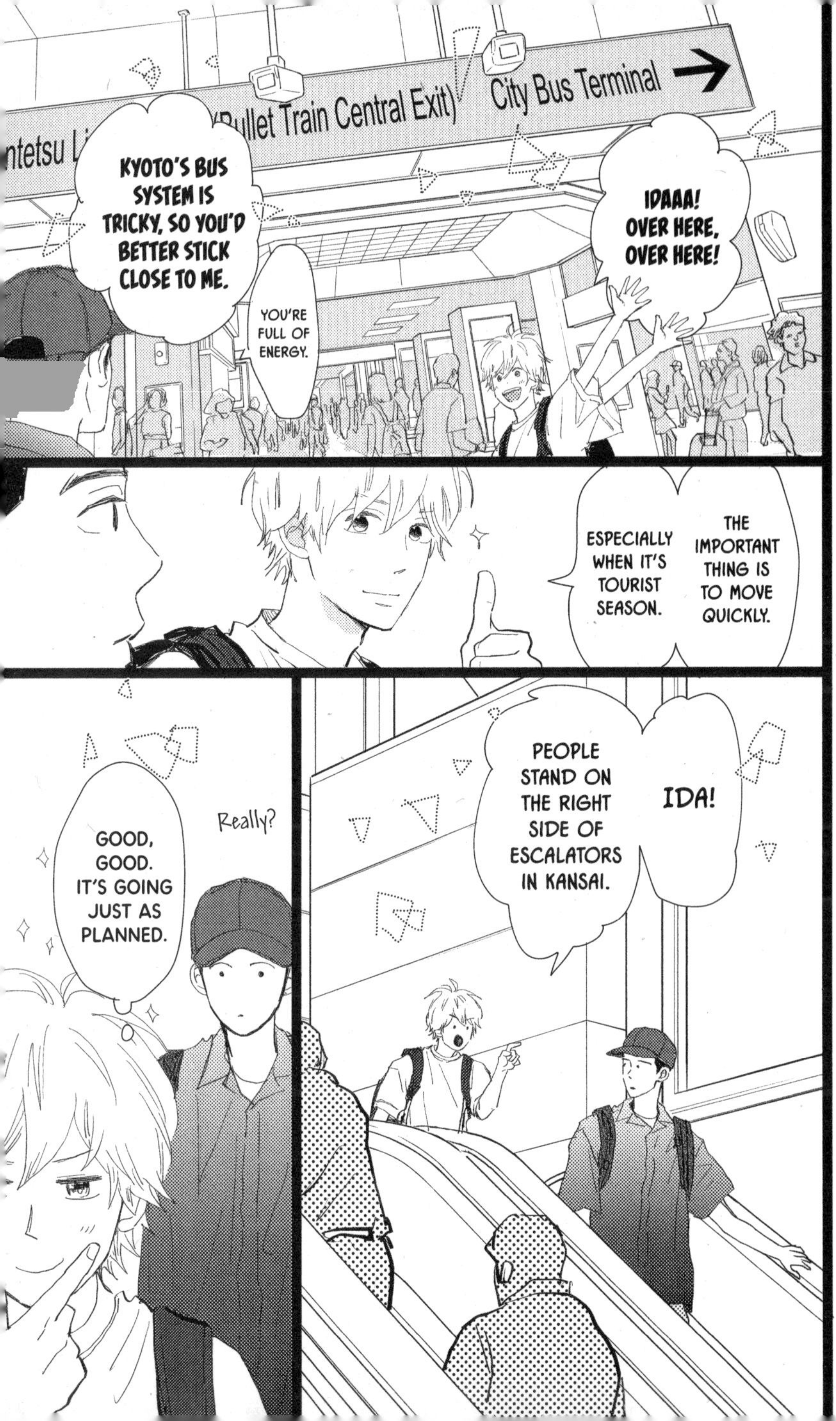
ntetsu Li
Bullet Train Central Exit)
City Bus Terminal
IDAAA! OVER HERE, OVER HERE!
KYOTO'S BUS SYSTEM IS TRICKY, SO YOU'D BETTER STICK CLOSE TO ME.
YOU'RE FULL OF ENERGY.
THE IMPORTANT THING IS TO MOVE QUICKLY.
ESPECIALLY WHEN IT'S TOURIST SEASON.
IDA!
PEOPLE STAND ON THE RIGHT SIDE OF ESCALATORS IN KANSAI.
Really?
GOOD, GOOD. IT'S GOING JUST AS PLANNED.

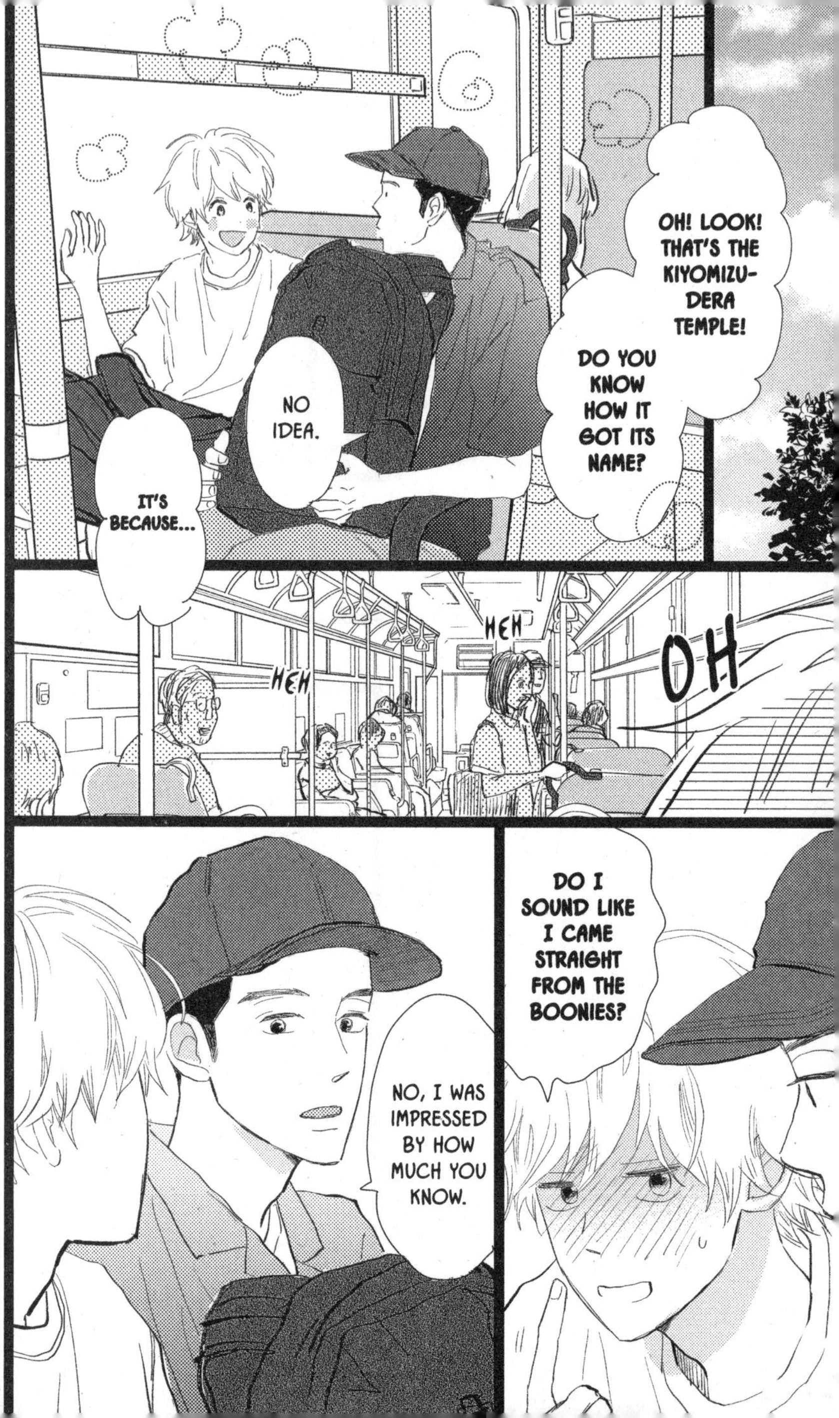
OH! LOOK! THAT'S THE KIYOMIZU-DERA TEMPLE!
DO YOU KNOW HOW IT GOT ITS NAME?
NO IDEA.
IT'S BECAUSE...
OH
HEH
HEH
DO I SOUND LIKE I CAME STRAIGHT FROM THE BOONIES?
NO, I WAS IMPRESSED BY HOW MUCH YOU KNOW.

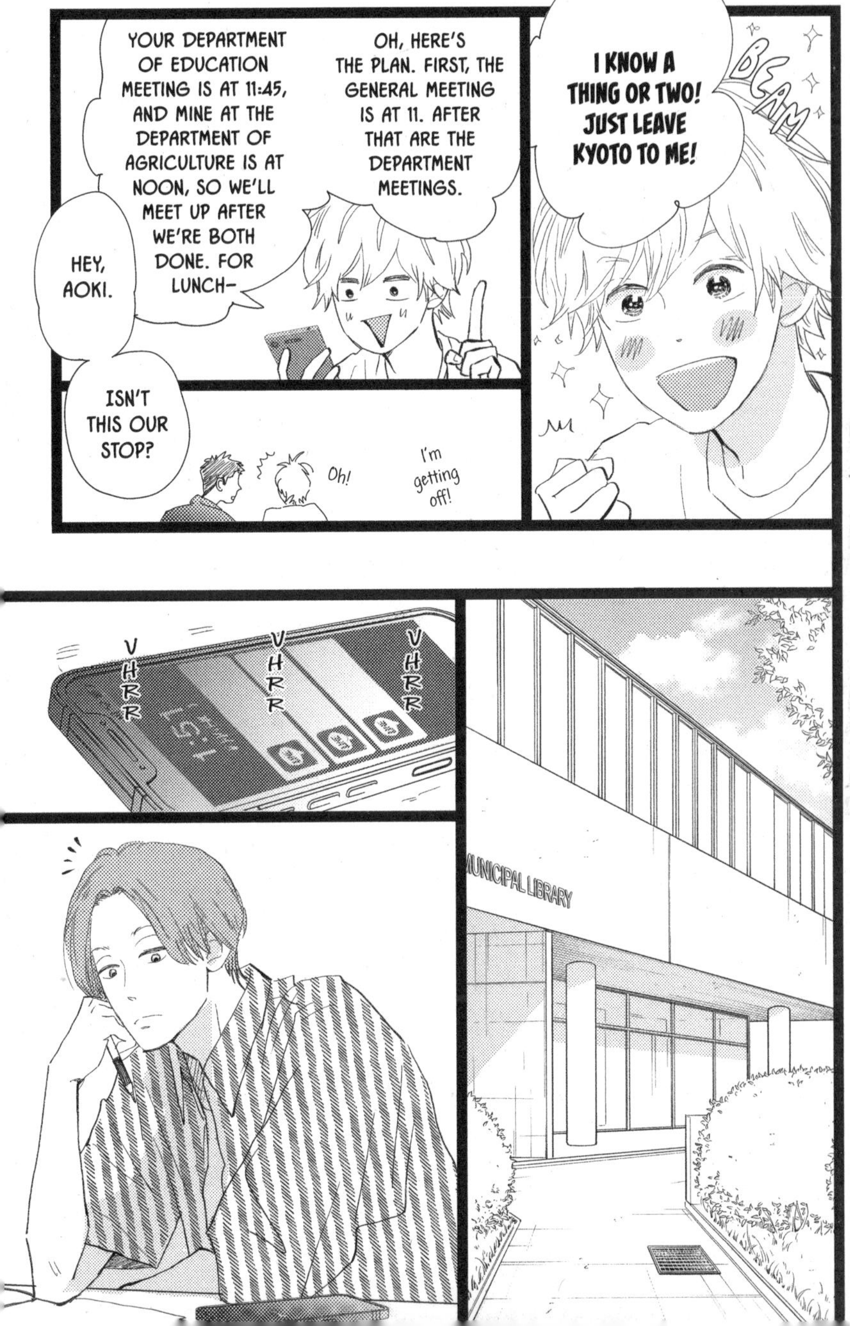
I KNOW A THING OR TWO! JUST LEAVE KYOTO TO ME!
BEAM
OH, HERE'S THE PLAN. FIRST, THE GENERAL MEETING IS AT 11. AFTER THAT ARE THE DEPARTMENT MEETINGS.
YOUR DEPARTMENT OF EDUCATION MEETING IS AT 11:45, AND MINE AT THE DEPARTMENT OF AGRICULTURE IS AT NOON, SO WE'LL MEET UP AFTER WE'RE BOTH DONE. FOR LUNCH-
HEY, AOKI.
I'm getting off!
Oh!
ISN'T THIS OUR STOP?
MUNICIPAL LIBRARY
VHRR
VHRR
VHRR

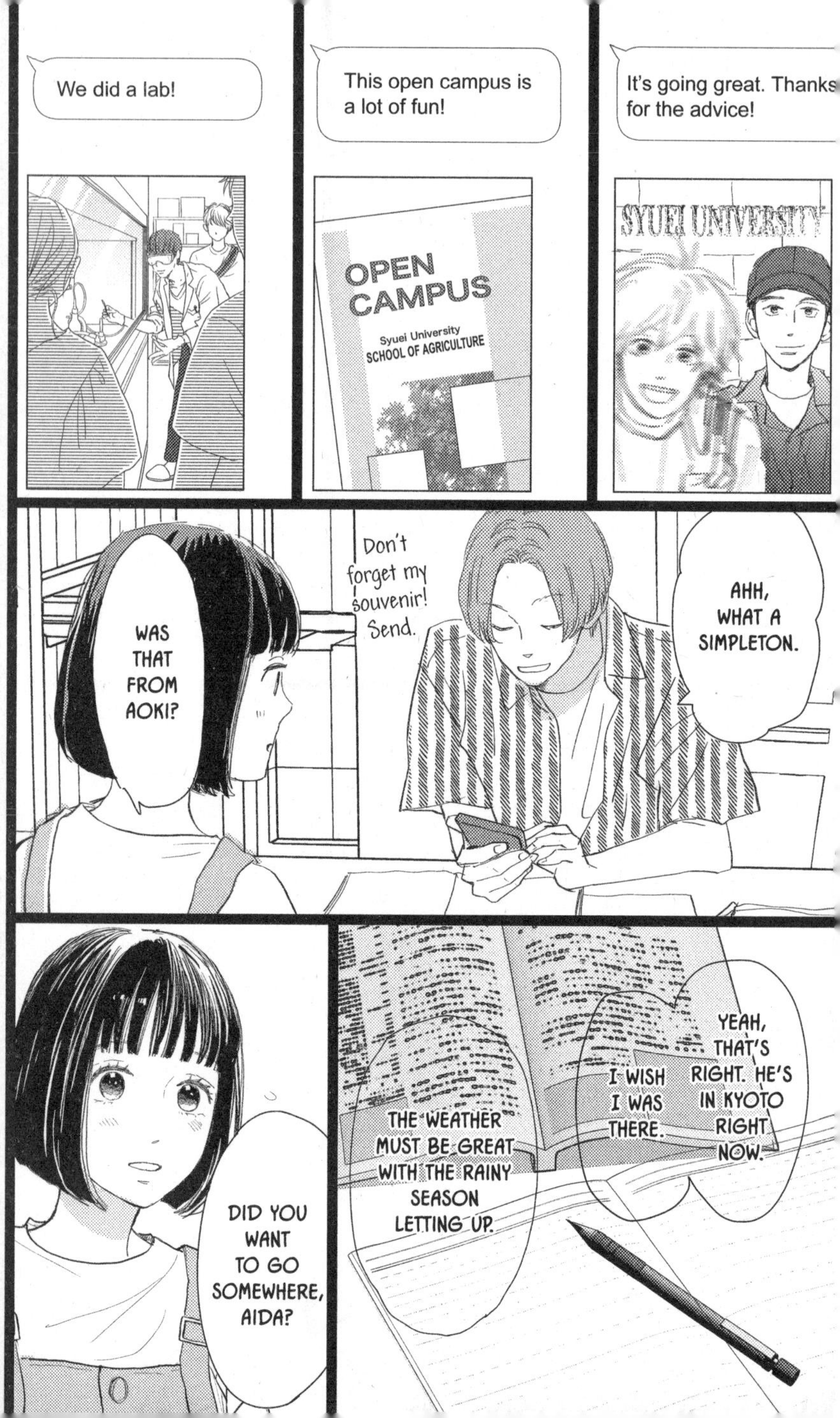
It's going great. Thanks for the advice!
SYUEI UNIVERSITY
This open campus is a lot of fun!
OPEN CAMPUS
Syuei University
SCHOOL OF AGRICULTURE
We did a lab!
AHH, WHAT A SIMPLETON.
Don't forget my souvenir! Send.
WAS THAT FROM AOKI?
YEAH, THAT'S RIGHT. HE'S IN KYOTO RIGHT NOW.
I WISH I WAS THERE.
THE WEATHER MUST BE GREAT WITH THE RAINY SEASON LETTING UP.
DID YOU WANT TO GO SOMEWHERE, AIDA?

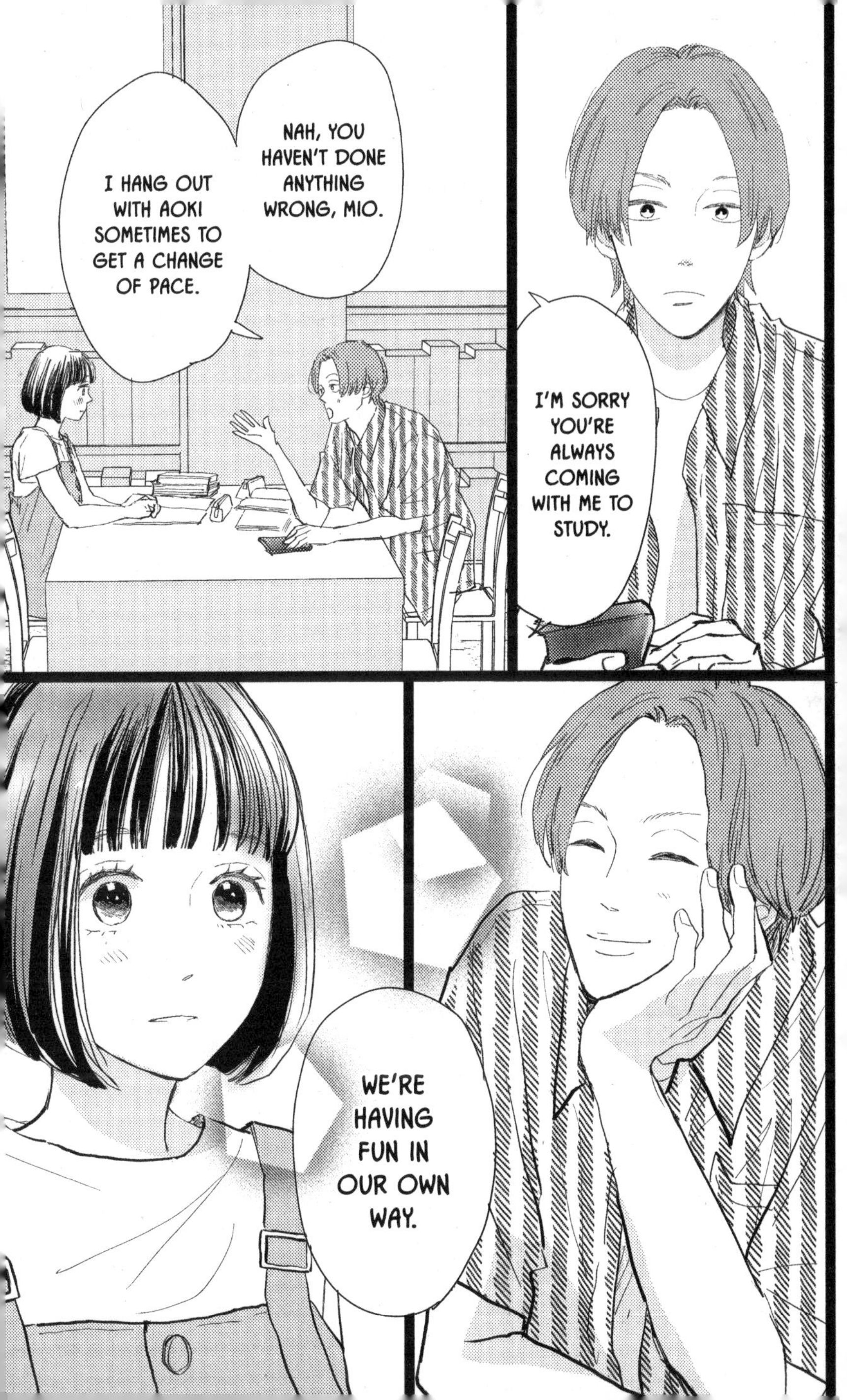
I'M SORRY YOU'RE ALWAYS COMING WITH ME TO STUDY.
NAH, YOU HAVEN'T DONE ANYTHING WRONG, MIO.
I HANG OUT WITH AOKI SOMETIMES TO GET A CHANGE OF PACE.
WE'RE HAVING FUN IN OUR OWN WAY.

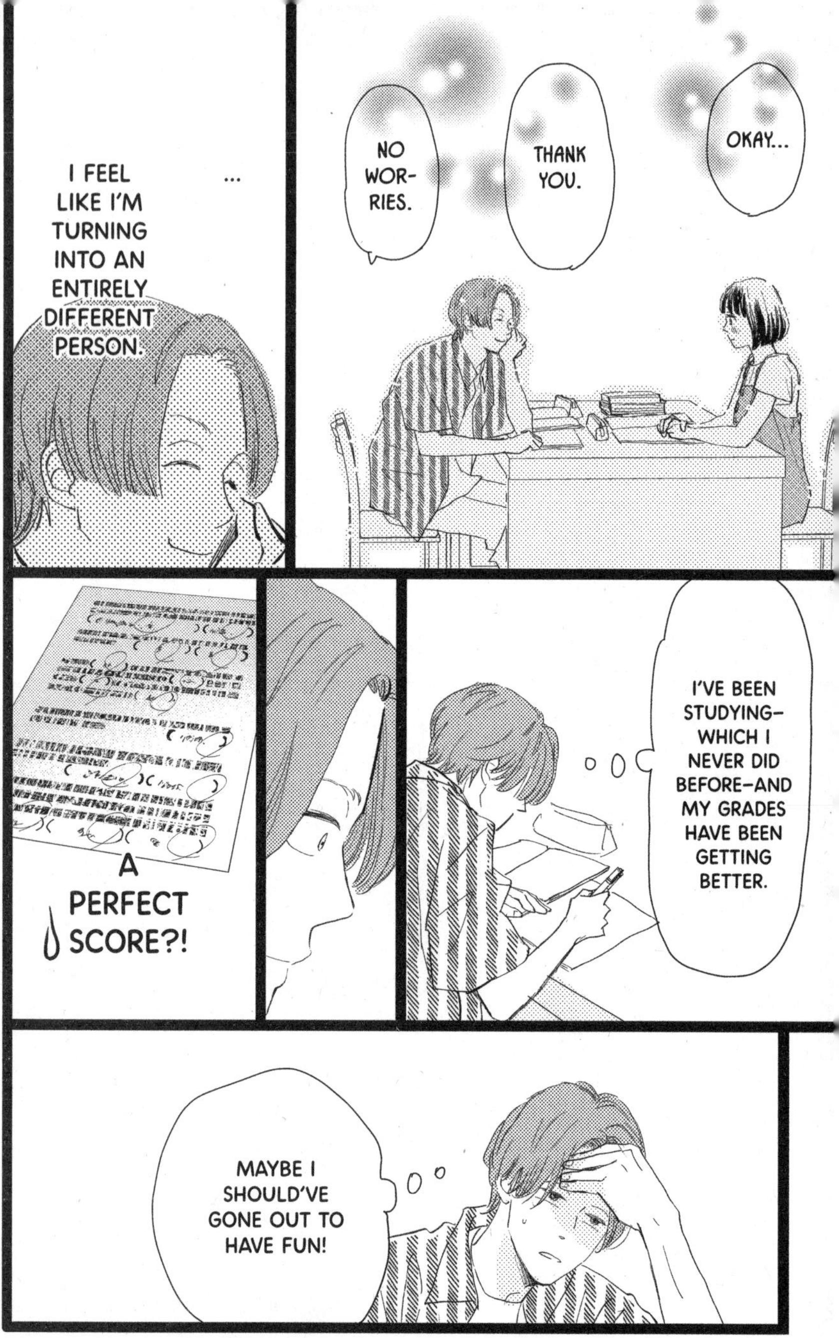
OKAY...
THANK YOU.
NO WORRIES.
...
I FEEL LIKE I'M TURNING INTO AN ENTIRELY DIFFERENT PERSON.
I'VE BEEN STUDYING—WHICH I NEVER DID BEFORE—AND MY GRADES HAVE BEEN GETTING BETTER.
A PERFECT SCORE?!
MAYBE I SHOULD'VE GONE OUT TO HAVE FUN!

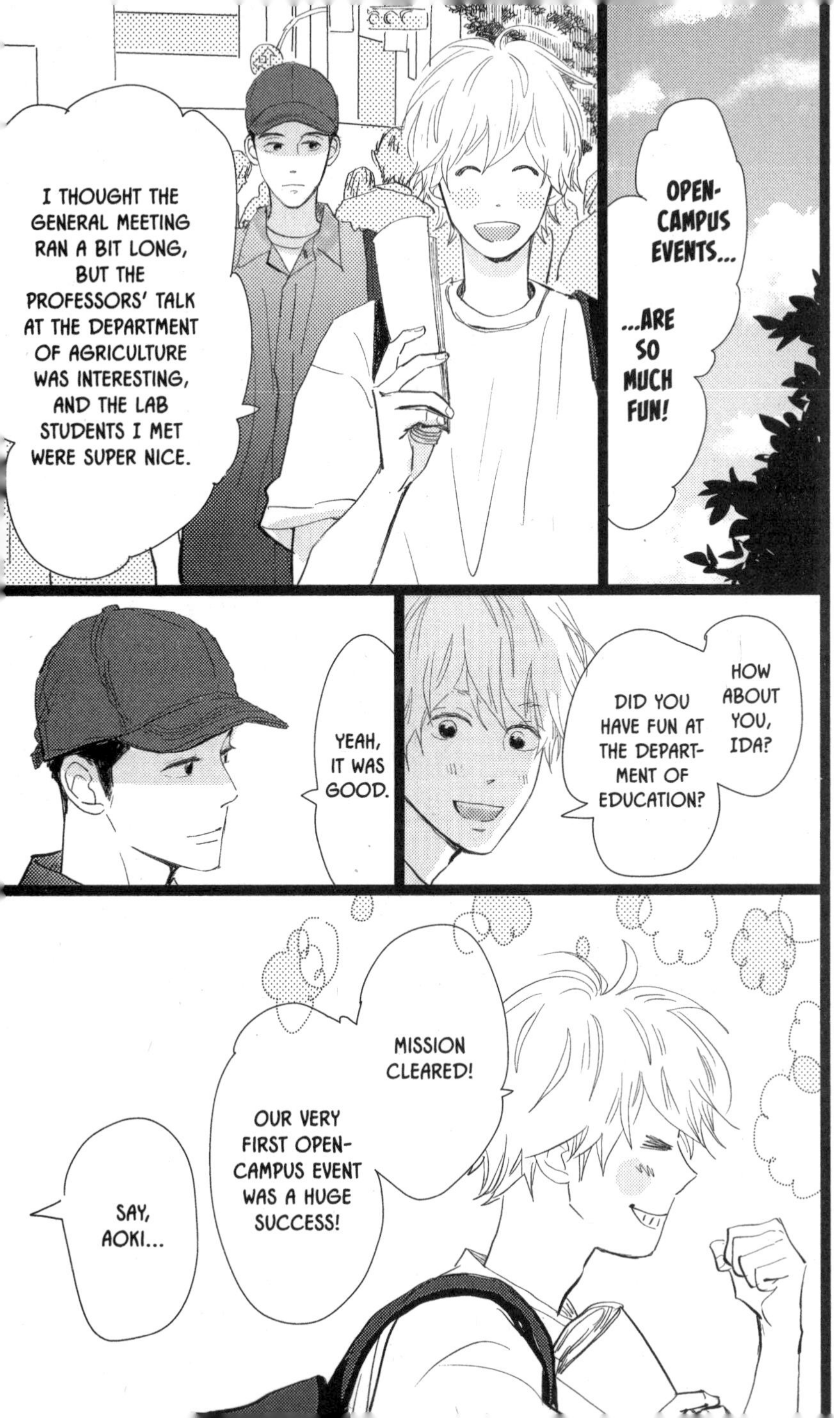
OPEN-CAMPUS EVENTS...
...ARE SO MUCH FUN!
I THOUGHT THE GENERAL MEETING RAN A BIT LONG, BUT THE PROFESSORS' TALK AT THE DEPARTMENT OF AGRICULTURE WAS INTERESTING, AND THE LAB STUDENTS I MET WERE SUPER NICE.
HOW ABOUT YOU, IDA?
DID YOU HAVE FUN AT THE DEPARTMENT OF EDUCATION?
YEAH, IT WAS GOOD.
MISSION CLEARED!
OUR VERY FIRST OPEN-CAMPUS EVENT WAS A HUGE SUCCESS!
SAY, AOKI...

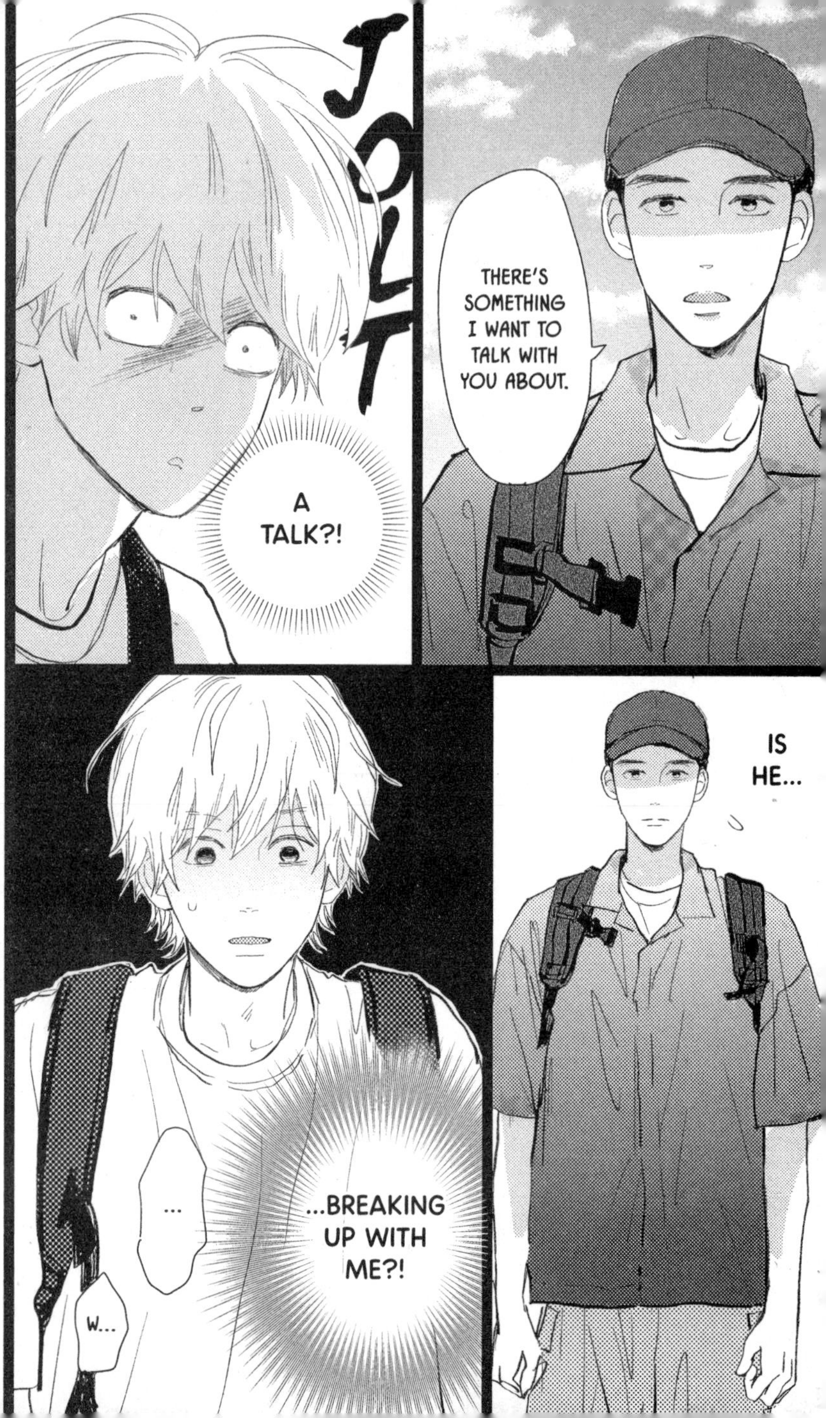
THERE'S SOMETHING I WANT TO TALK WITH YOU ABOUT.
JOLT
A TALK?!
IS HE...
...BREAKING UP WITH ME?!
...
W...

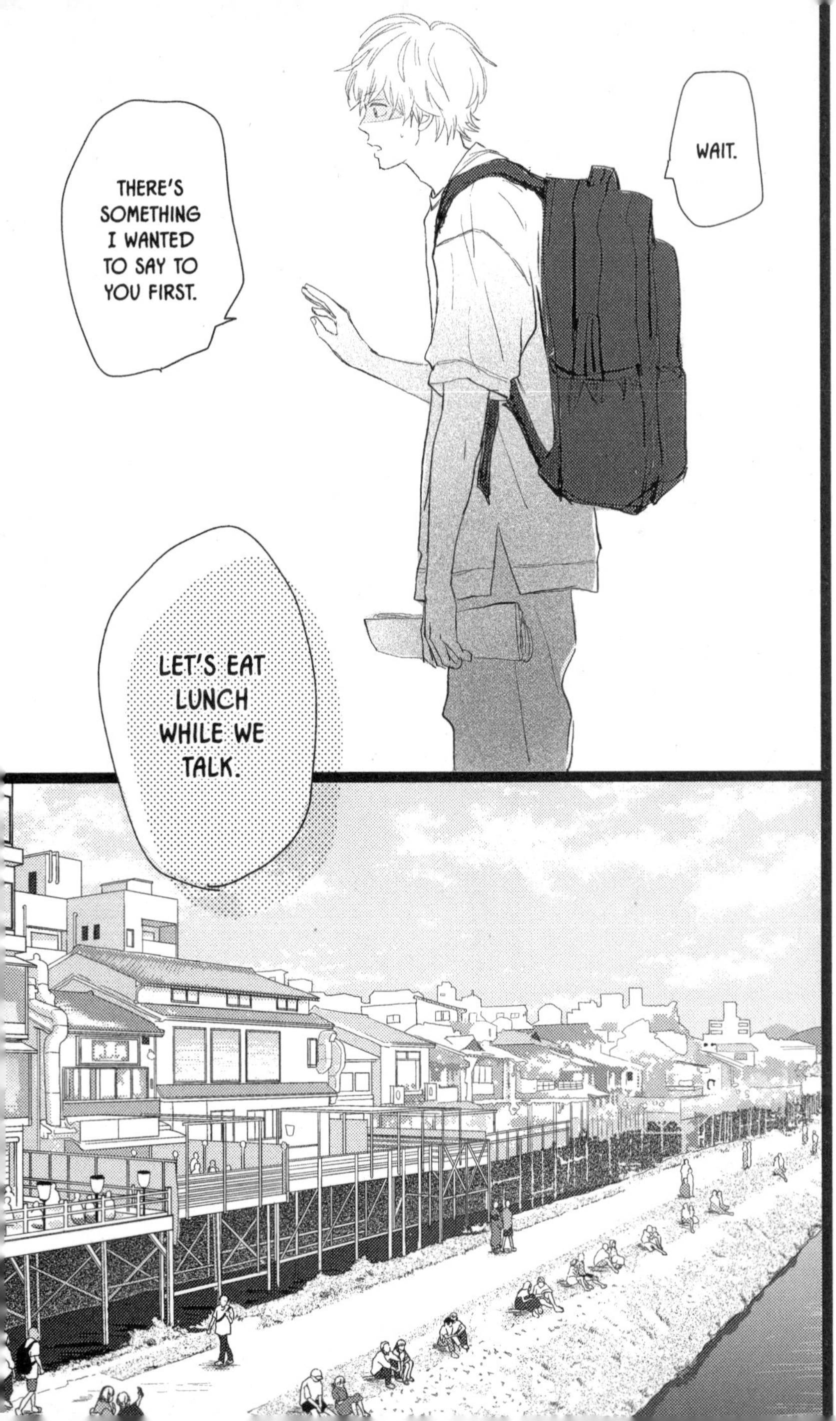
WAIT.
THERE'S SOMETHING I WANTED TO SAY TO YOU FIRST.
LET'S EAT LUNCH WHILE WE TALK.

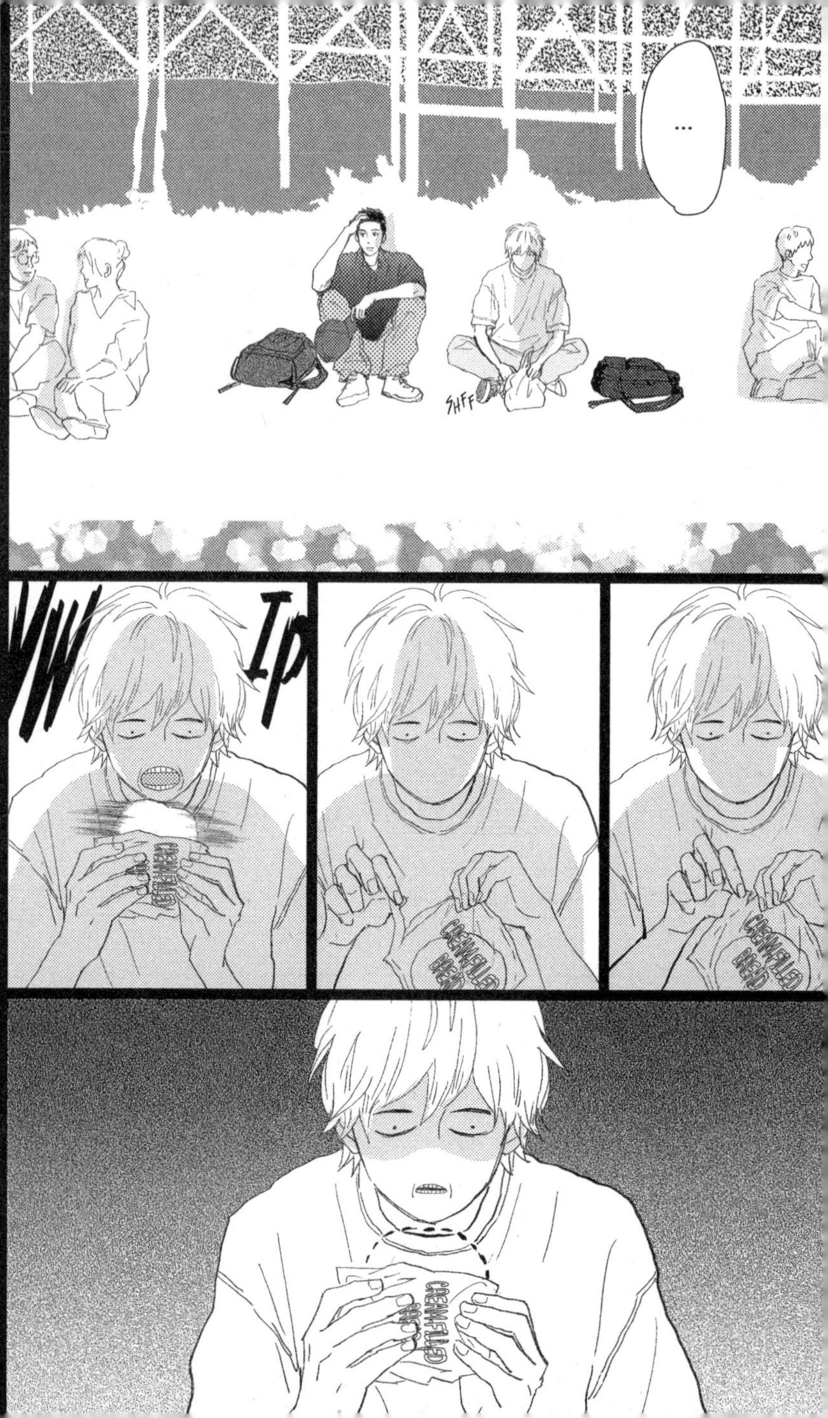
...
SHFF
CREAM-FILLED BREAD
CREAM-FILLED BREAD
CREAM-FILLED
CREAM-FILLED BREAD

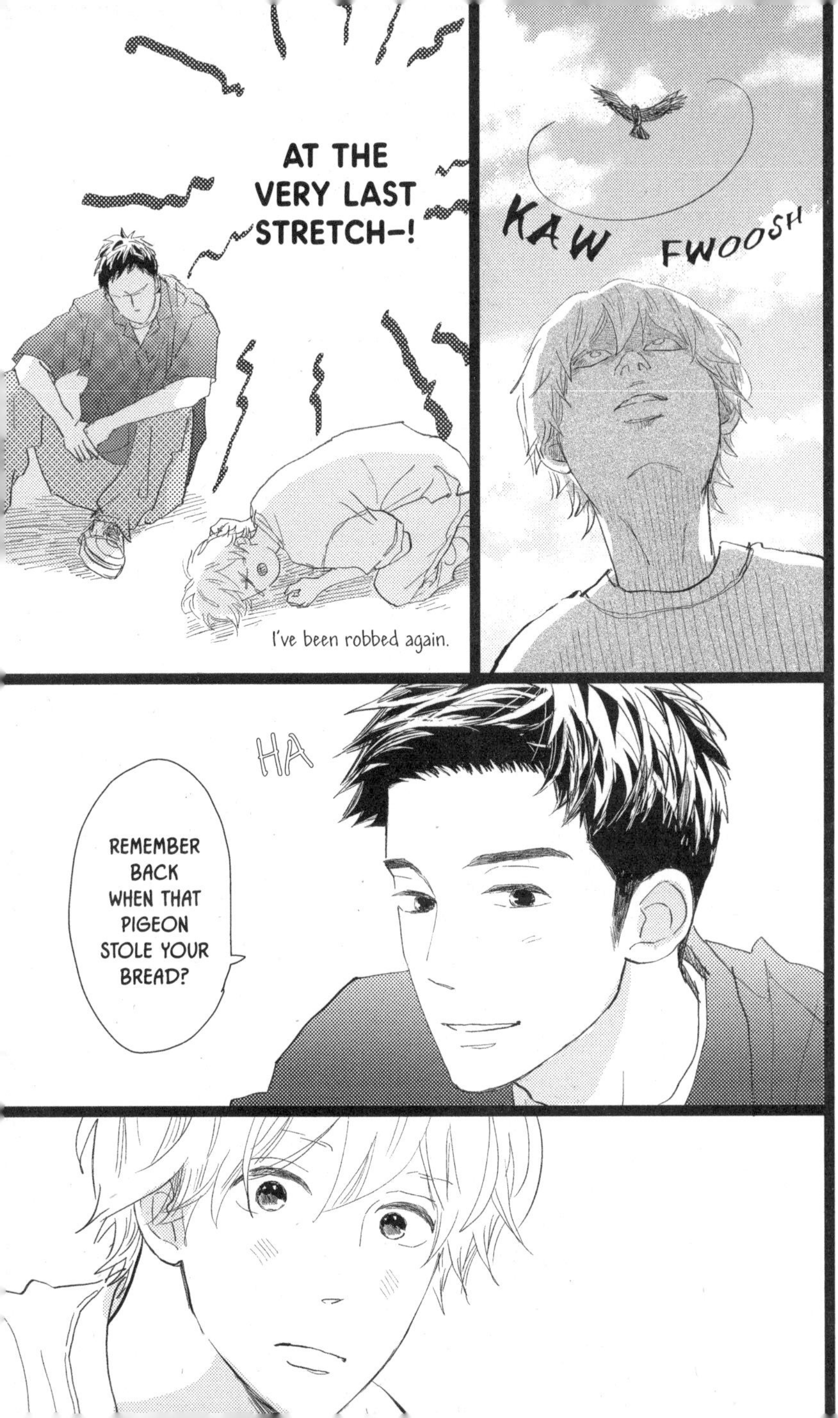
KAW
FWOOSH
AT THE VERY LAST STRETCH–!
I've been robbed again.
HA
REMEMBER BACK WHEN THAT PIGEON STOLE YOUR BREAD?

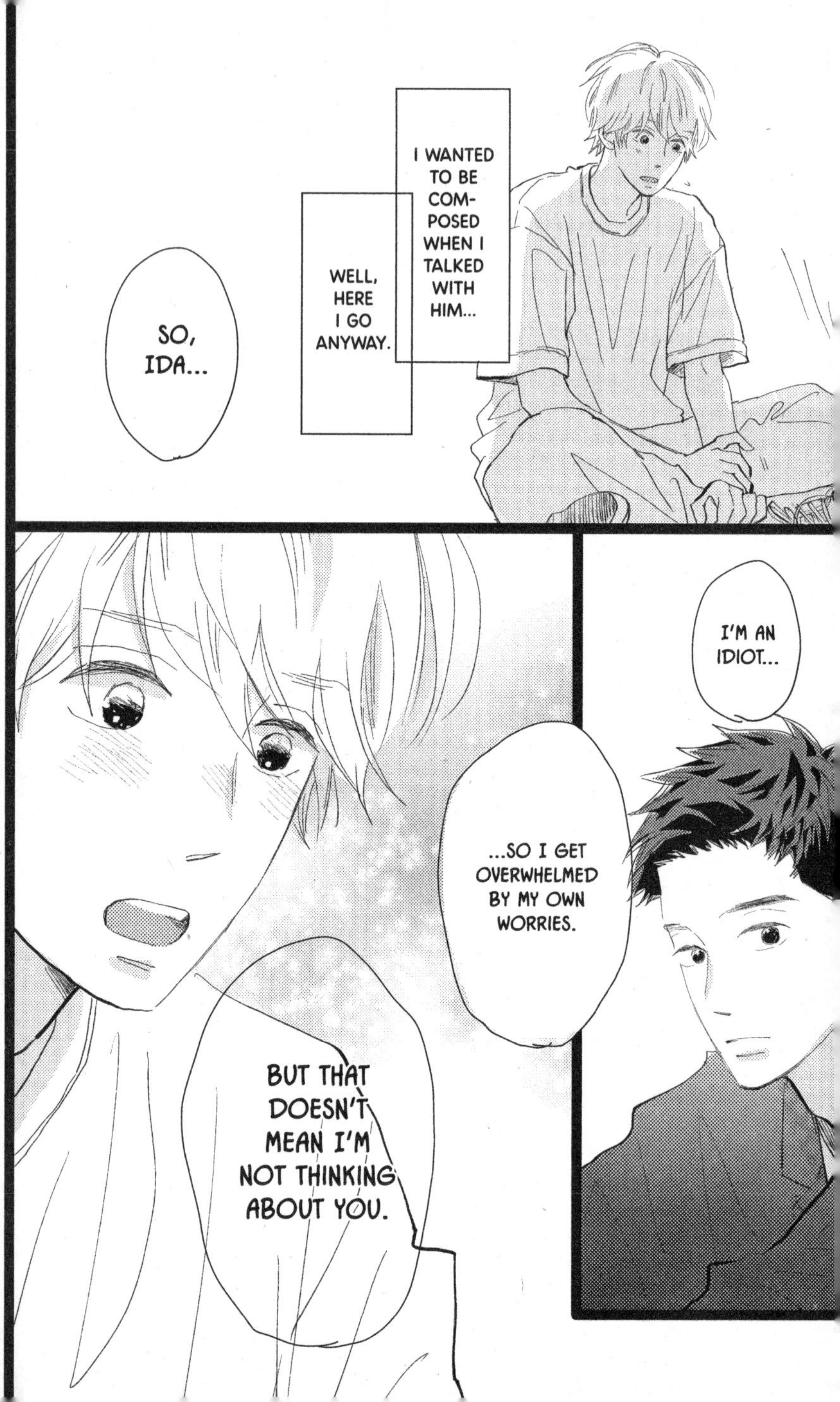
I WANTED TO BE COMPOSED WHEN I TALKED WITH HIM...
WELL, HERE I GO ANYWAY.
SO, IDA...
I'M AN IDIOT...
...SO I GET OVERWHELMED BY MY OWN WORRIES.
BUT THAT DOESN'T MEAN I'M NOT THINKING ABOUT YOU.

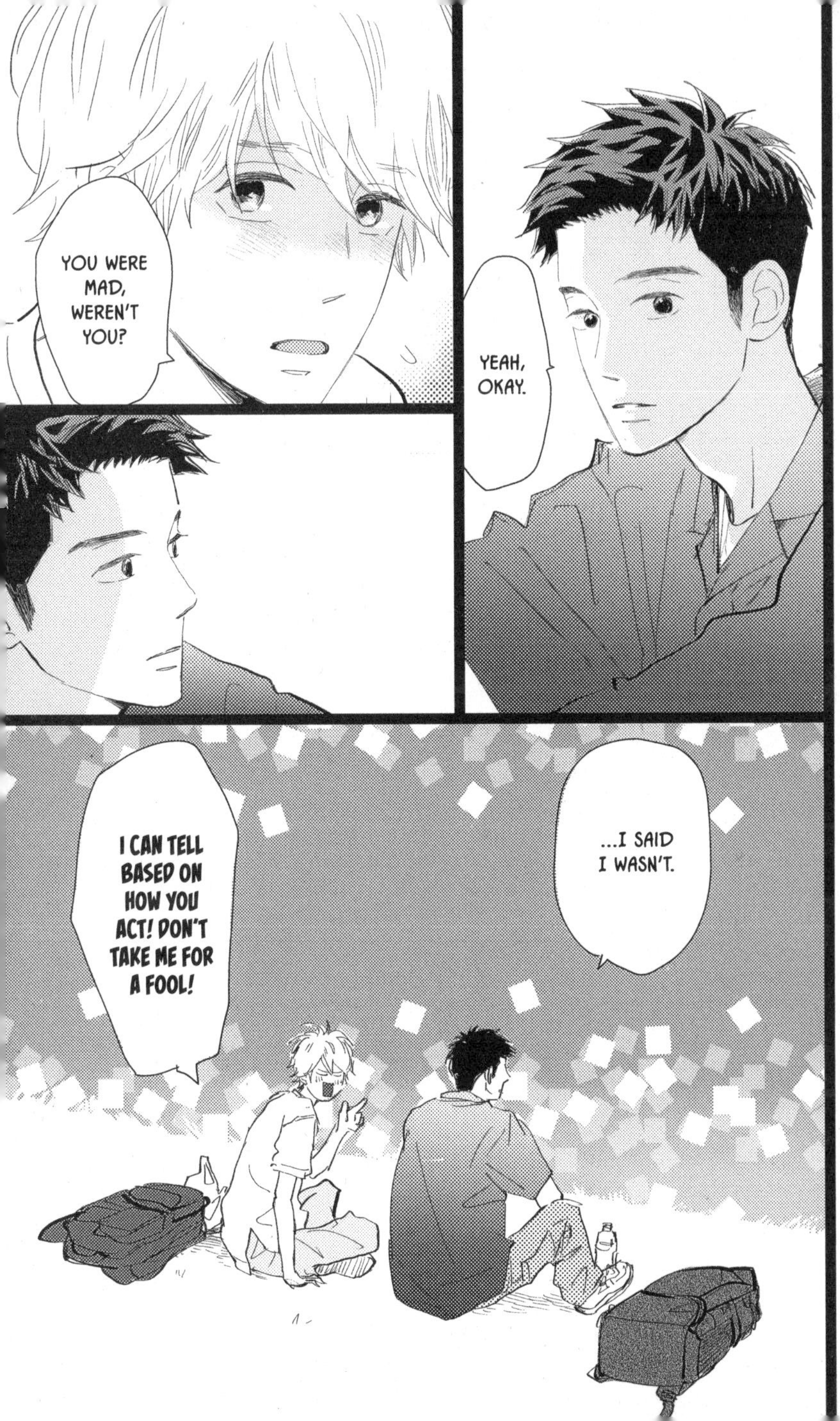
YEAH, OKAY.
YOU WERE MAD, WEREN'T YOU?
...I SAID I WASN'T.
I CAN TELL BASED ON HOW YOU ACT! DON'T TAKE ME FOR A FOOL!

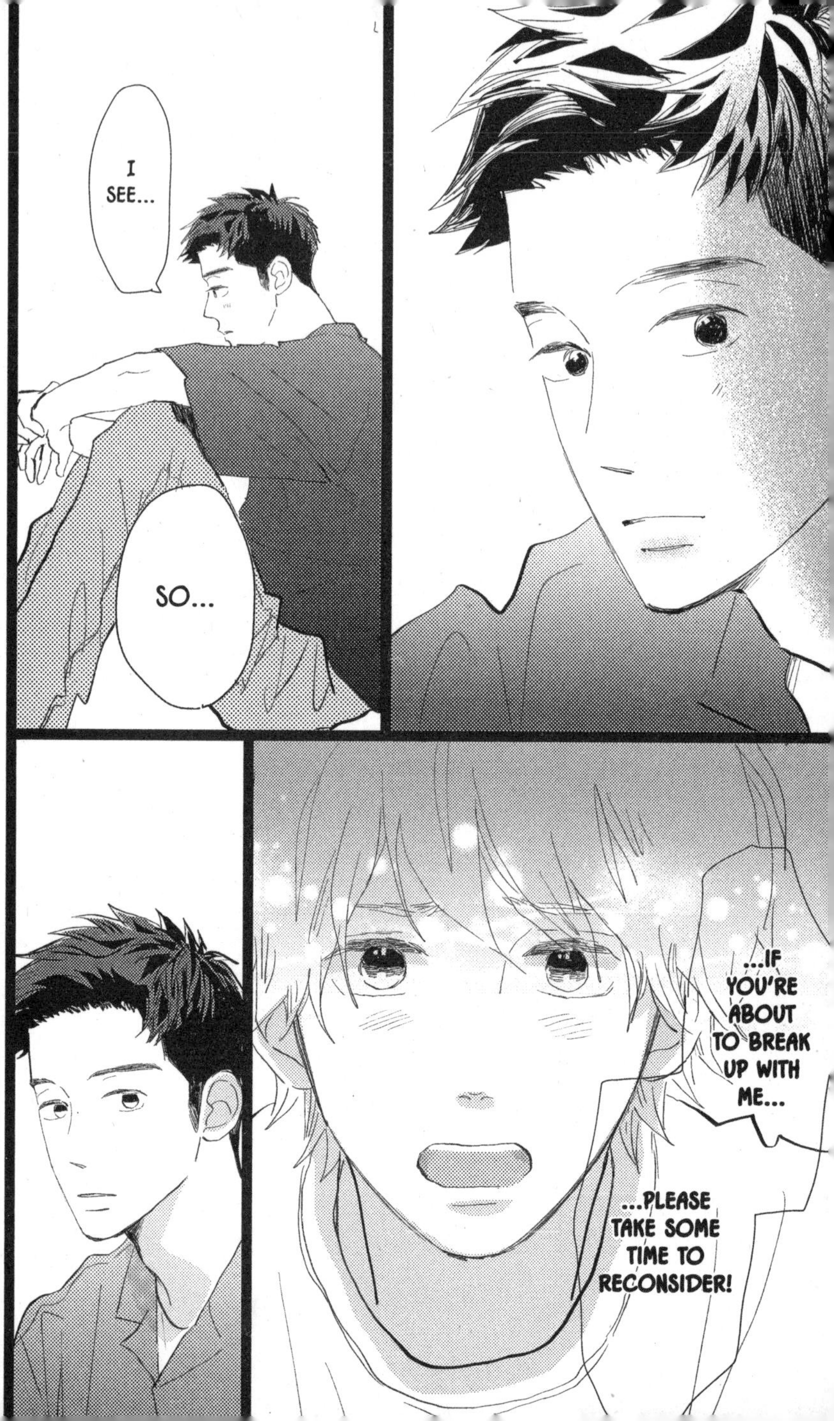
I SEE...
SO...
...IF YOU'RE ABOUT TO BREAK UP WITH ME...
...PLEASE TAKE SOME TIME TO RECONSIDER!

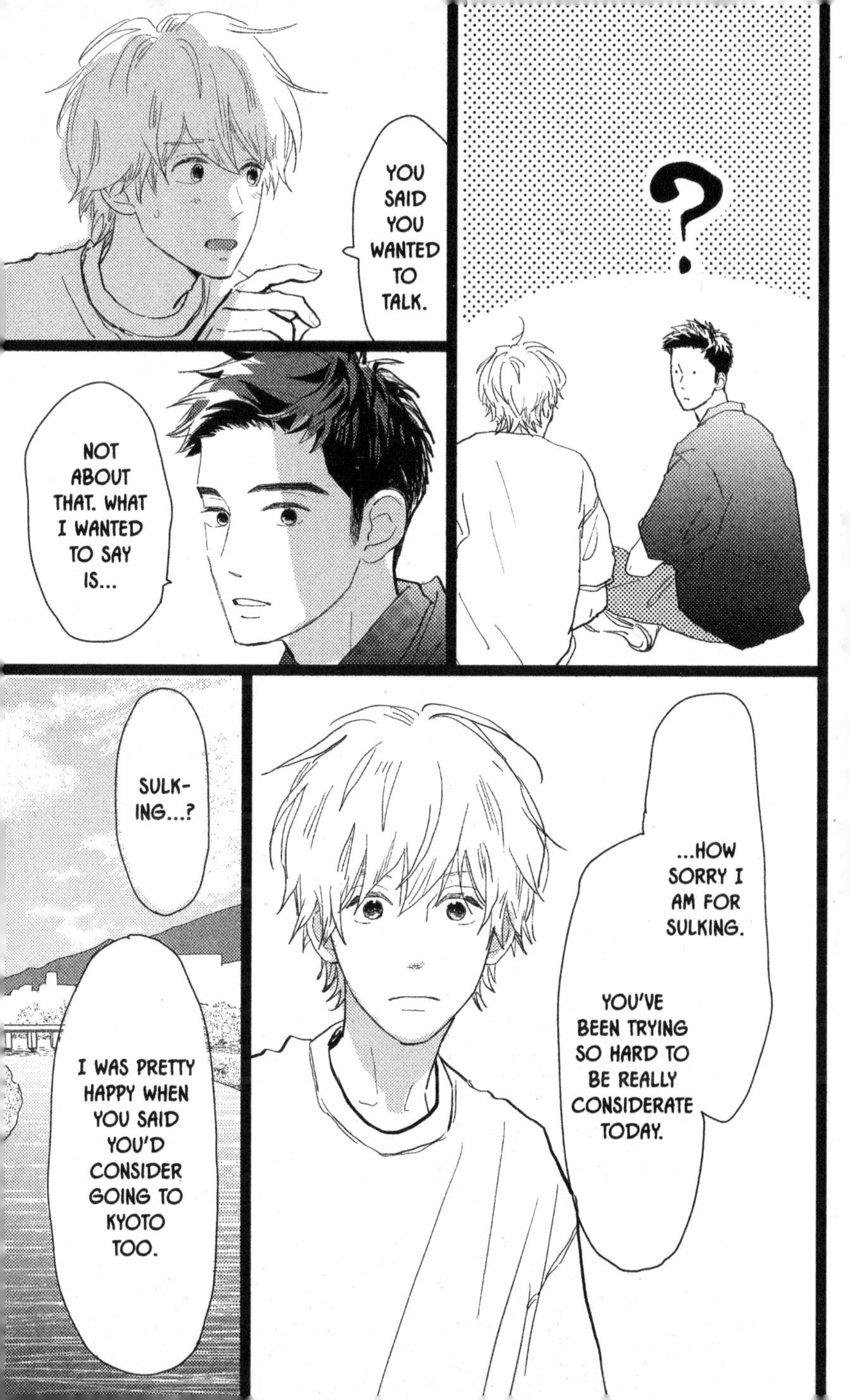
?
YOU SAID YOU WANTED TO TALK.
NOT ABOUT THAT. WHAT I WANTED TO SAY IS...
...HOW SORRY I AM FOR SULKING.
YOU'VE BEEN TRYING SO HARD TO BE REALLY CONSIDERATE TODAY.
SULK-ING...?
I WAS PRETTY HAPPY WHEN YOU SAID YOU'D CONSIDER GOING TO KYOTO TOO.

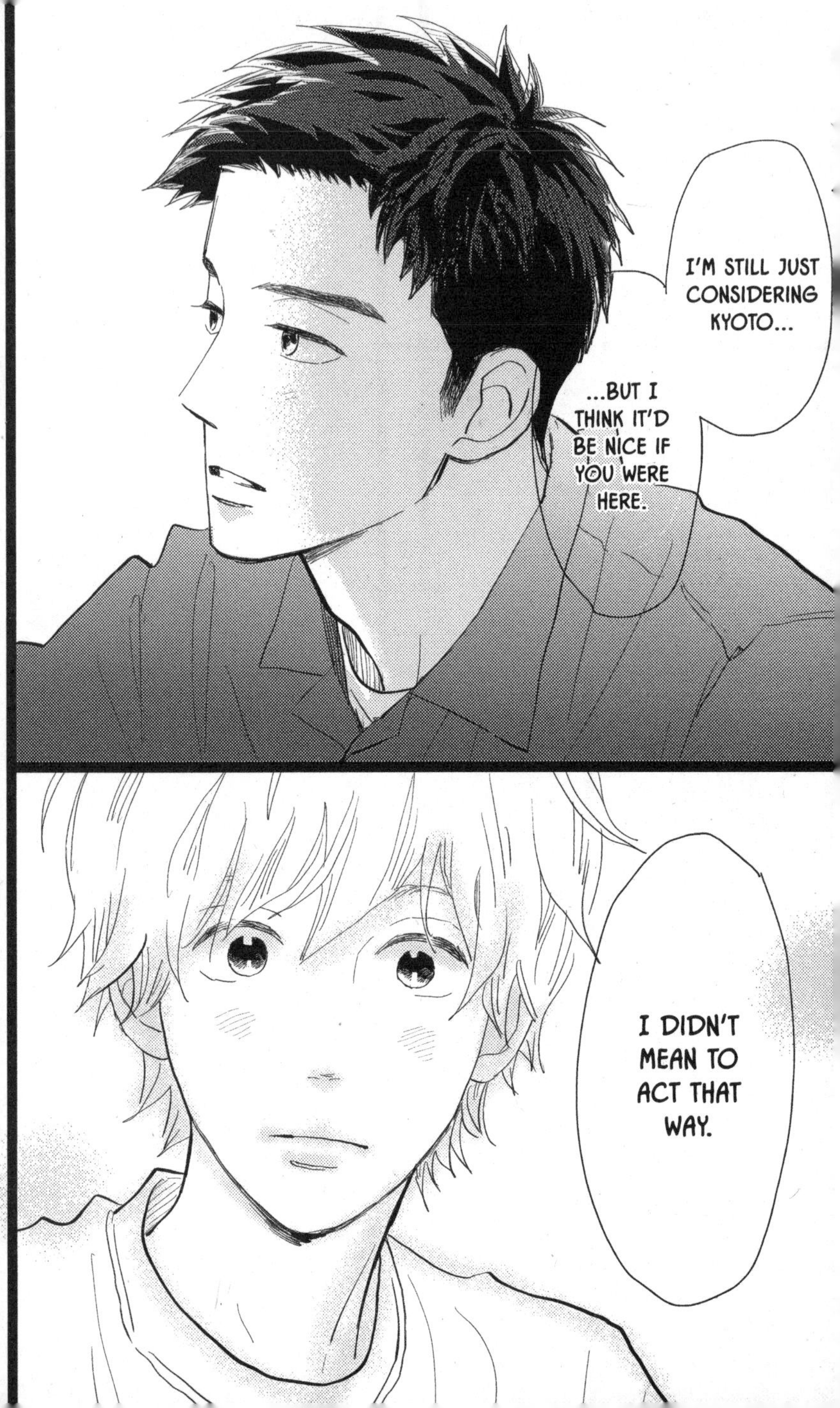
I'M STILL JUST CONSIDERING KYOTO...
...BUT I THINK IT'D BE NICE IF YOU WERE HERE.
I DIDN'T MEAN TO ACT THAT WAY.

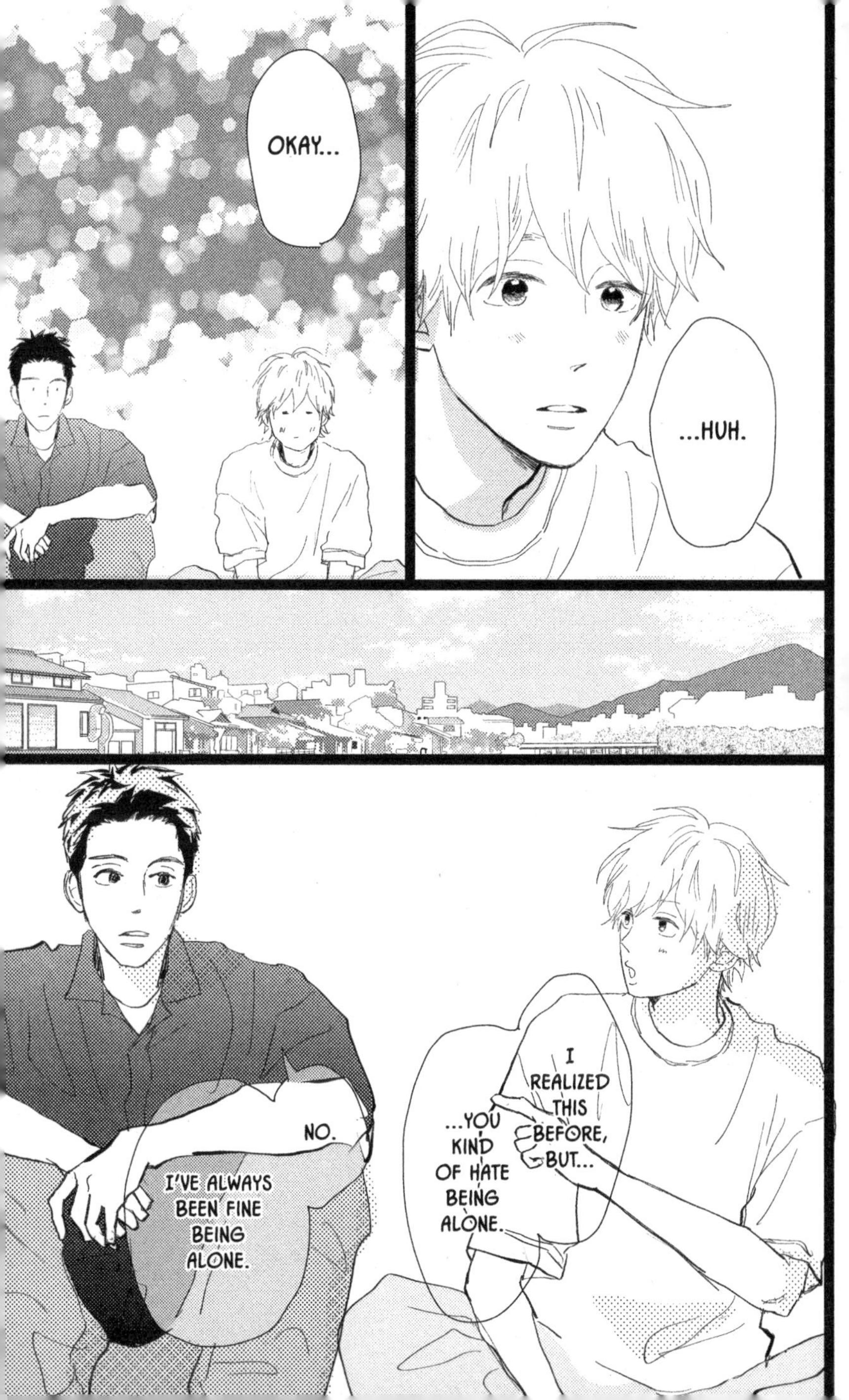
...HUH.
OKAY...
I REALIZED THIS BEFORE, BUT...
...YOU KIND OF HATE BEING ALONE.
NO.
I'VE ALWAYS BEEN FINE BEING ALONE.

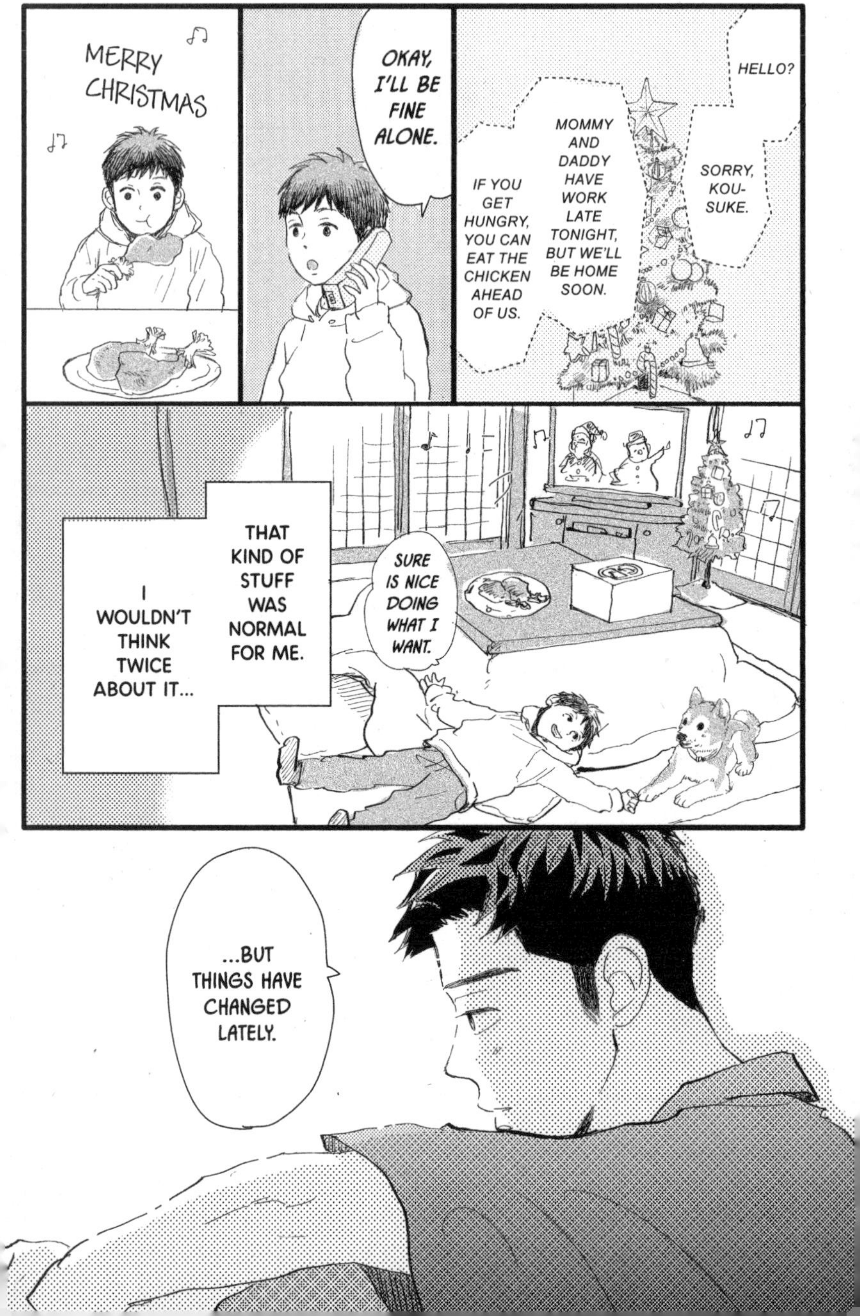
HELLO?
SORRY, KOU-SUKE.
MOMMY AND DADDY HAVE WORK LATE TONIGHT, BUT WE'LL BE HOME SOON.
IF YOU GET HUNGRY, YOU CAN EAT THE CHICKEN AHEAD OF US.
OKAY, I'LL BE FINE ALONE.
MERRY CHRISTMAS
SURE IS NICE DOING WHAT I WANT.
THAT KIND OF STUFF WAS NORMAL FOR ME.
I WOULDN'T THINK TWICE ABOUT IT...
...BUT THINGS HAVE CHANGED LATELY.

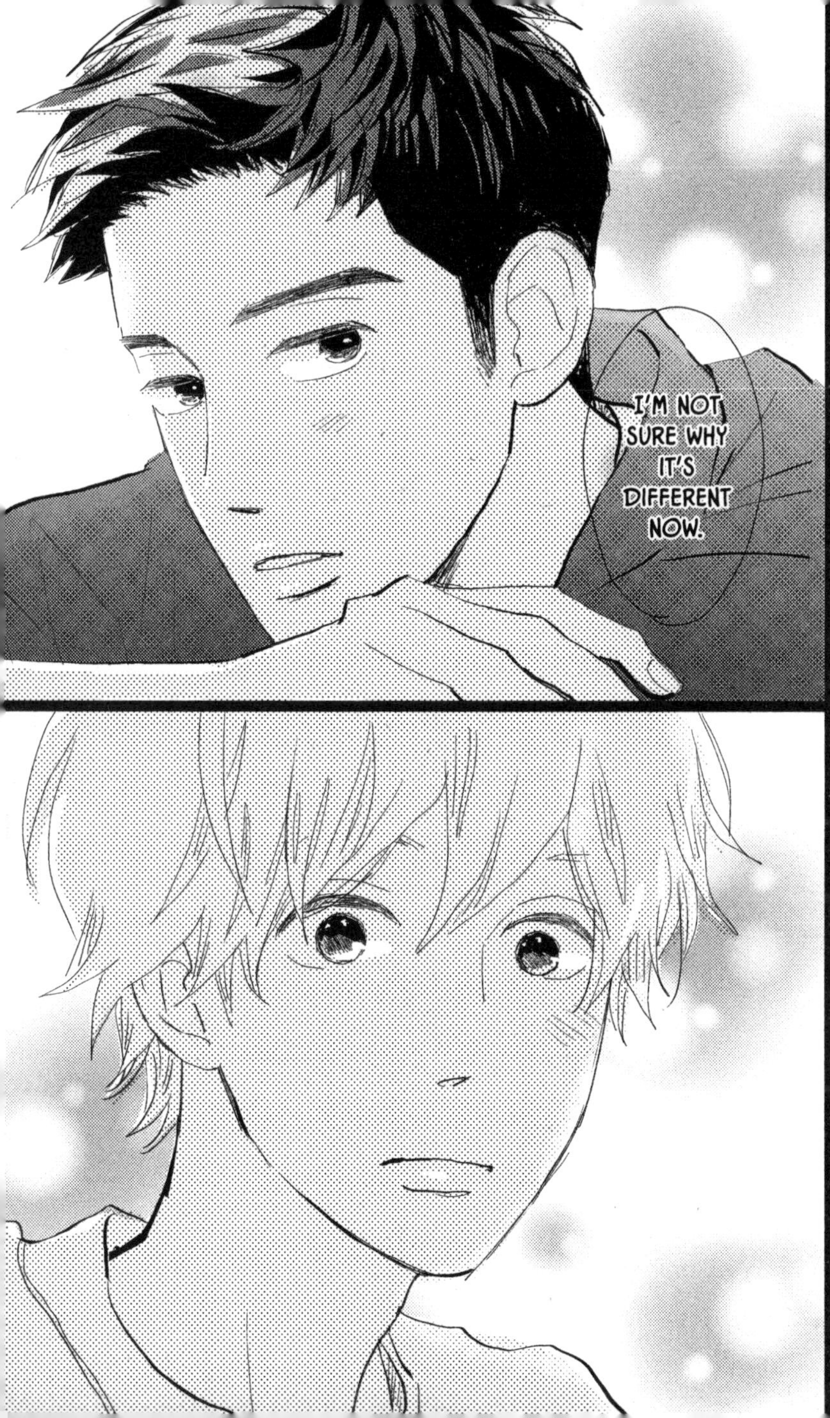
I'M NOT SURE WHY IT'S DIFFERENT NOW.

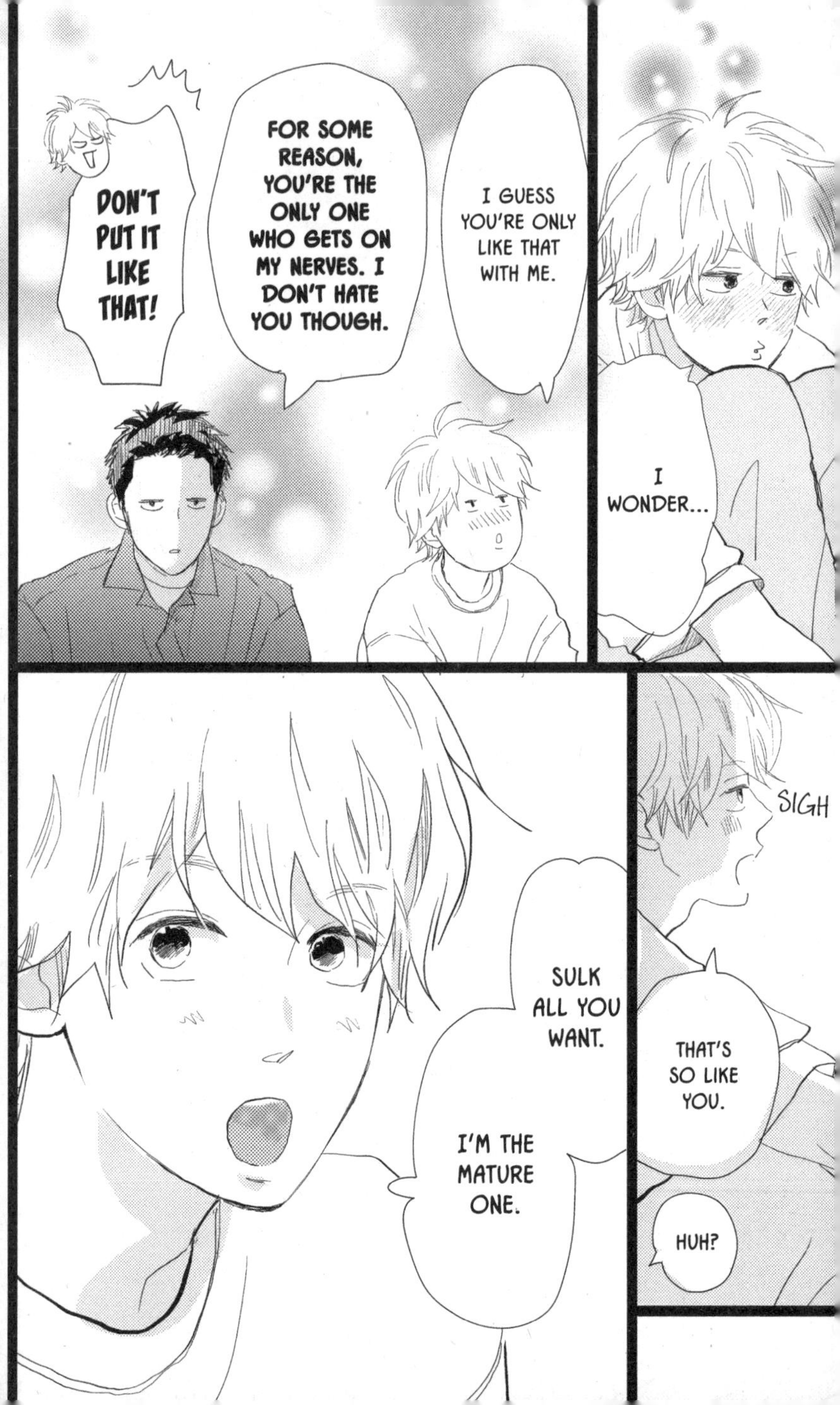
I WONDER...
I GUESS YOU'RE ONLY LIKE THAT WITH ME.
FOR SOME REASON, YOU'RE THE ONLY ONE WHO GETS ON MY NERVES. I DON'T HATE YOU THOUGH.
DON'T PUT IT LIKE THAT!
SIGH
THAT'S SO LIKE YOU.
HUH?
SULK ALL YOU WANT.
I'M THE MATURE ONE.

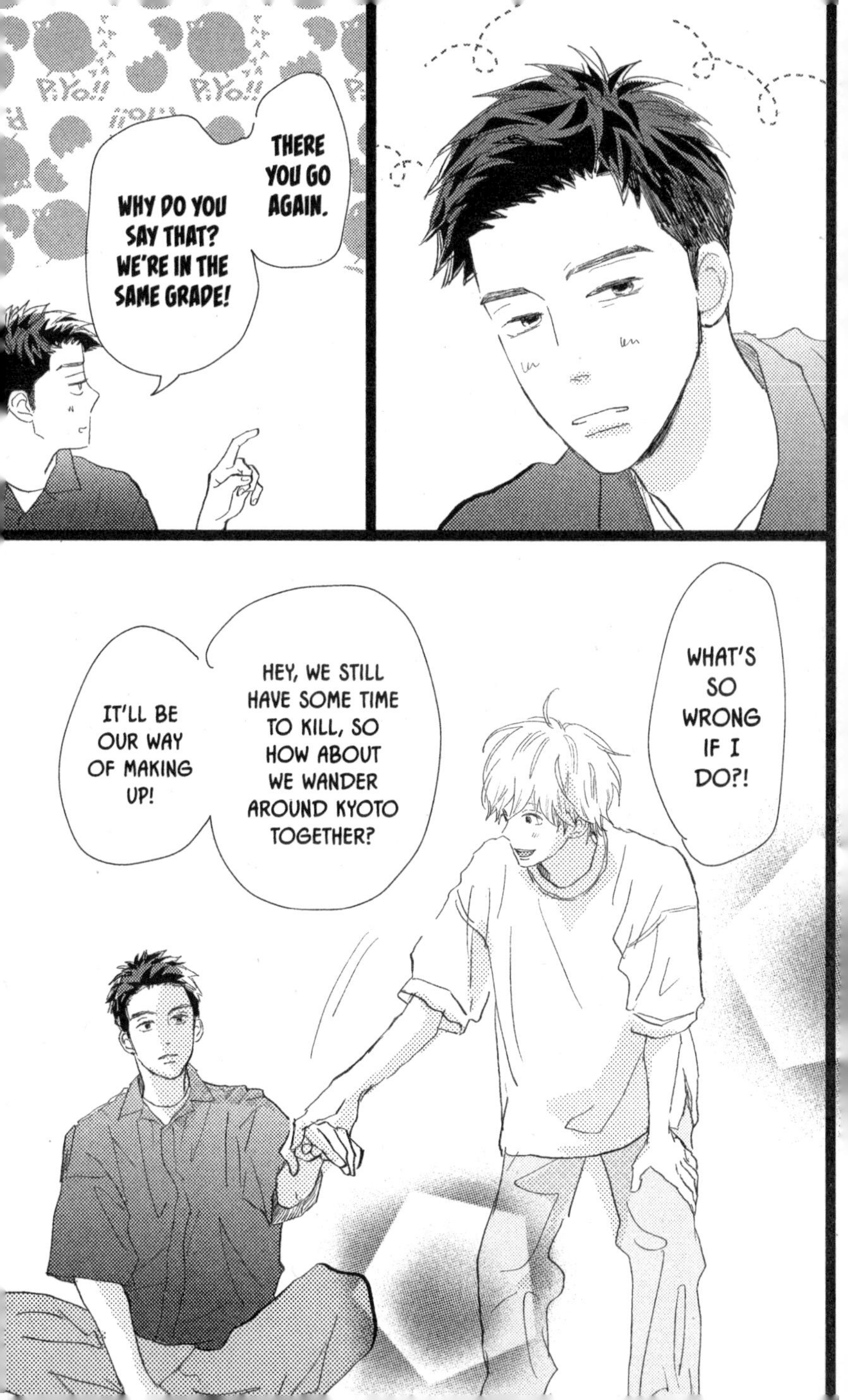
PiYo!! PiYo!!
THERE YOU GO AGAIN.
WHY DO YOU SAY THAT? WE'RE IN THE SAME GRADE!
WHAT'S SO WRONG IF I DO?!
HEY, WE STILL HAVE SOME TIME TO KILL, SO HOW ABOUT WE WANDER AROUND KYOTO TOGETHER?
IT'LL BE OUR WAY OF MAKING UP!

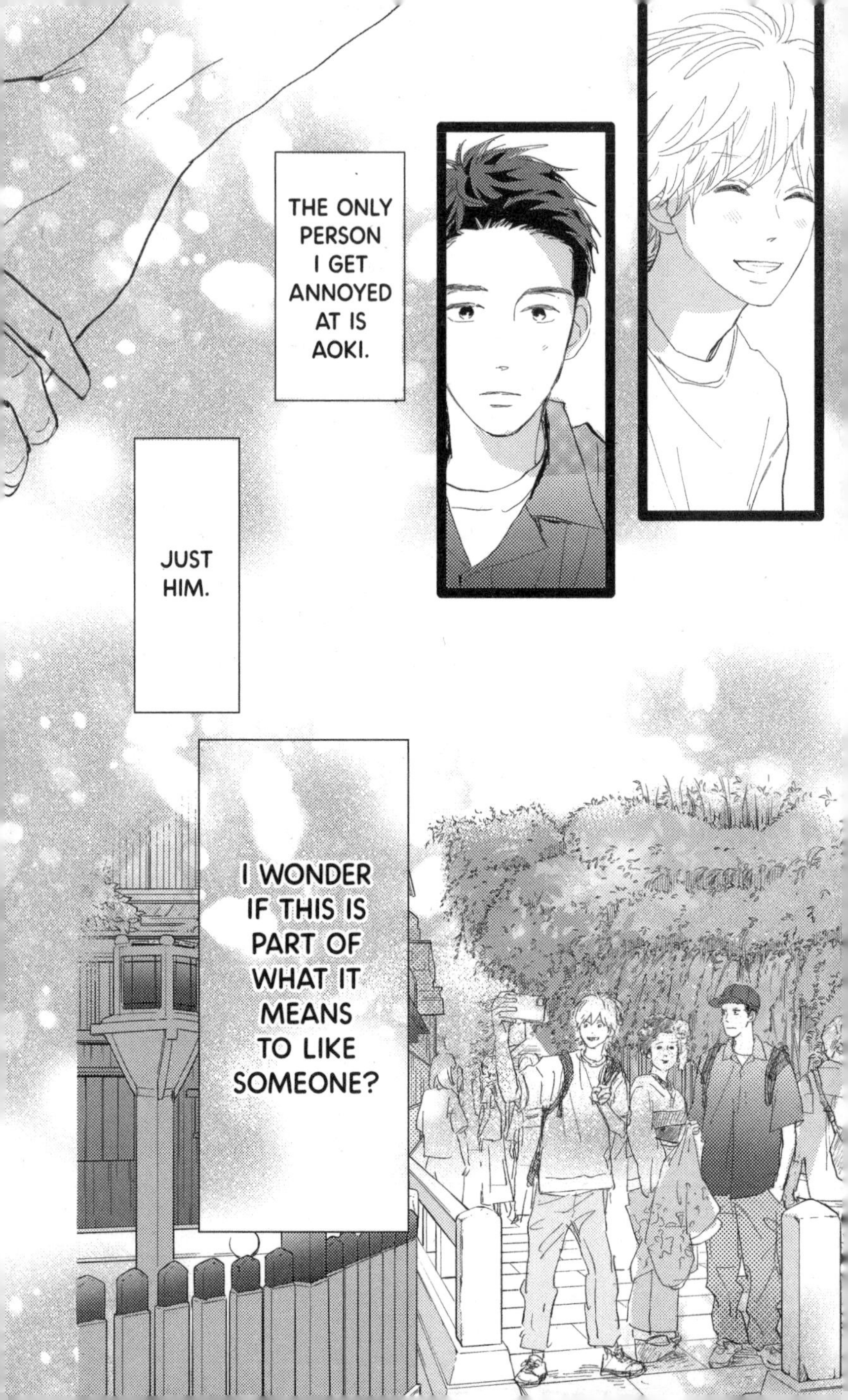
THE ONLY PERSON I GET ANNOYED AT IS AOKI.
JUST HIM.
I WONDER IF THIS IS PART OF WHAT IT MEANS TO LIKE SOMEONE?

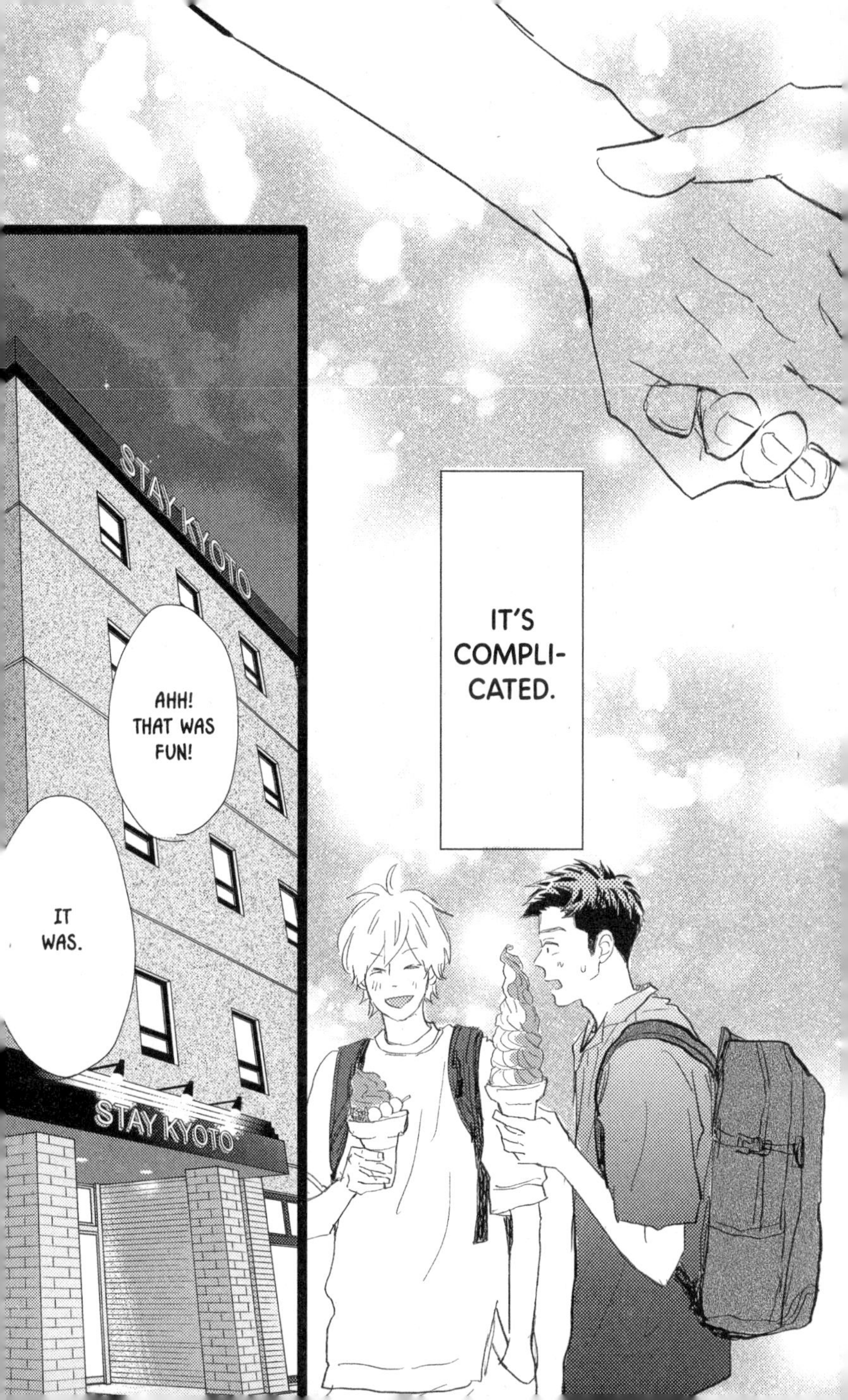
IT'S COMPLICATED.
STAY KYOTO
AHH! THAT WAS FUN!
IT WAS.
STAY KYOTO

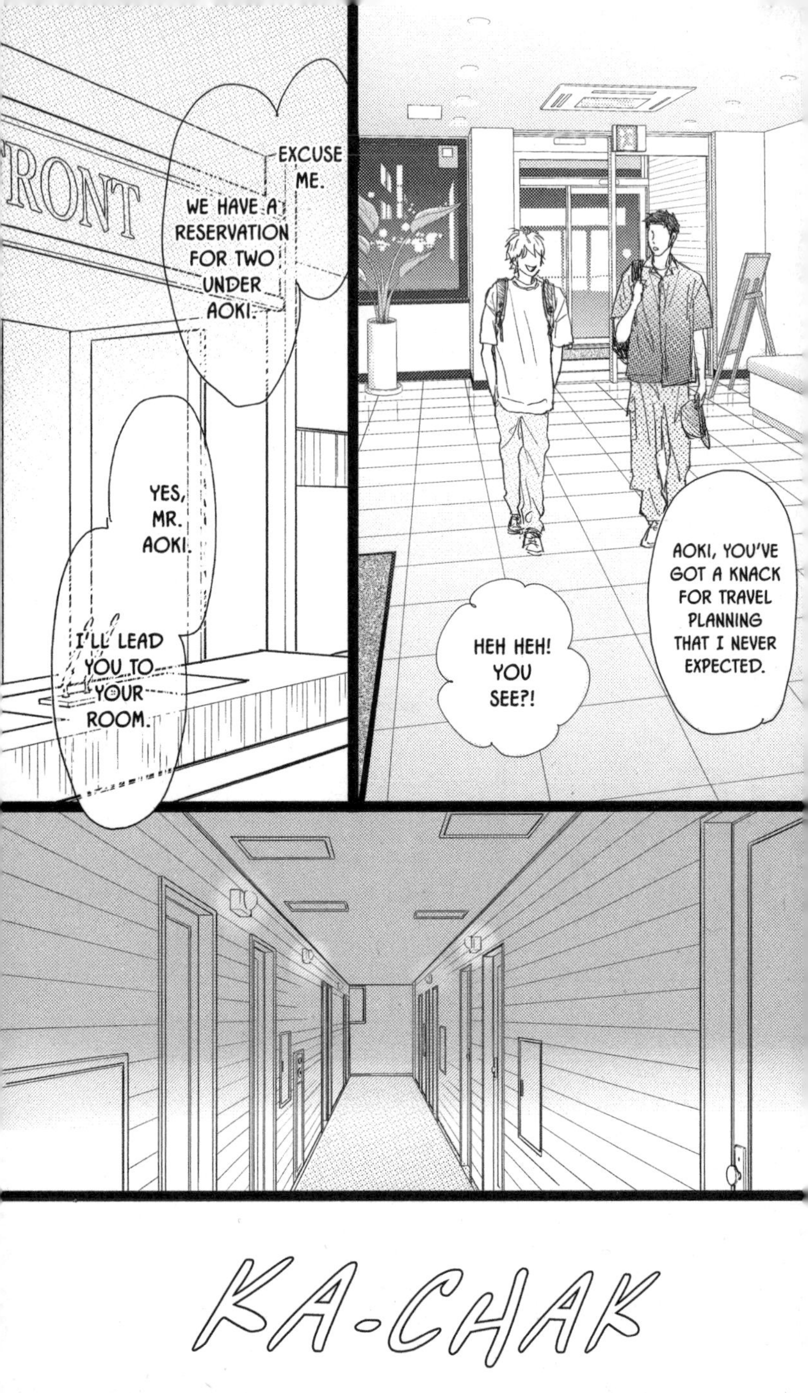
AOKI, YOU'VE GOT A KNACK FOR TRAVEL PLANNING THAT I NEVER EXPECTED.
HEH HEH! YOU SEE?!
FRONT
EXCUSE ME.
WE HAVE A RESERVATION FOR TWO UNDER AOKI.
YES, MR. AOKI.
I'LL LEAD YOU TO YOUR ROOM.
KA-CHAK

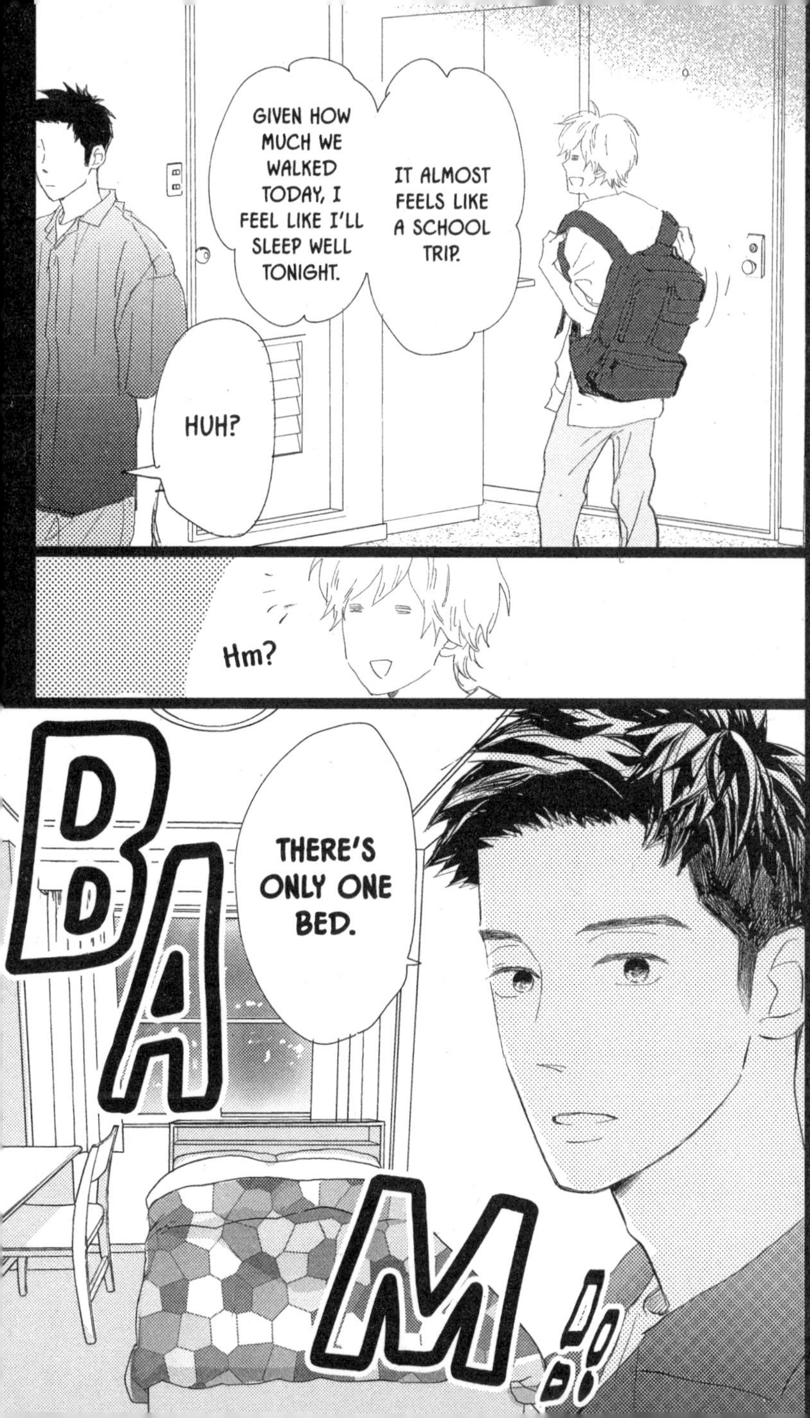
IT ALMOST FEELS LIKE A SCHOOL TRIP.
GIVEN HOW MUCH WE WALKED TODAY, I FEEL LIKE I'LL SLEEP WELL TONIGHT.
HUH?
Hm?
THERE'S ONLY ONE BED.
BAM!!

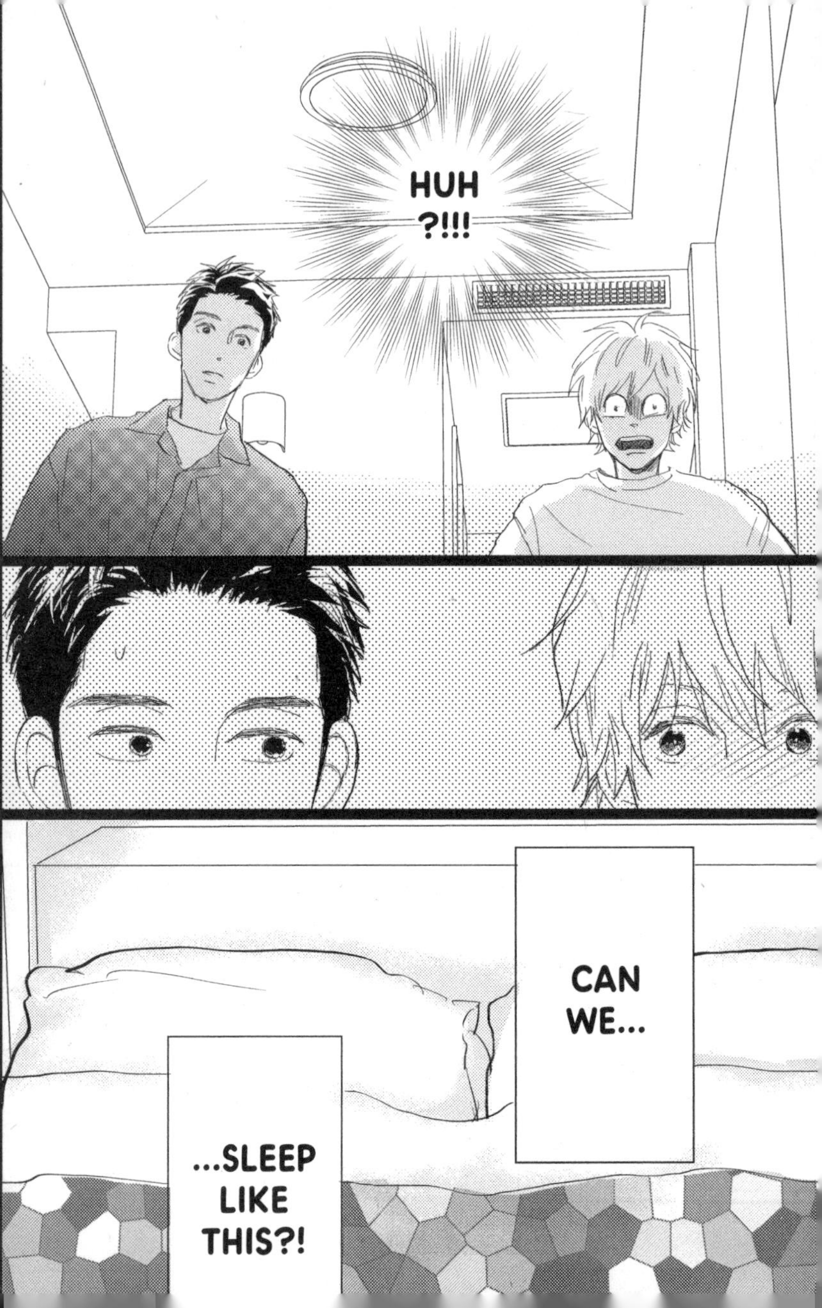
HUH ?!!!
CAN WE...
...SLEEP LIKE THIS?!

My Love
Mix-Up!

Chapter 27

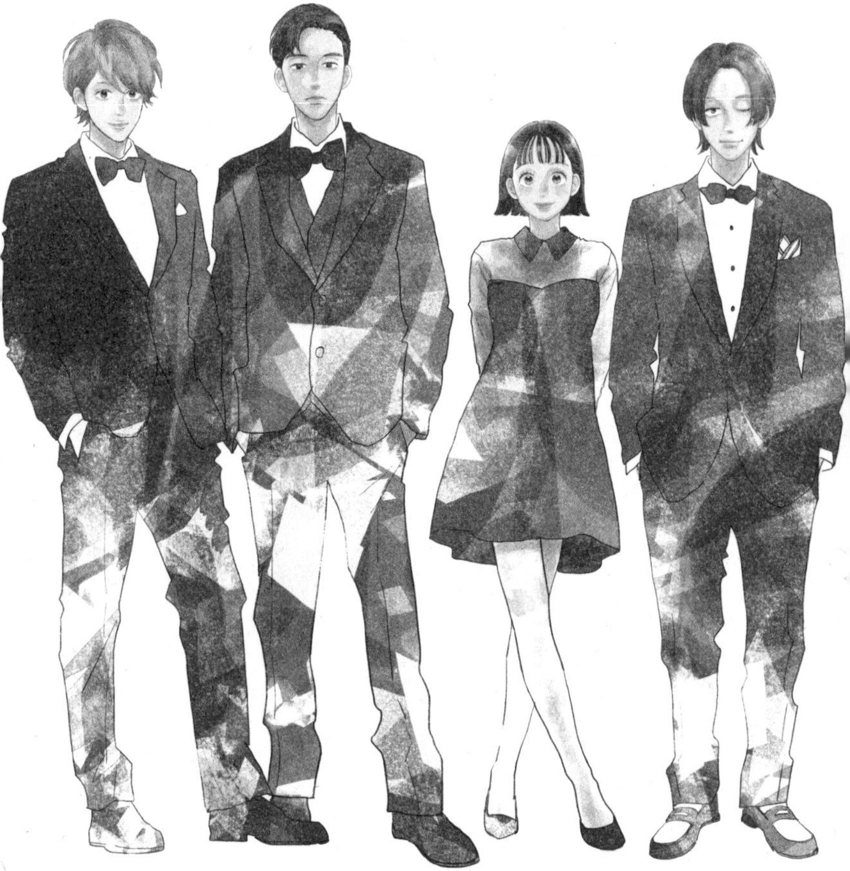

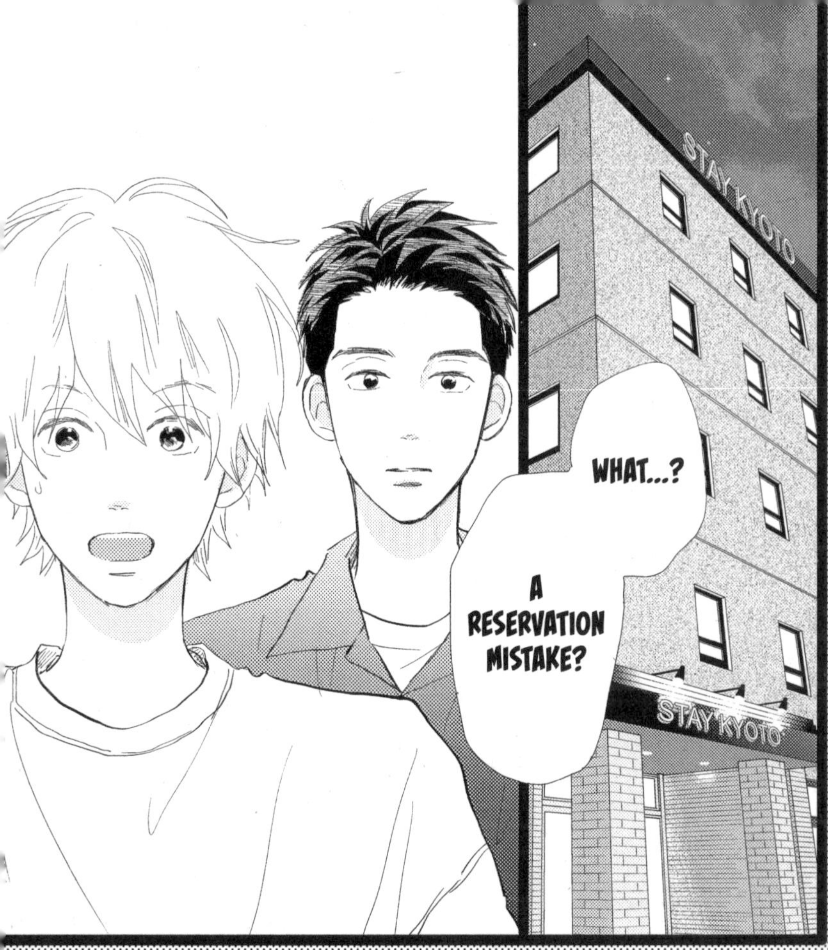
STAY KYOTO
WHAT...?
A RESERVATION MISTAKE?
STAY KYOTO

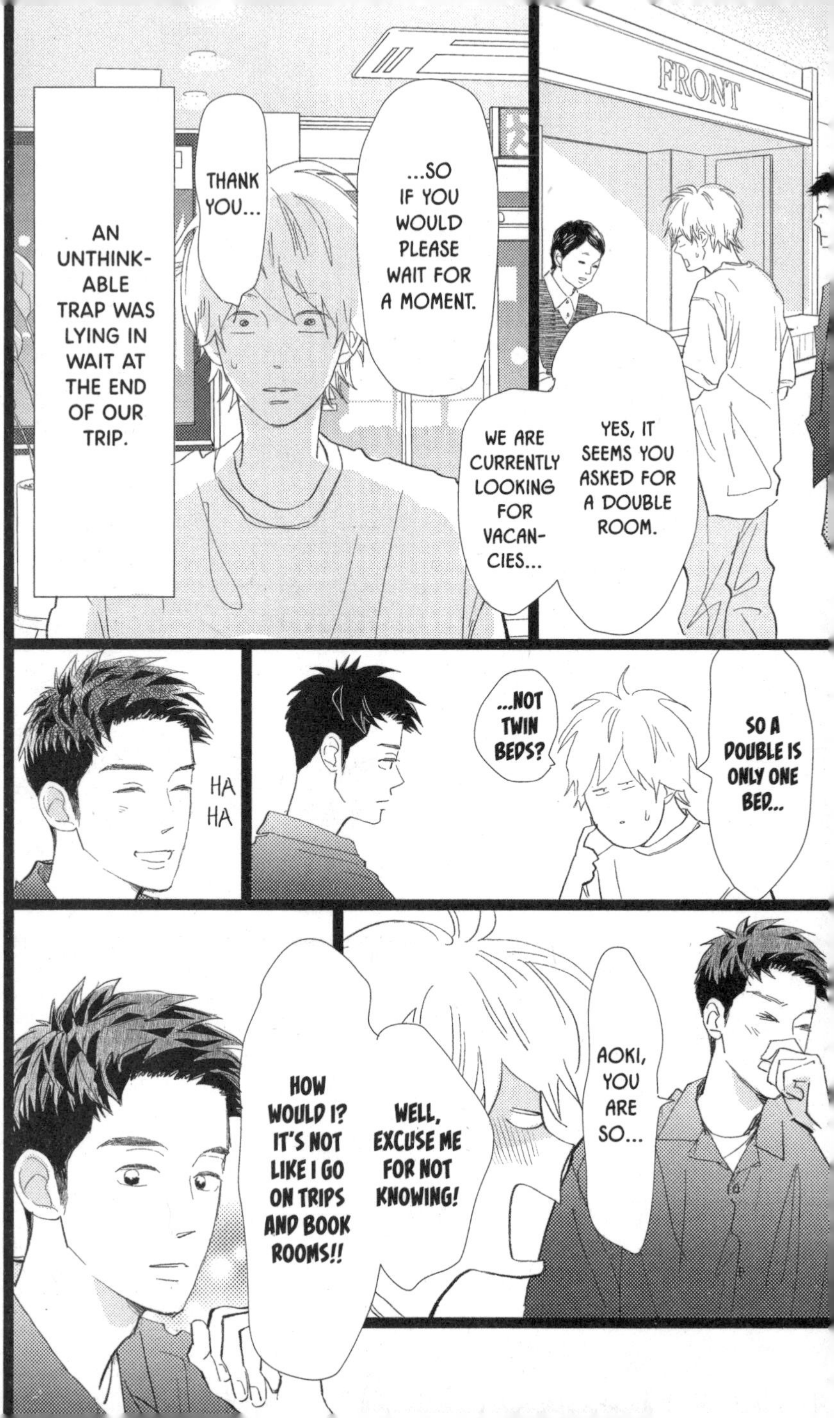
FRONT
YES, IT SEEMS YOU ASKED FOR A DOUBLE ROOM.
WE ARE CURRENTLY LOOKING FOR VACANCIES...
...SO IF YOU WOULD PLEASE WAIT FOR A MOMENT.
THANK YOU...
AN UNTHINKABLE TRAP WAS LYING IN WAIT AT THE END OF OUR TRIP.
SO A DOUBLE IS ONLY ONE BED...
...NOT TWIN BEDS?
HA HA
AOKI, YOU ARE SO...
WELL, EXCUSE ME FOR NOT KNOWING!
HOW WOULD I? IT'S NOT LIKE I GO ON TRIPS AND BOOK ROOMS!!

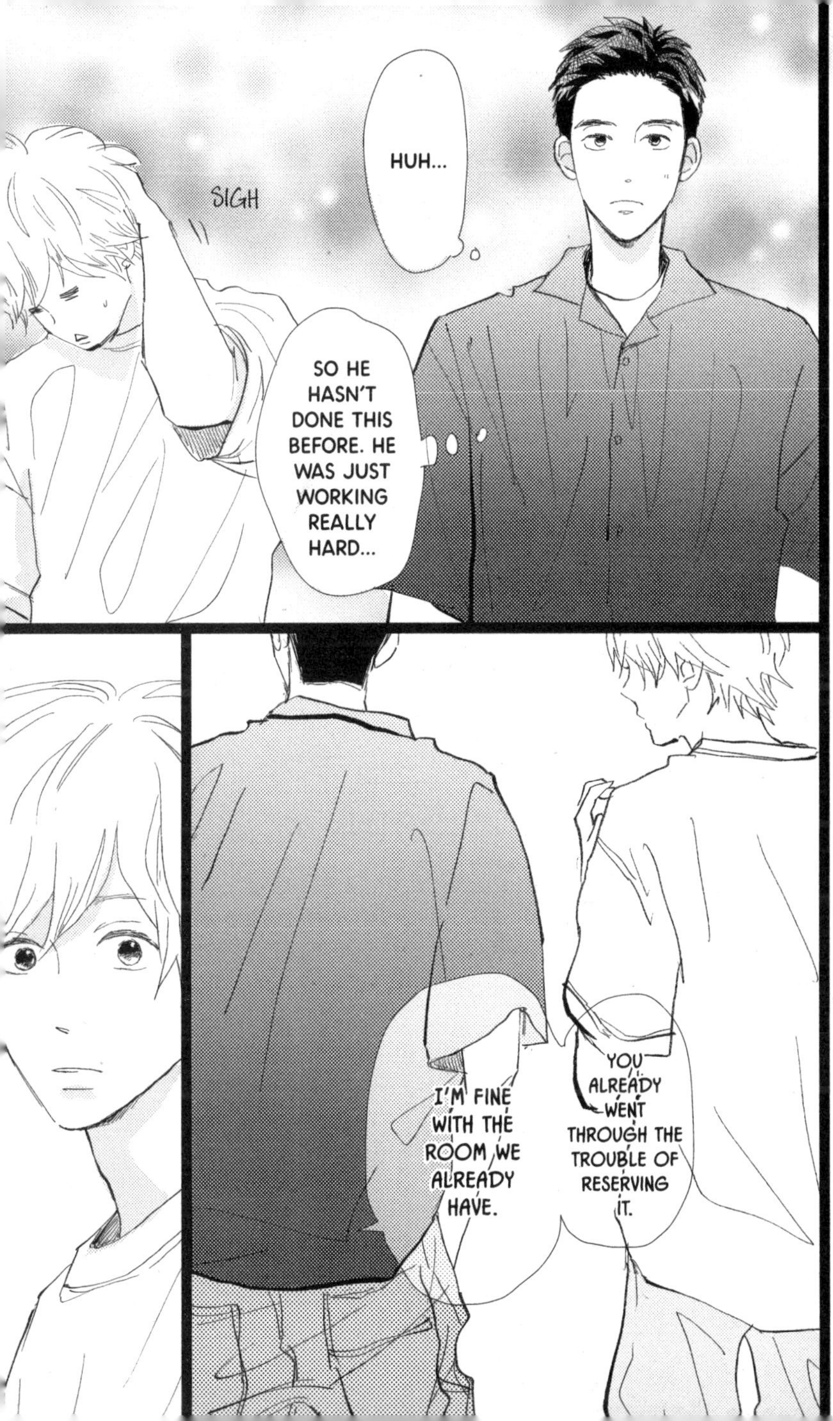
HUH...
SIGH
SO HE HASN'T DONE THIS BEFORE. HE WAS JUST WORKING REALLY HARD...
YOU ALREADY WENT THROUGH THE TROUBLE OF RESERVING IT.
I'M FINE WITH THE ROOM WE ALREADY HAVE.

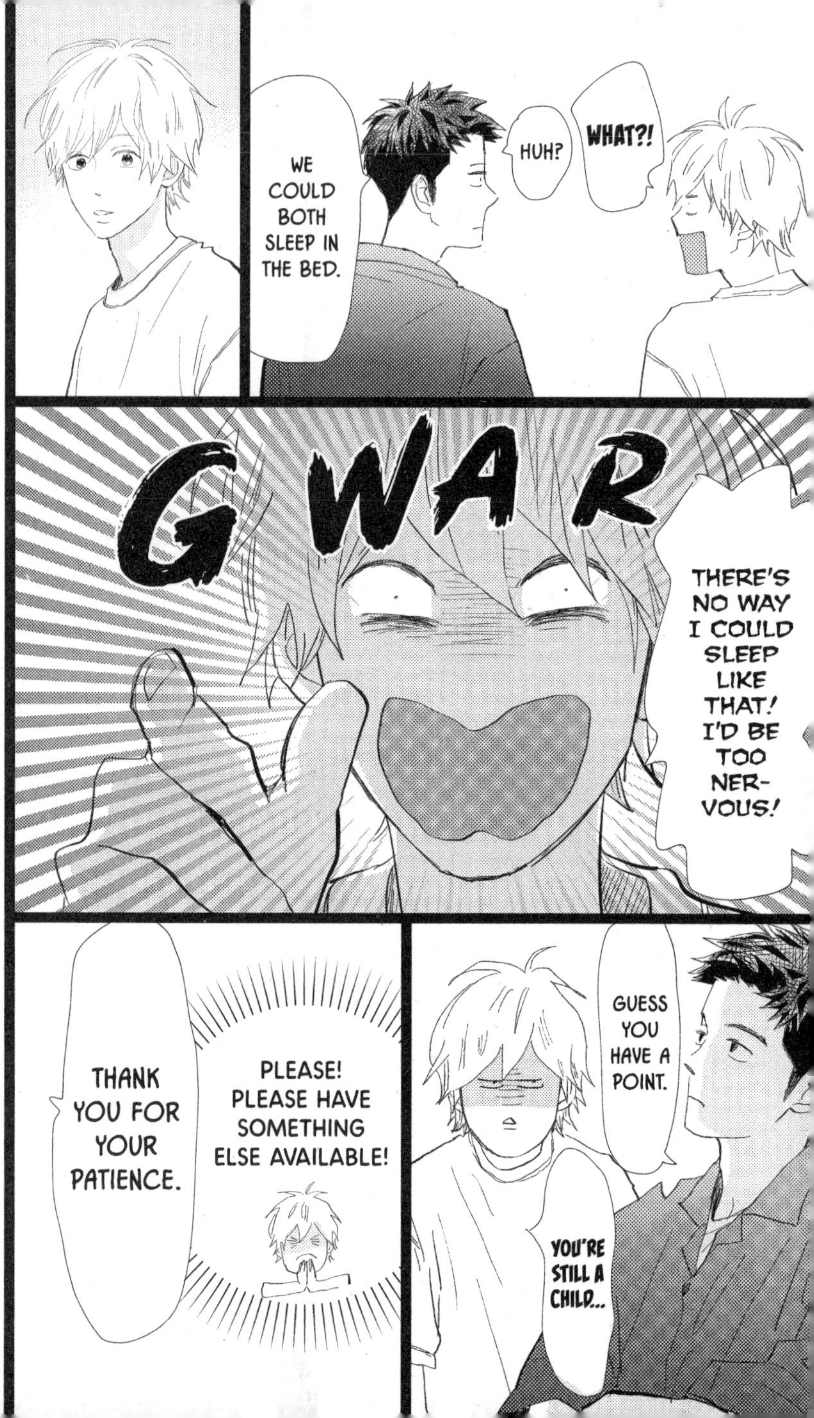
WE COULD BOTH SLEEP IN THE BED.
HUH?
WHAT?!
GWAR
THERE'S NO WAY I COULD SLEEP LIKE THAT! I'D BE TOO NERVOUS!
GUESS YOU HAVE A POINT.
YOU'RE STILL A CHILD...
PLEASE! PLEASE HAVE SOMETHING ELSE AVAILABLE!
THANK YOU FOR YOUR PATIENCE.

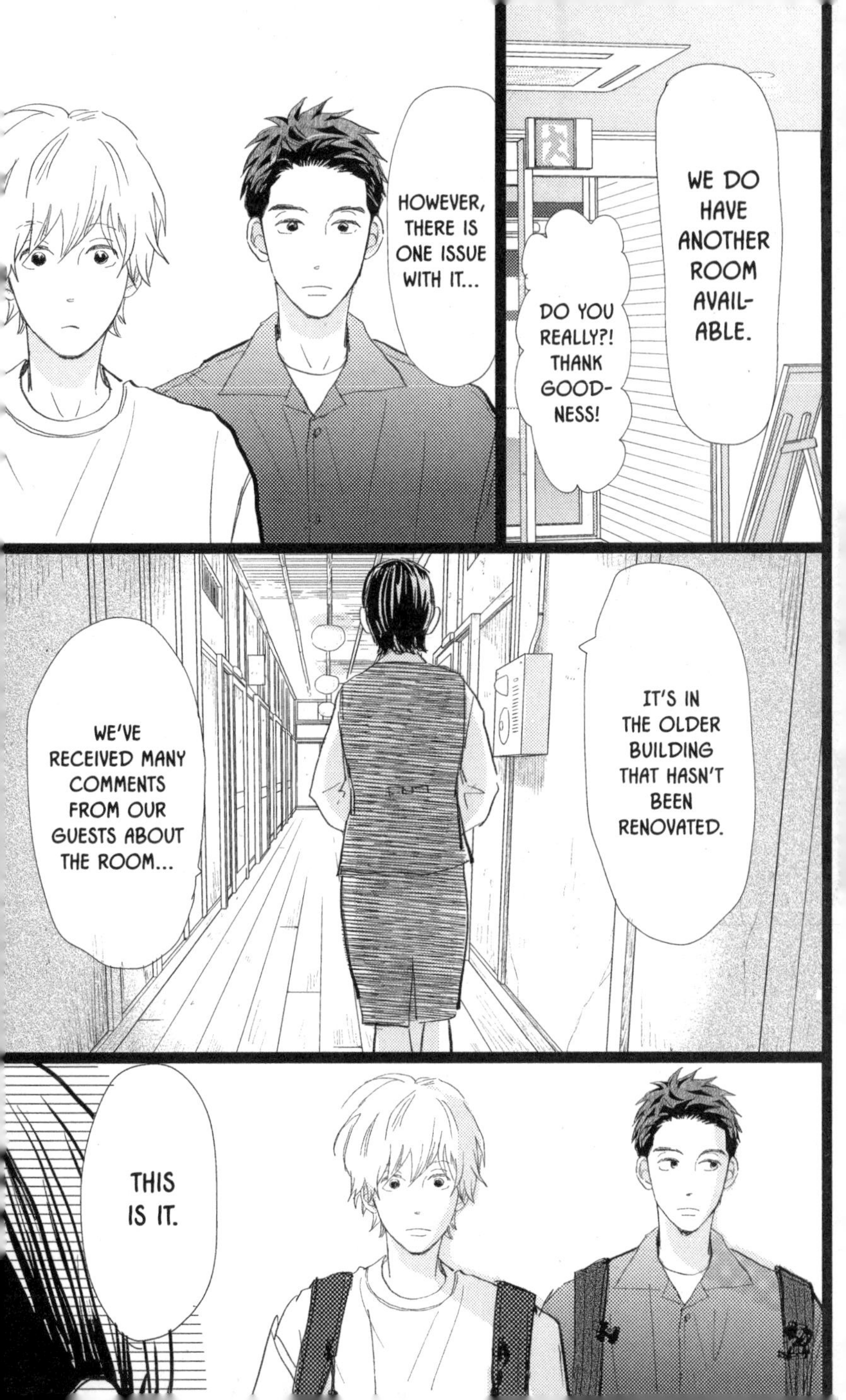
WE DO HAVE ANOTHER ROOM AVAIL-ABLE.
DO YOU REALLY?! THANK GOOD-NESS!
HOWEVER, THERE IS ONE ISSUE WITH IT...
IT'S IN THE OLDER BUILDING THAT HASN'T BEEN RENOVATED.
WE'VE RECEIVED MANY COMMENTS FROM OUR GUESTS ABOUT THE ROOM...
THIS IS IT.

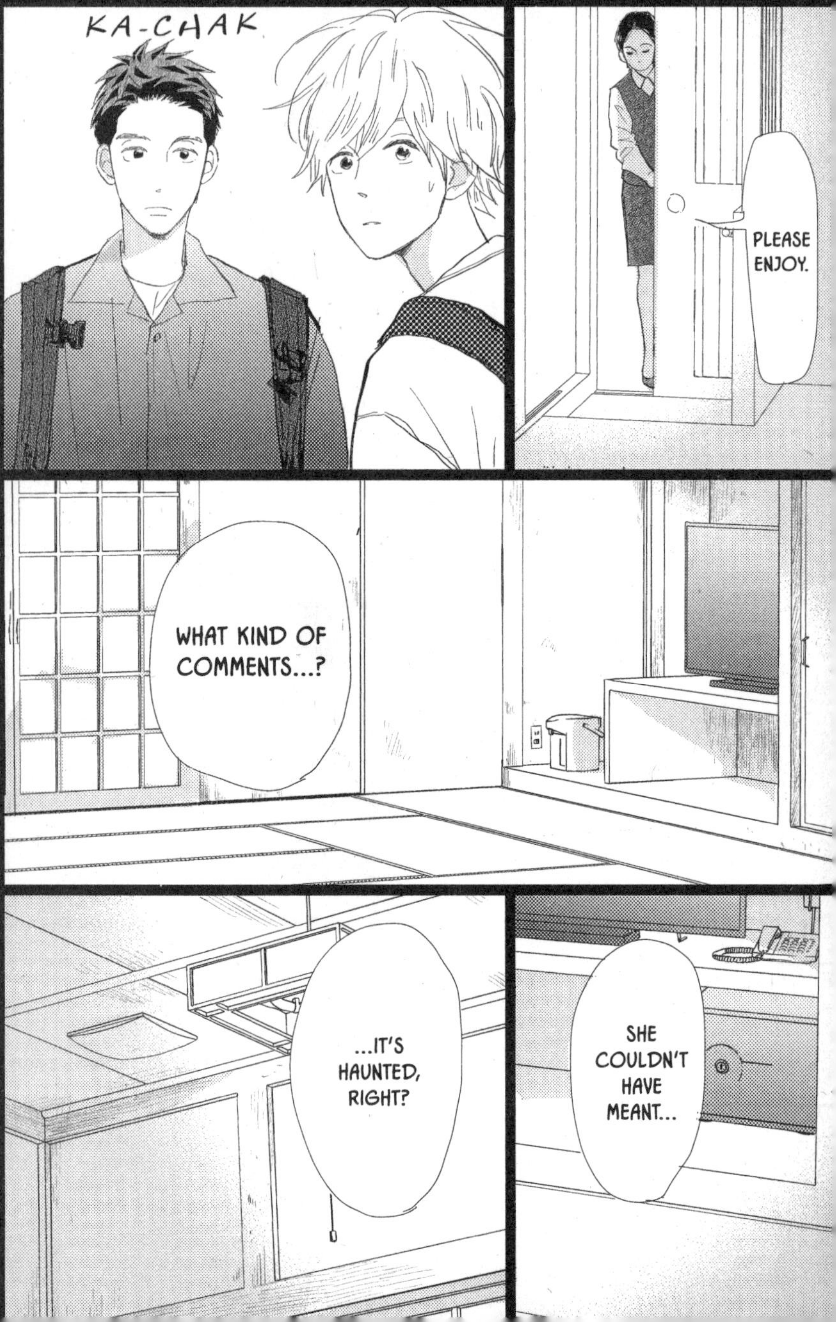
PLEASE ENJOY.
KA-CHAK
WHAT KIND OF COMMENTS...?
SHE COULDN'T HAVE MEANT...
...IT'S HAUNTED, RIGHT?

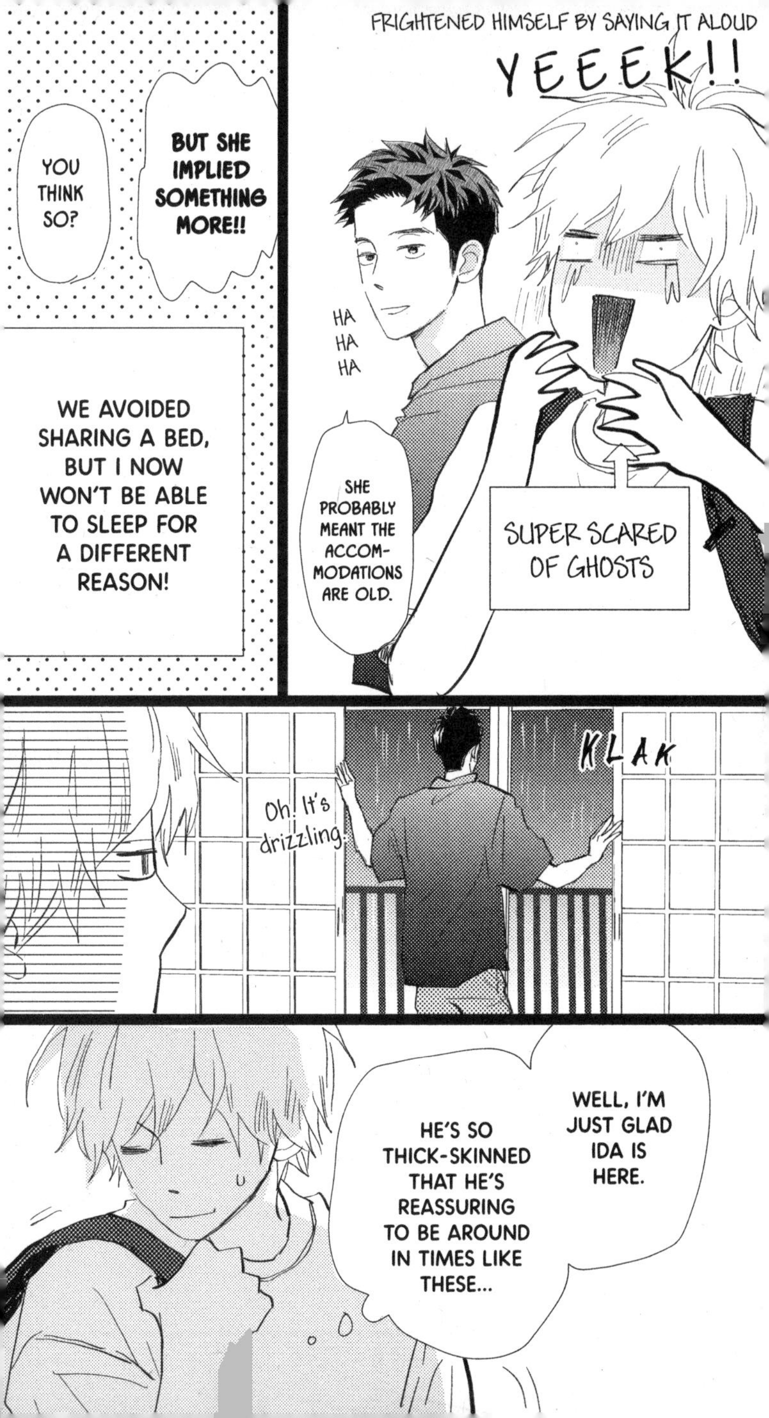
FRIGHTENED HIMSELF BY SAYING IT ALOUD
YEEEK!!
HA HA HA
SHE PROBABLY MEANT THE ACCOMMODATIONS ARE OLD.
SUPER SCARED OF GHOSTS
BUT SHE IMPLIED SOMETHING MORE!!
YOU THINK SO?
WE AVOIDED SHARING A BED, BUT I NOW WON'T BE ABLE TO SLEEP FOR A DIFFERENT REASON!
KLAK
Oh! It's drizzling.
WELL, I'M JUST GLAD IDA IS HERE.
HE'S SO THICK-SKINNED THAT HE'S REASSURING TO BE AROUND IN TIMES LIKE THESE...

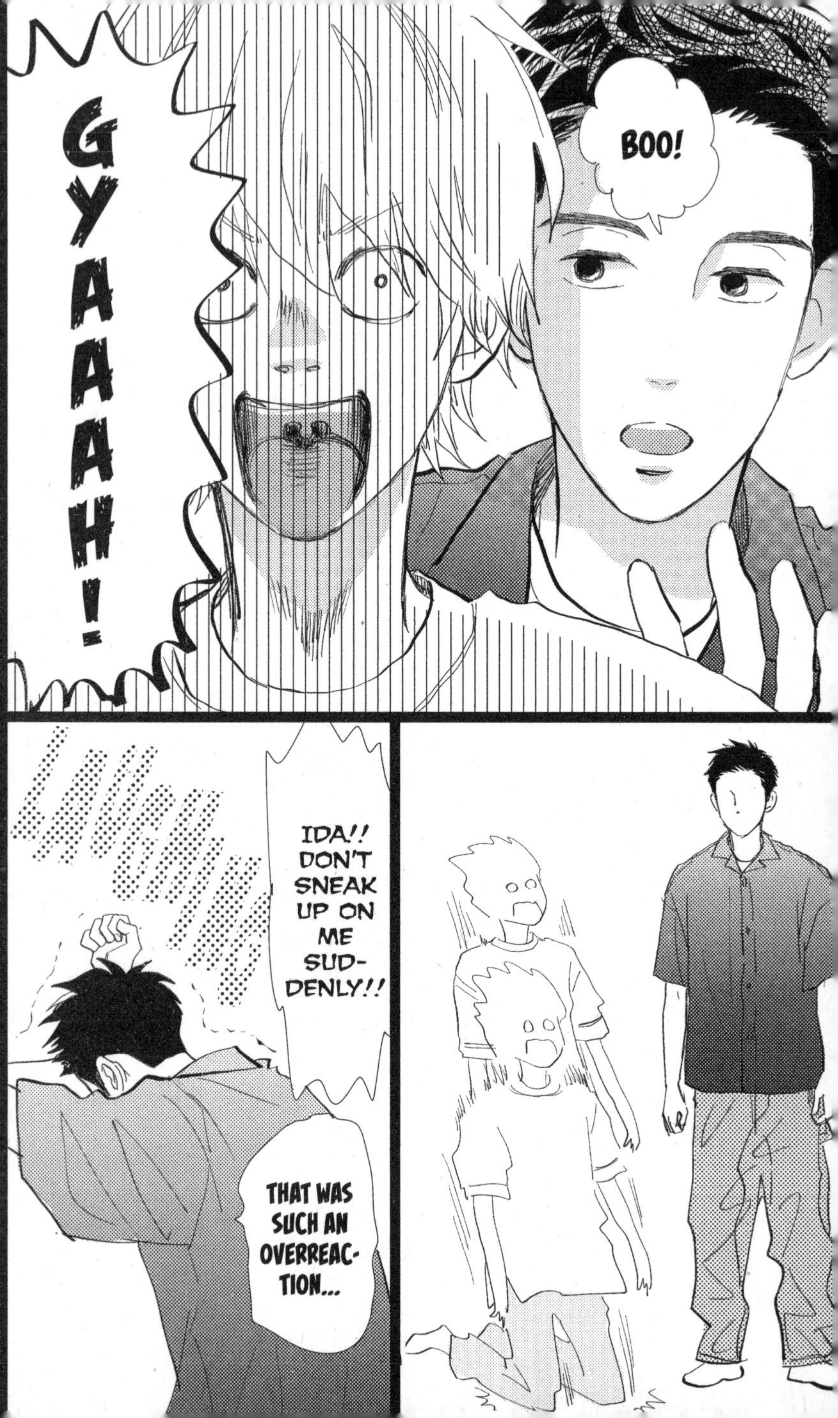
BOO!
GYAAAH!
IDA!! DON'T SNEAK UP ON ME SUD-DENLY!!
THAT WAS SUCH AN OVERREAC-TION...

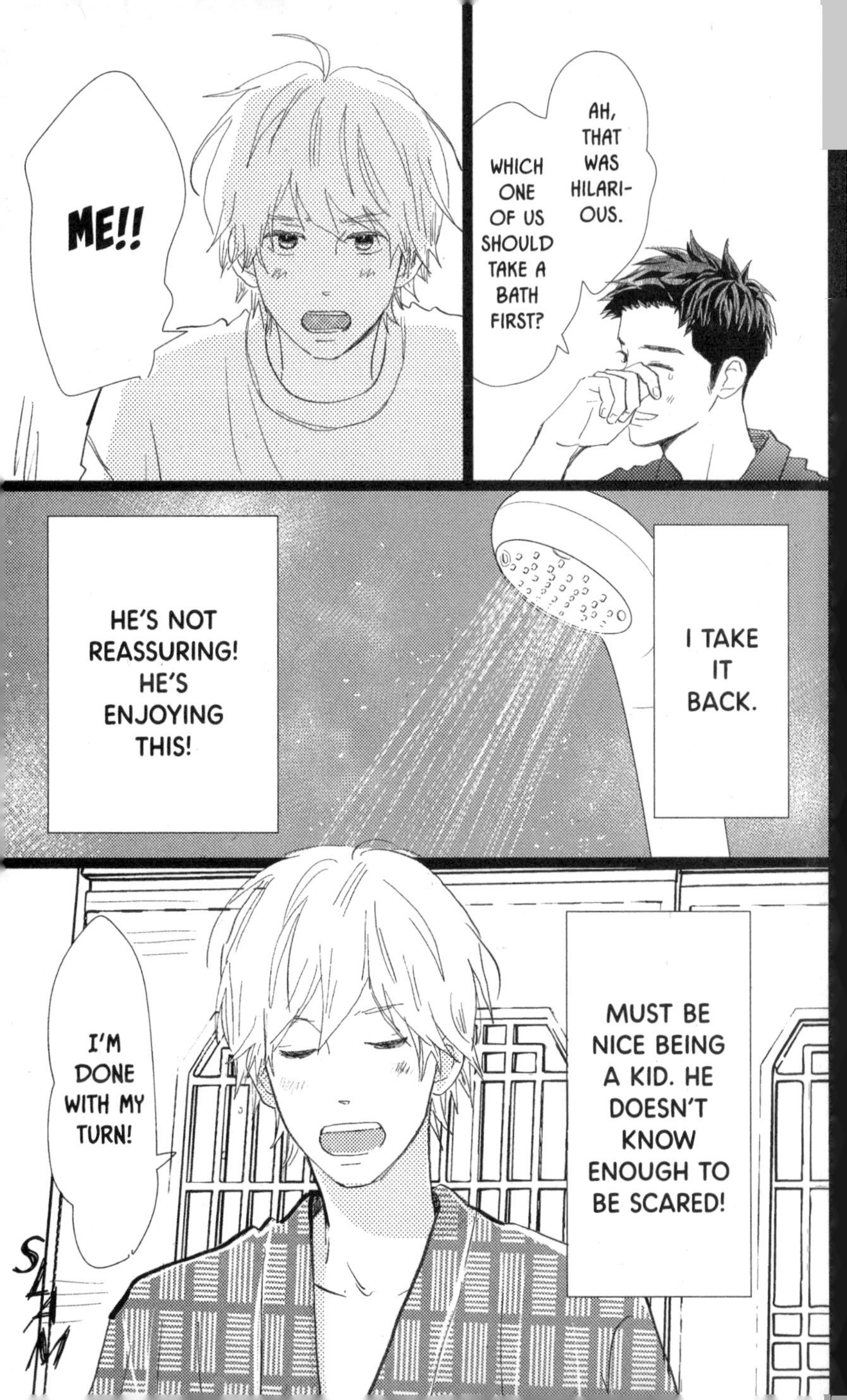
AH, THAT WAS HILARI-OUS.
WHICH ONE OF US SHOULD TAKE A BATH FIRST?
ME!!
I TAKE IT BACK.
HE'S NOT REASSURING! HE'S ENJOYING THIS!
MUST BE NICE BEING A KID. HE DOESN'T KNOW ENOUGH TO BE SCARED!
I'M DONE WITH MY TURN!
SLAM

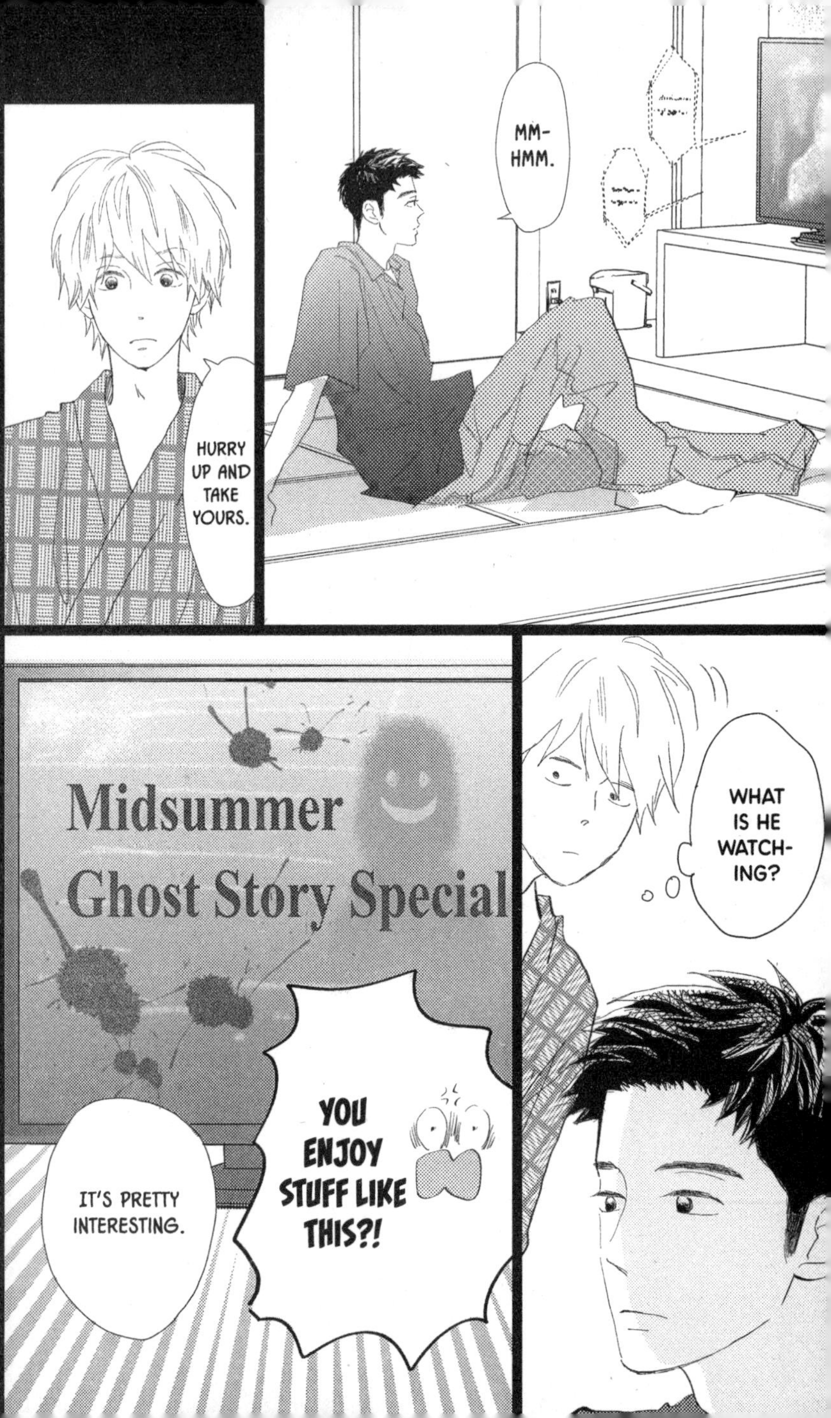
MM-HMM.
HURRY UP AND TAKE YOURS.
WHAT IS HE WATCHING?
Midsummer Ghost Story Special
YOU ENJOY STUFF LIKE THIS?!
IT'S PRETTY INTERESTING.

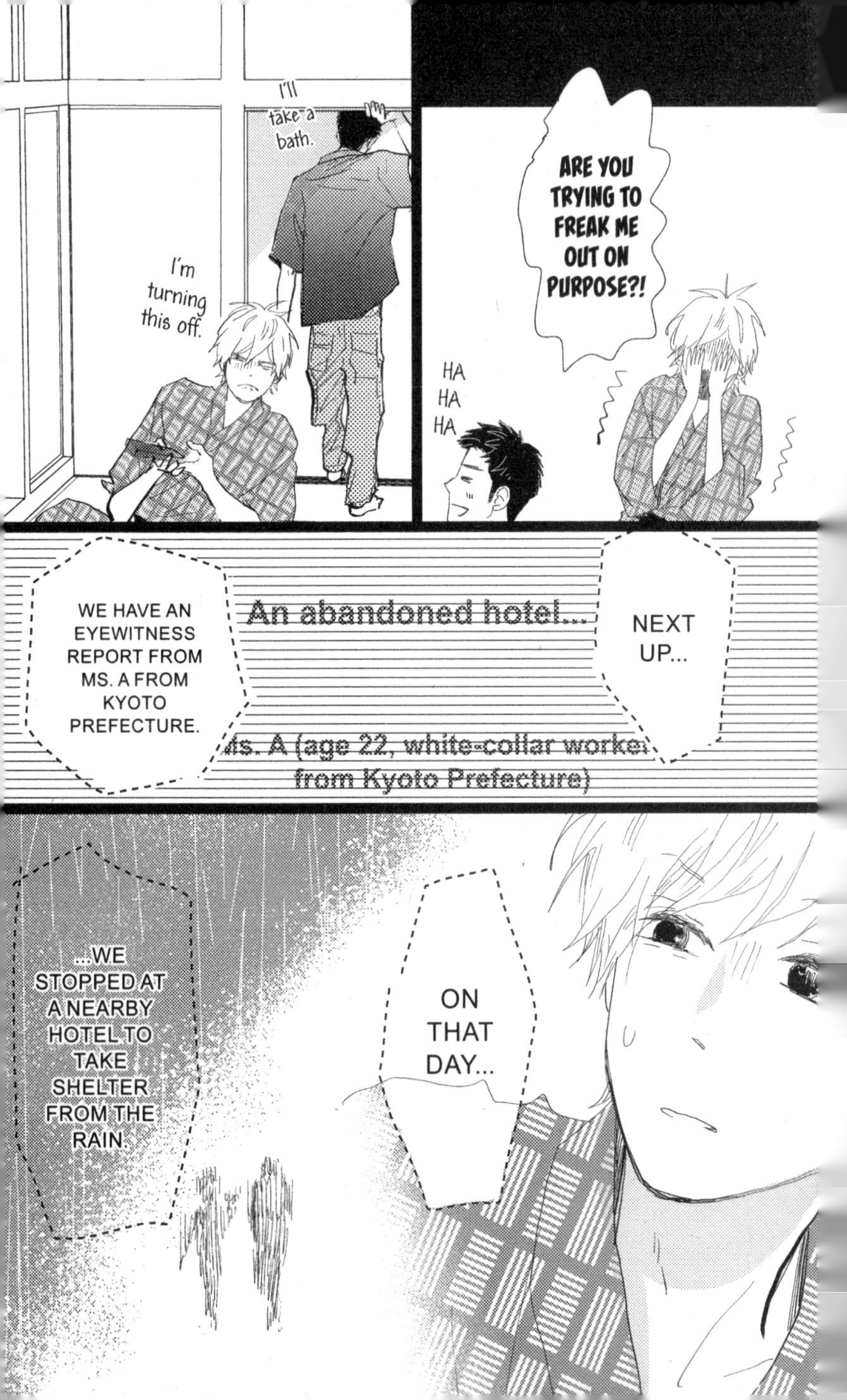
ARE YOU TRYING TO FREAK ME OUT ON PURPOSE?!
HA HA HA
I'll take a bath.
I'm turning this off.
NEXT UP...
An abandoned hotel...
WE HAVE AN EYEWITNESS REPORT FROM MS. A FROM KYOTO PREFECTURE.
Ms. A (age 22, white-collar worker from Kyoto Prefecture)
ON THAT DAY...
...WE STOPPED AT A NEARBY HOTEL TO TAKE SHELTER FROM THE RAIN.

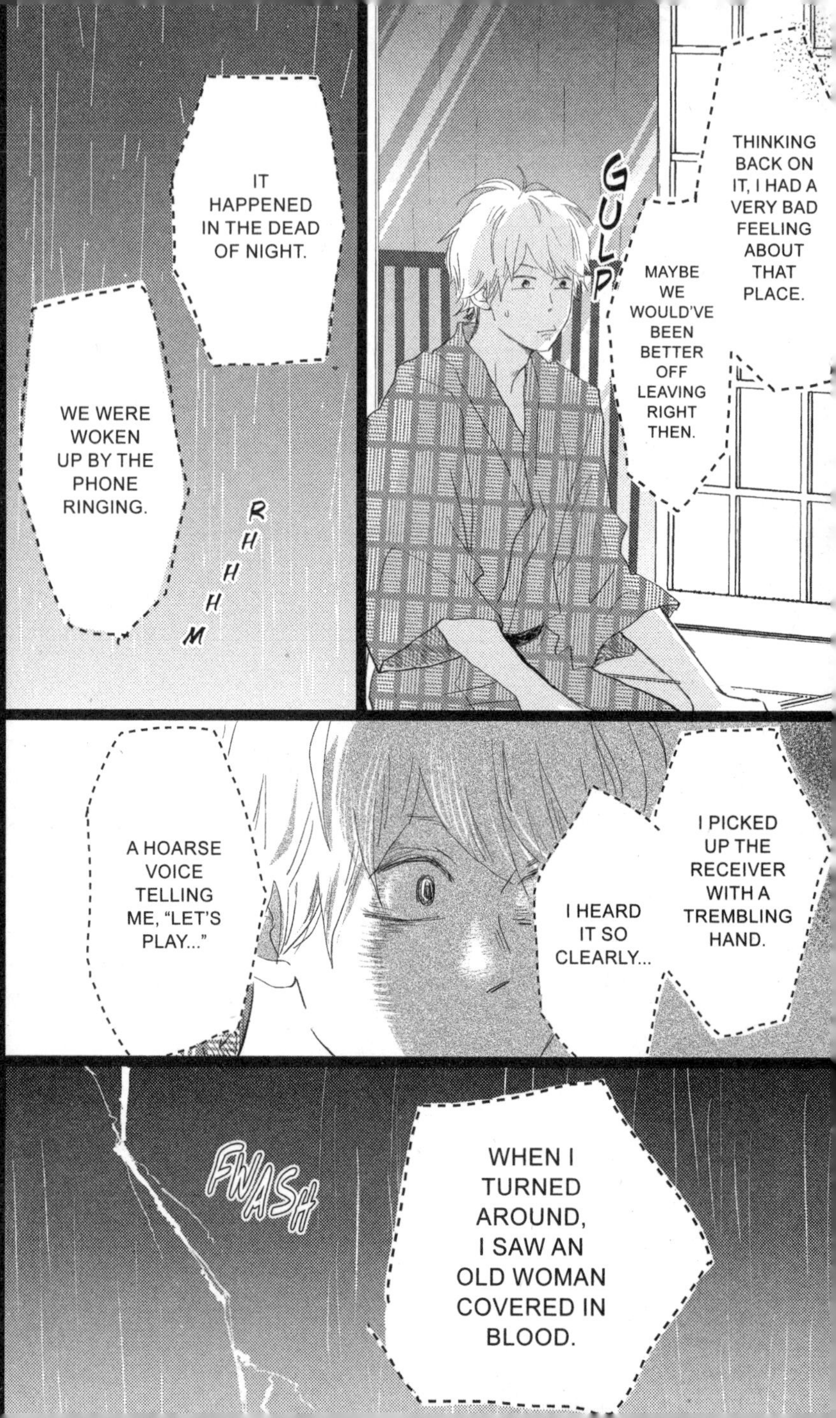
THINKING BACK ON IT, I HAD A VERY BAD FEELING ABOUT THAT PLACE.
GULP
MAYBE WE WOULD'VE BEEN BETTER OFF LEAVING RIGHT THEN.
IT HAPPENED IN THE DEAD OF NIGHT.
RHHHM
WE WERE WOKEN UP BY THE PHONE RINGING.
I PICKED UP THE RECEIVER WITH A TREMBLING HAND.
I HEARD IT SO CLEARLY...
A HOARSE VOICE TELLING ME, "LET'S PLAY..."
WHEN I TURNED AROUND, I SAW AN OLD WOMAN COVERED IN BLOOD.
FWASH

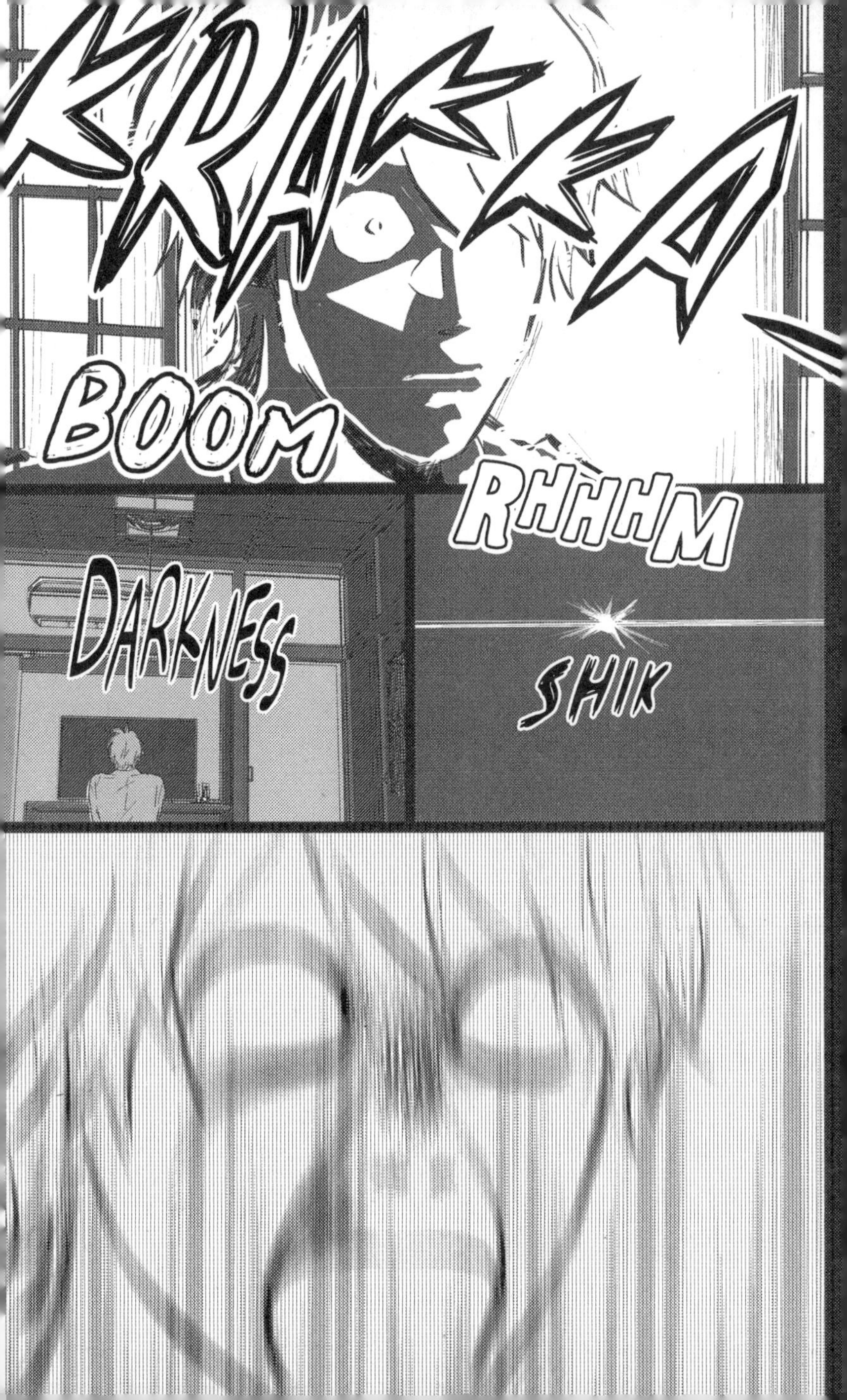
KRAKKA
BOOM
RHHHM
SHIK
DARKNESS

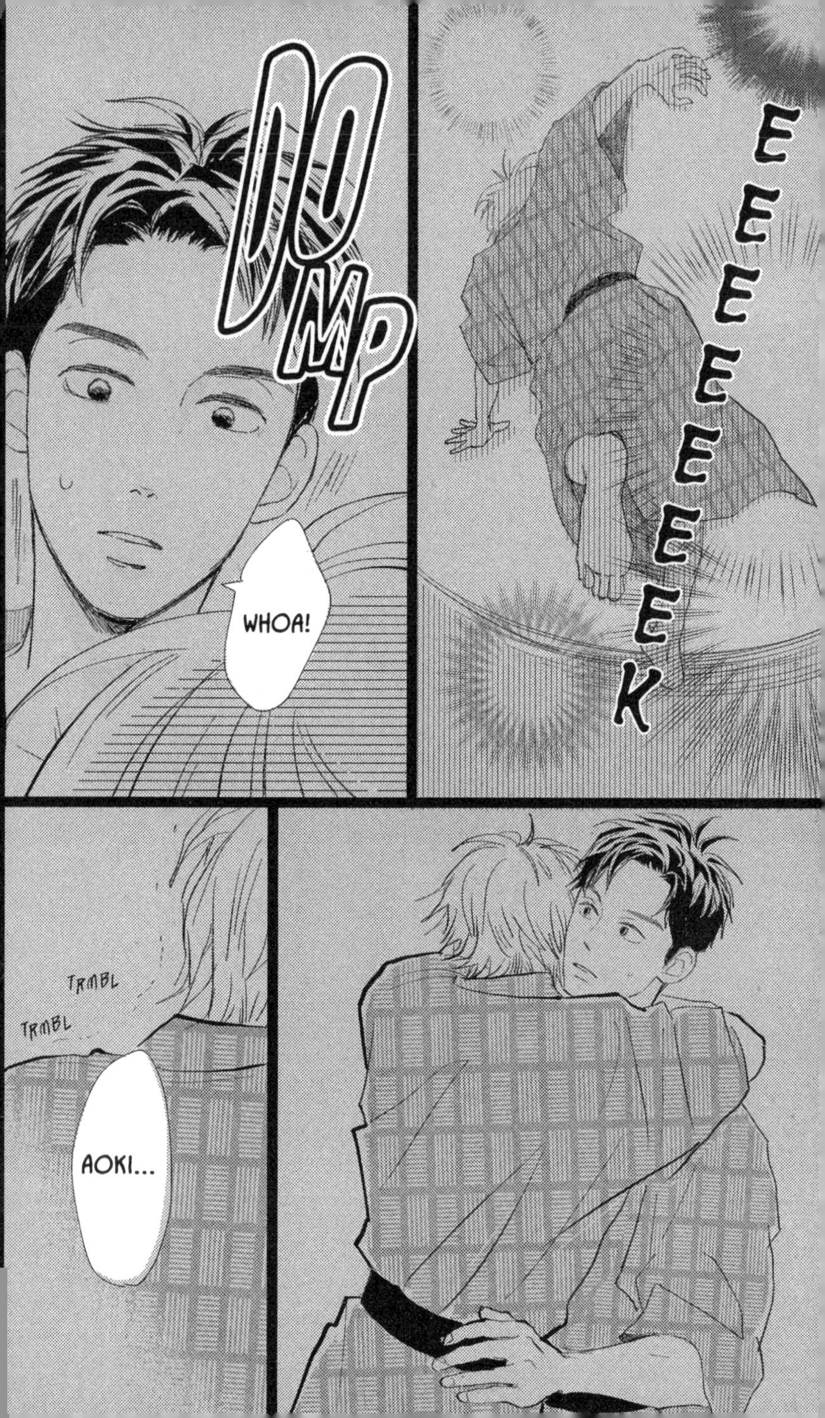
EEEEEEEK
DOMP
WHOA!
TRMBL
TRMBL
AOKI...

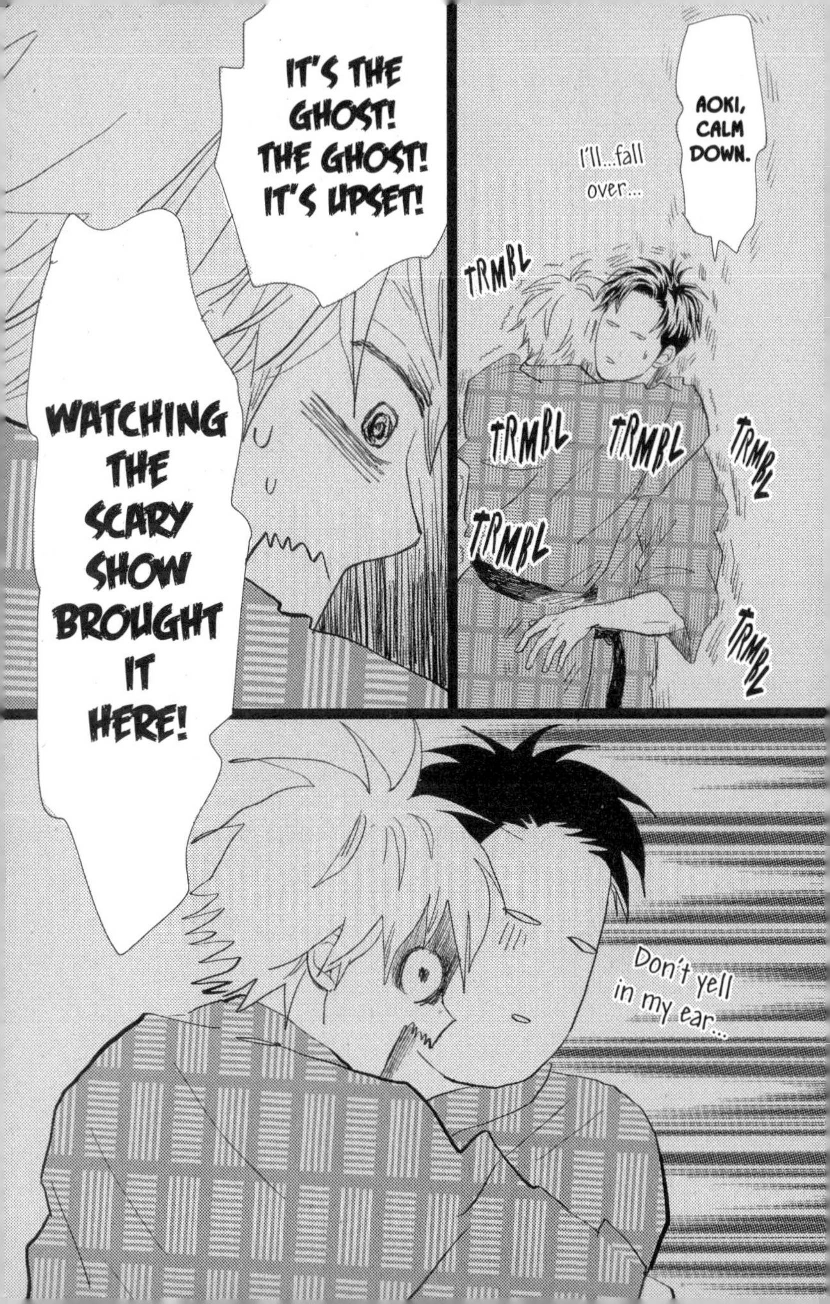
AOKI, CALM DOWN.
I'll...fall over...
TRMBL
TRMBL
TRMBL
TRMBL
TRMBL
TRMBL
IT'S THE GHOST! THE GHOST! IT'S UPSET!
WATCHING THE SCARY SHOW BROUGHT IT HERE!
Don't yell in my ear...

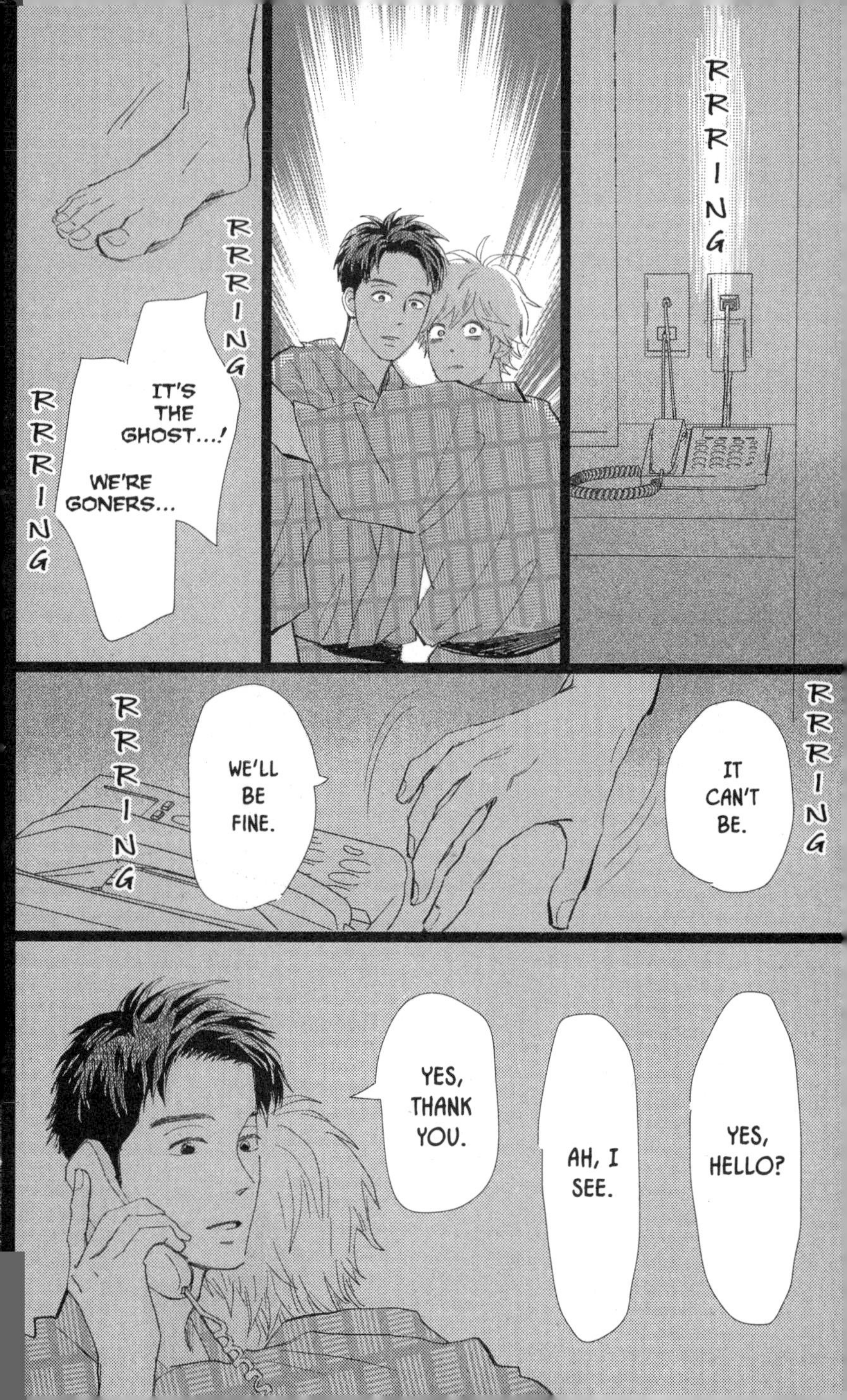
RRRING
RRRING
IT'S THE GHOST...!
WE'RE GONERS...
RRRING
RRRING
IT CAN'T BE.
WE'LL BE FINE.
RRRING
YES, HELLO?
AH, I SEE.
YES, THANK YOU.

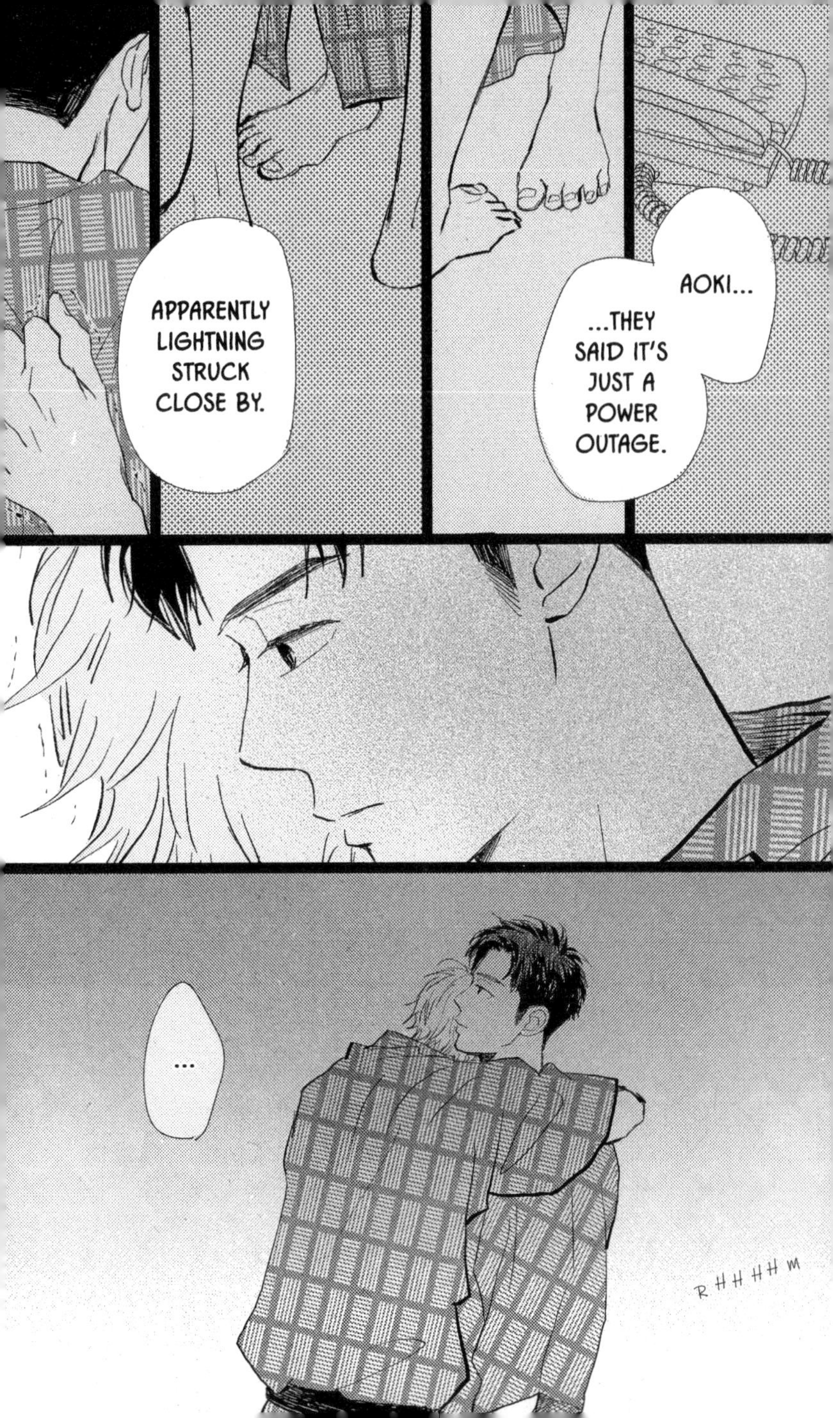
AOKI...
...THEY SAID IT'S JUST A POWER OUTAGE.
APPARENTLY LIGHTNING STRUCK CLOSE BY.
...
RHHHHM

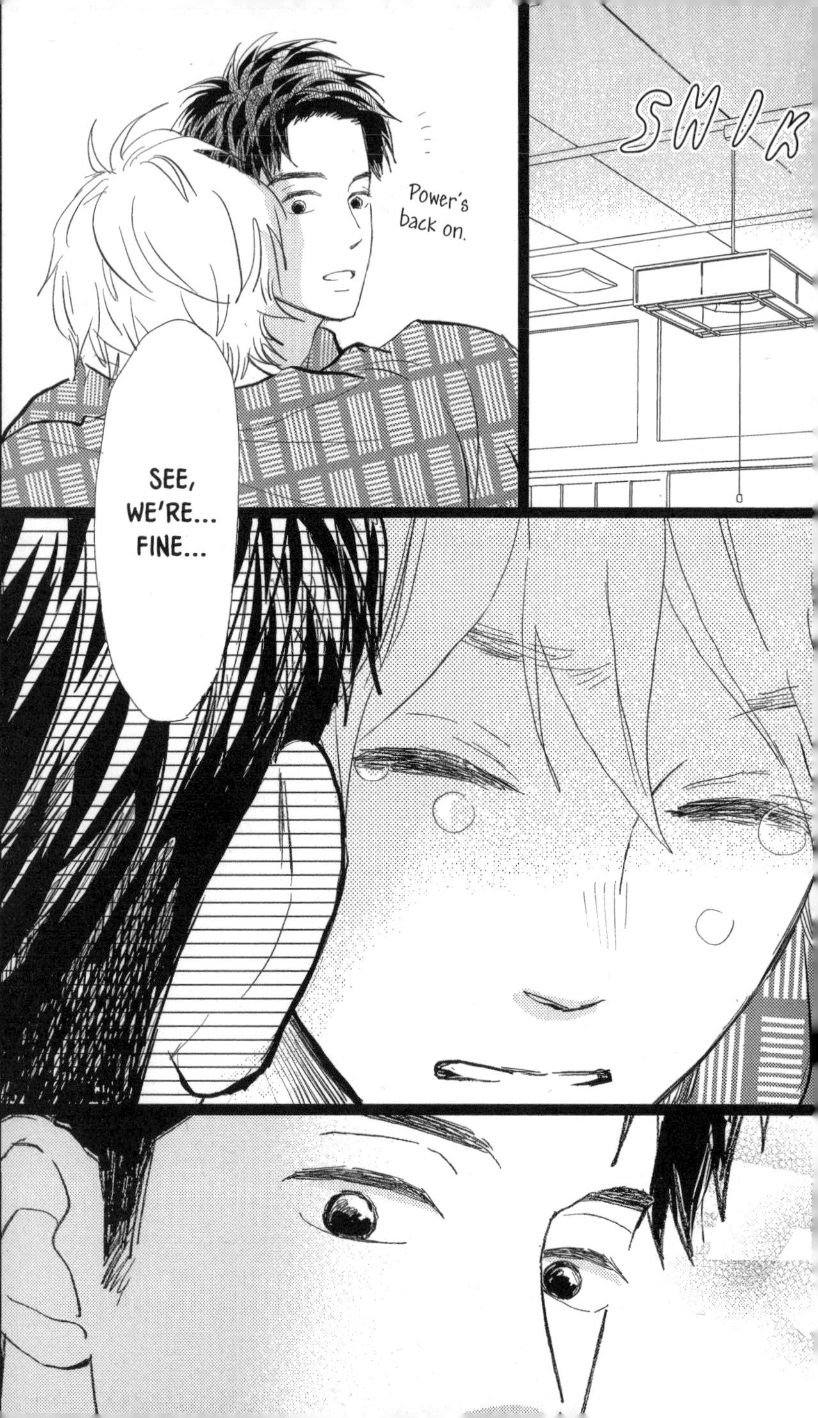
SHIK
Power's back on.
SEE, WE'RE... FINE...

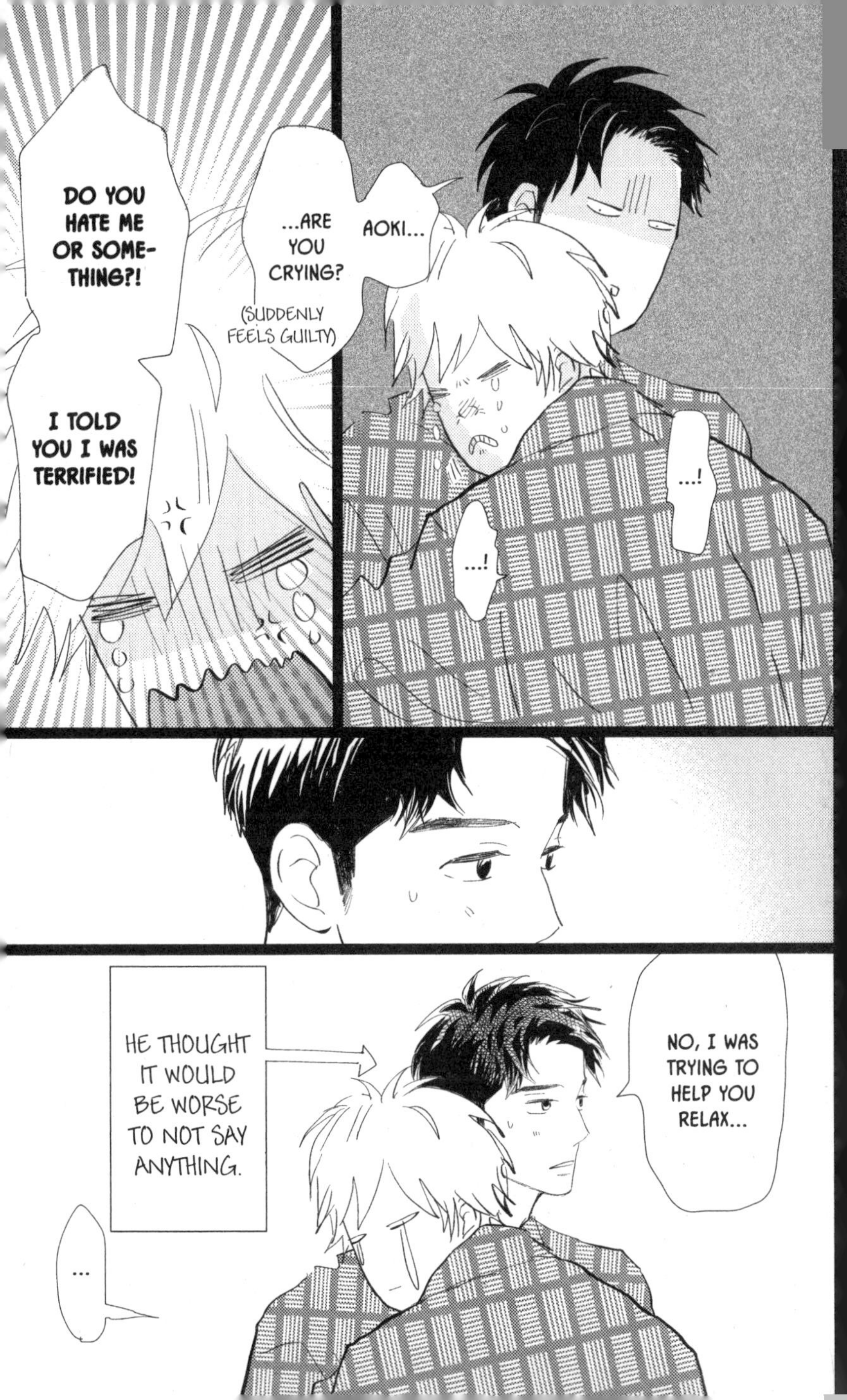
AOKI...
...ARE YOU CRYING?
(SUDDENLY FEELS GUILTY)
...!
...!
DO YOU HATE ME OR SOME-THING?!
I TOLD YOU I WAS TERRIFIED!
NO, I WAS TRYING TO HELP YOU RELAX...
HE THOUGHT IT WOULD BE WORSE TO NOT SAY ANYTHING.
...

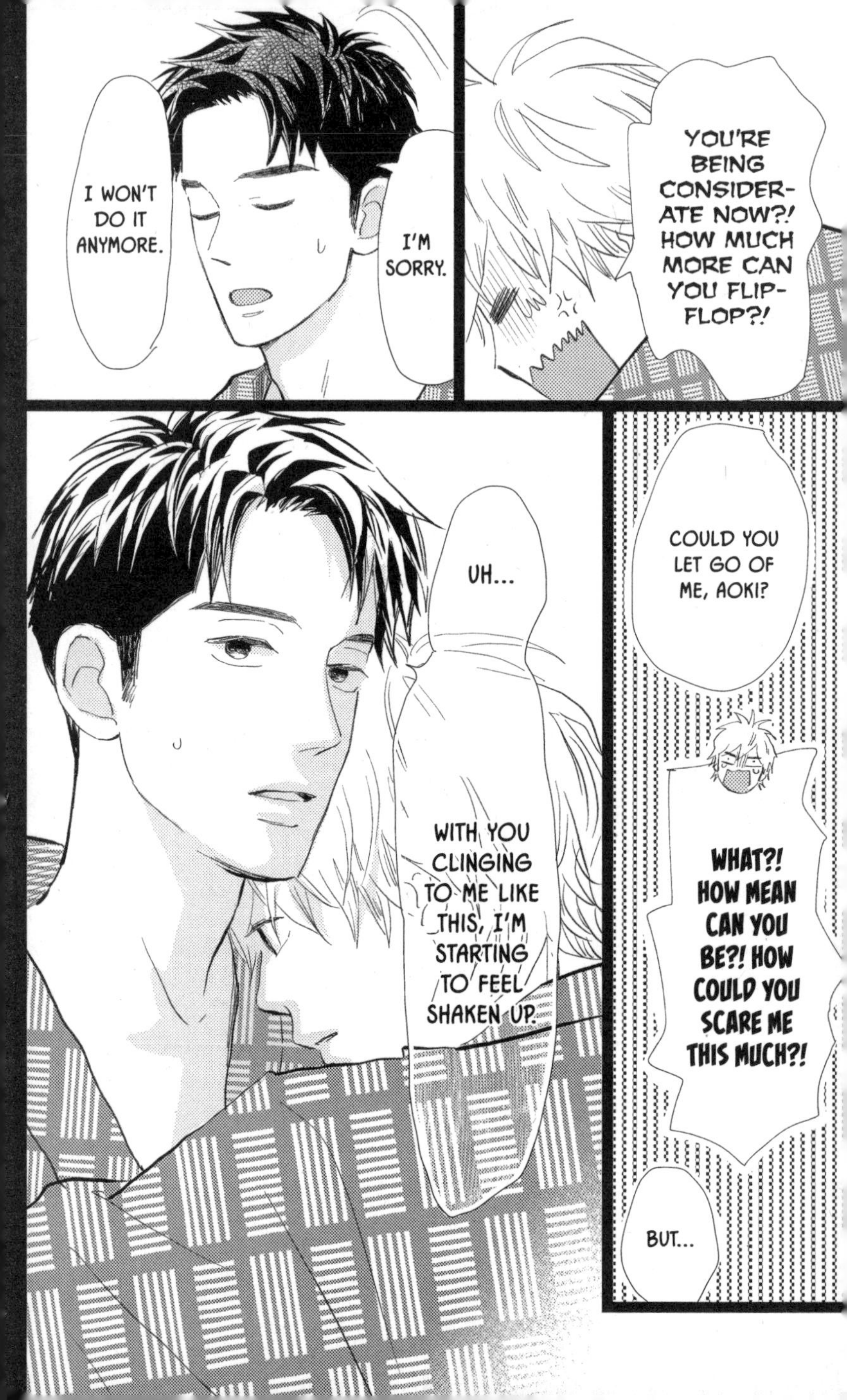
YOU'RE BEING CONSIDER-ATE NOW?! HOW MUCH MORE CAN YOU FLIP-FLOP?!
I'M SORRY.
I WON'T DO IT ANYMORE.
COULD YOU LET GO OF ME, AOKI?
WHAT?! HOW MEAN CAN YOU BE?! HOW COULD YOU SCARE ME THIS MUCH?!
BUT...
UH...
WITH YOU CLINGING TO ME LIKE THIS, I'M STARTING TO FEEL SHAKEN UP.

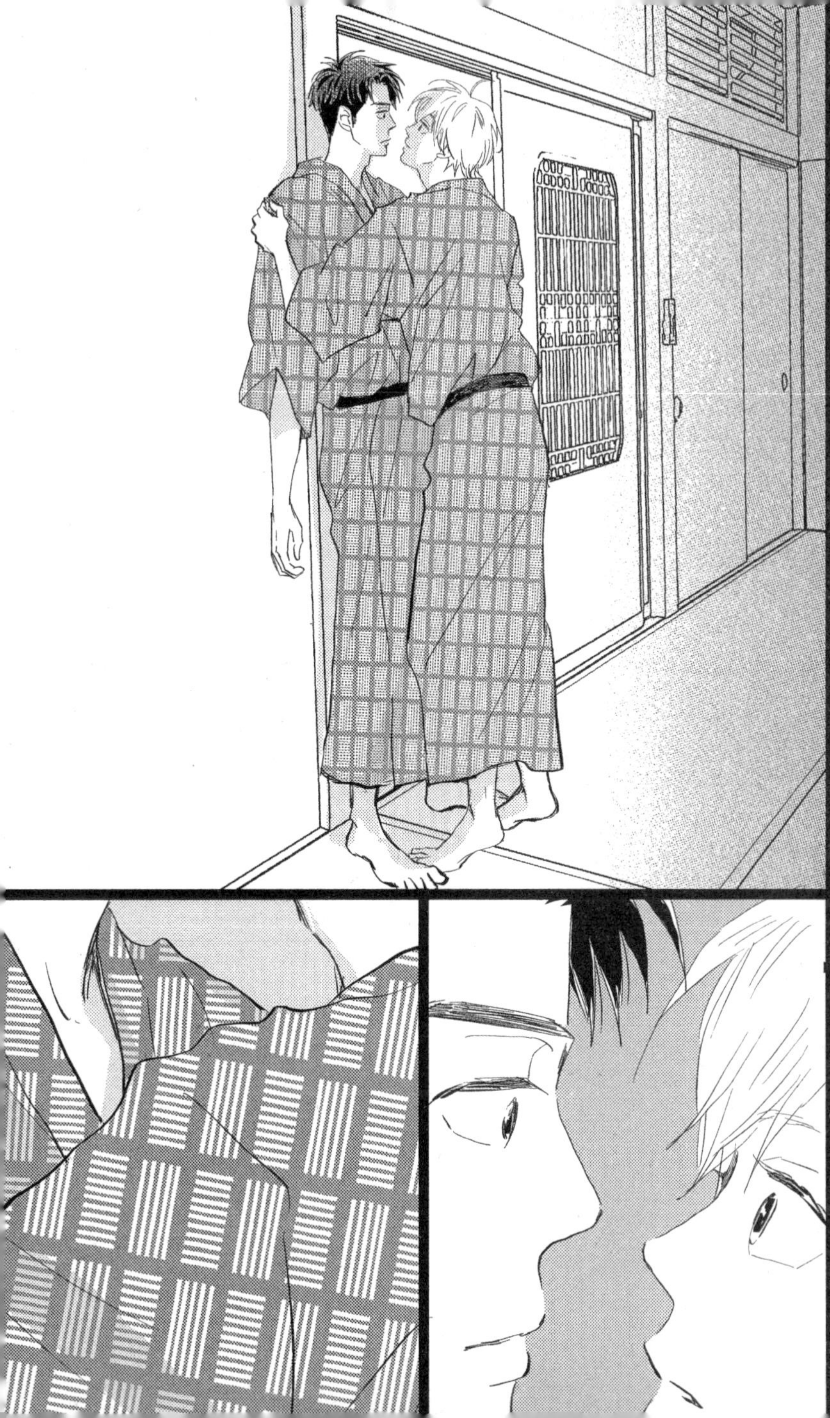

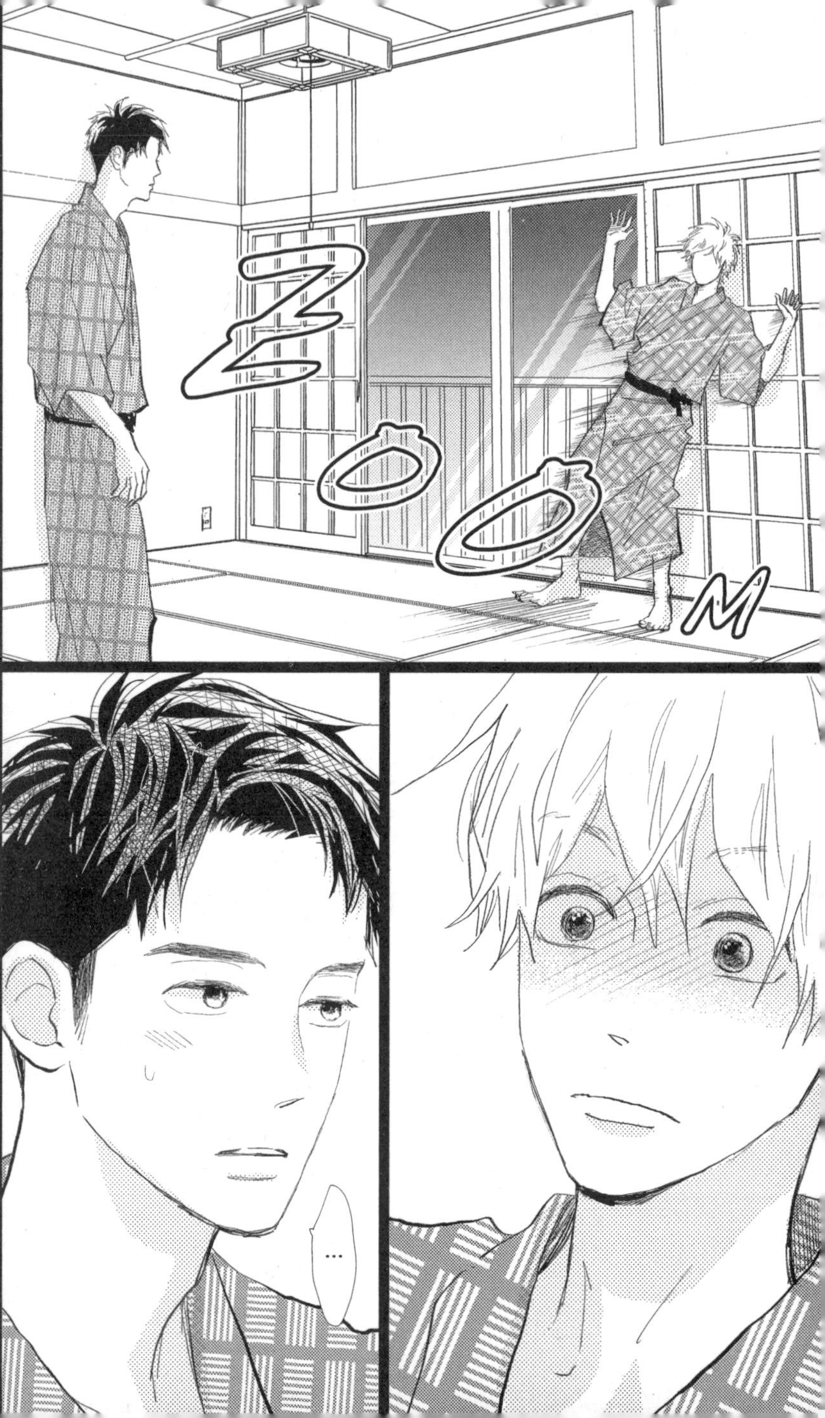
ZOOOM
...

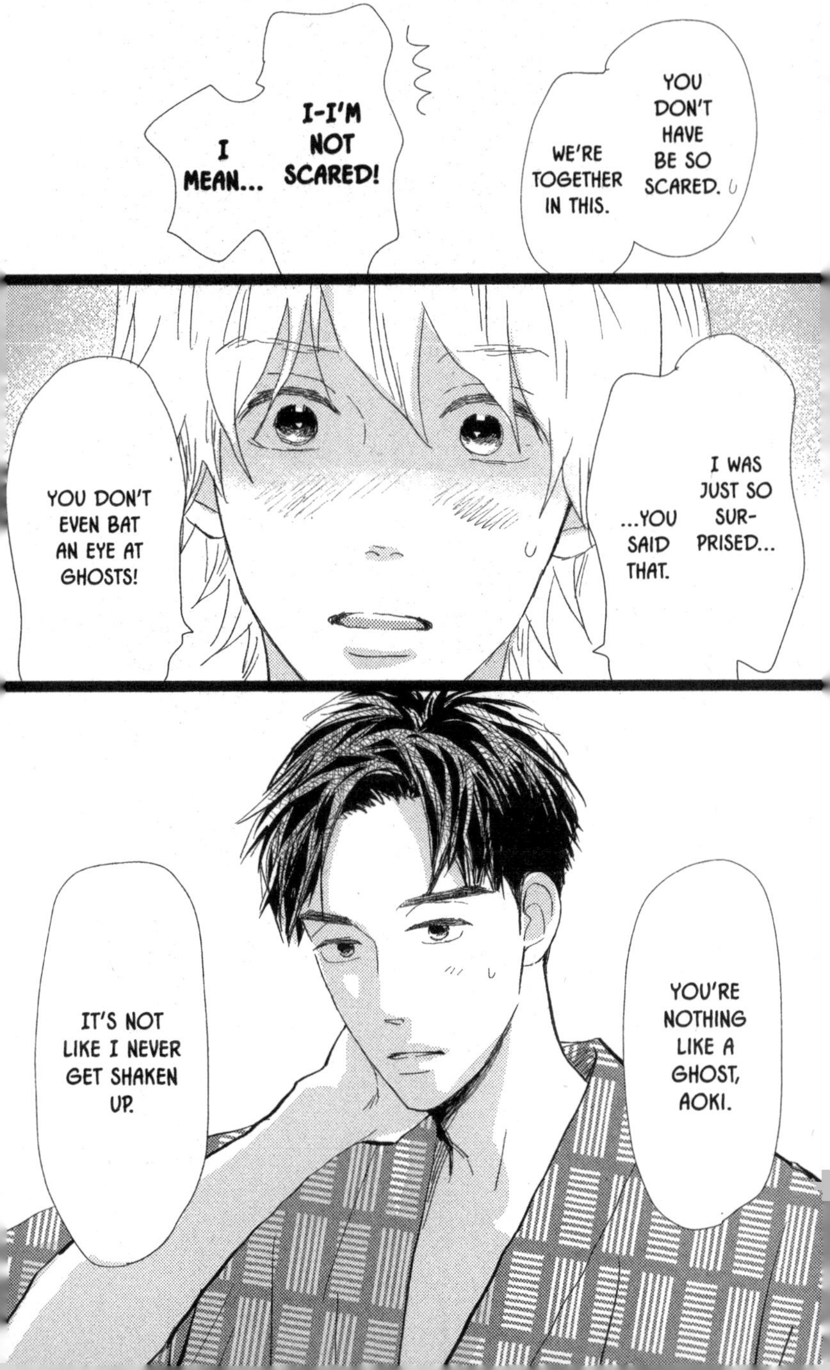
YOU DON'T HAVE BE SO SCARED.
WE'RE TOGETHER IN THIS.
I-I'M NOT SCARED!
I MEAN...
I WAS JUST SO SURPRISED...
...YOU SAID THAT.
YOU DON'T EVEN BAT AN EYE AT GHOSTS!
YOU'RE NOTHING LIKE A GHOST, AOKI.
IT'S NOT LIKE I NEVER GET SHAKEN UP.

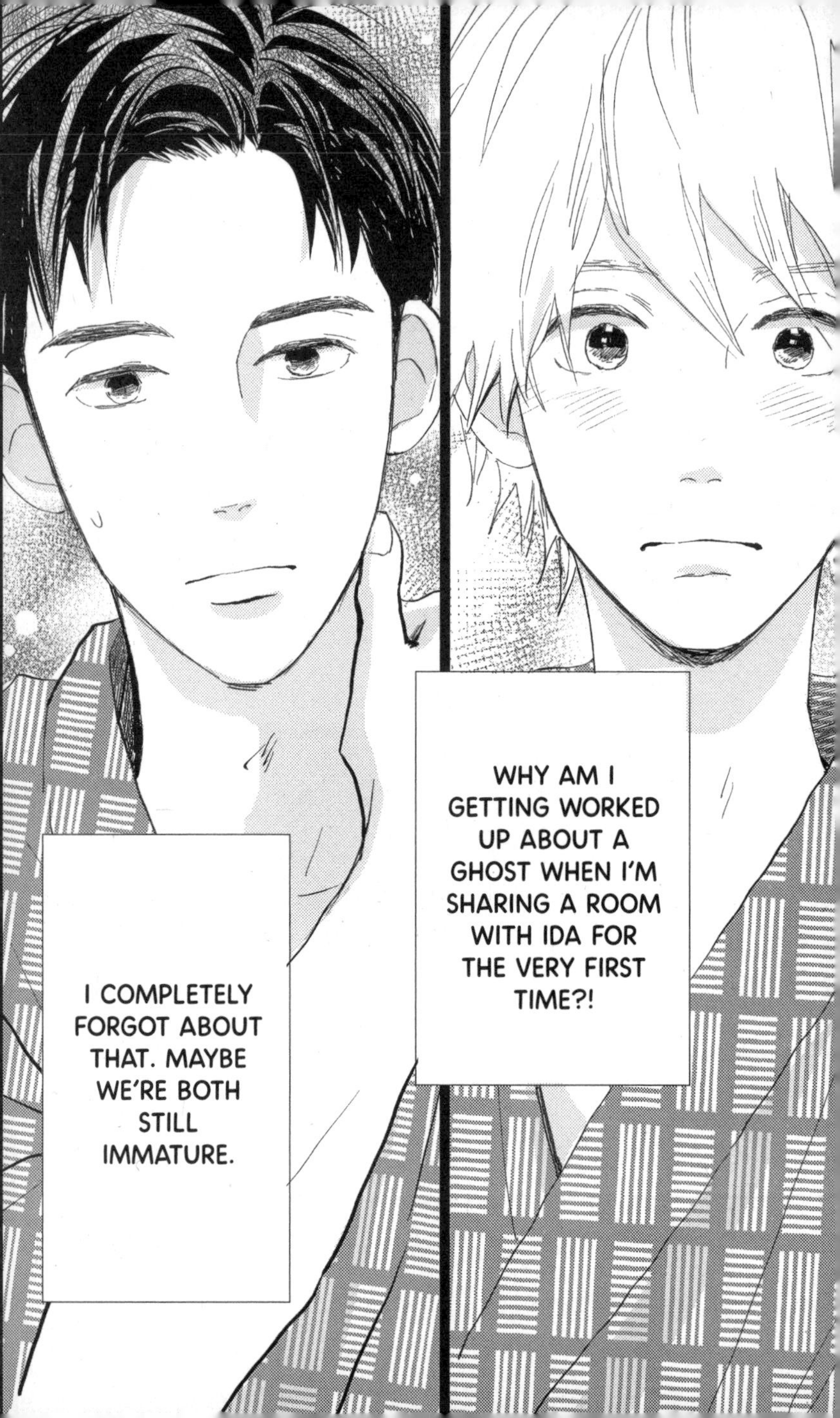
WHY AM I GETTING WORKED UP ABOUT A GHOST WHEN I'M SHARING A ROOM WITH IDA FOR THE VERY FIRST TIME?!
I COMPLETELY FORGOT ABOUT THAT. MAYBE WE'RE BOTH STILL IMMATURE.

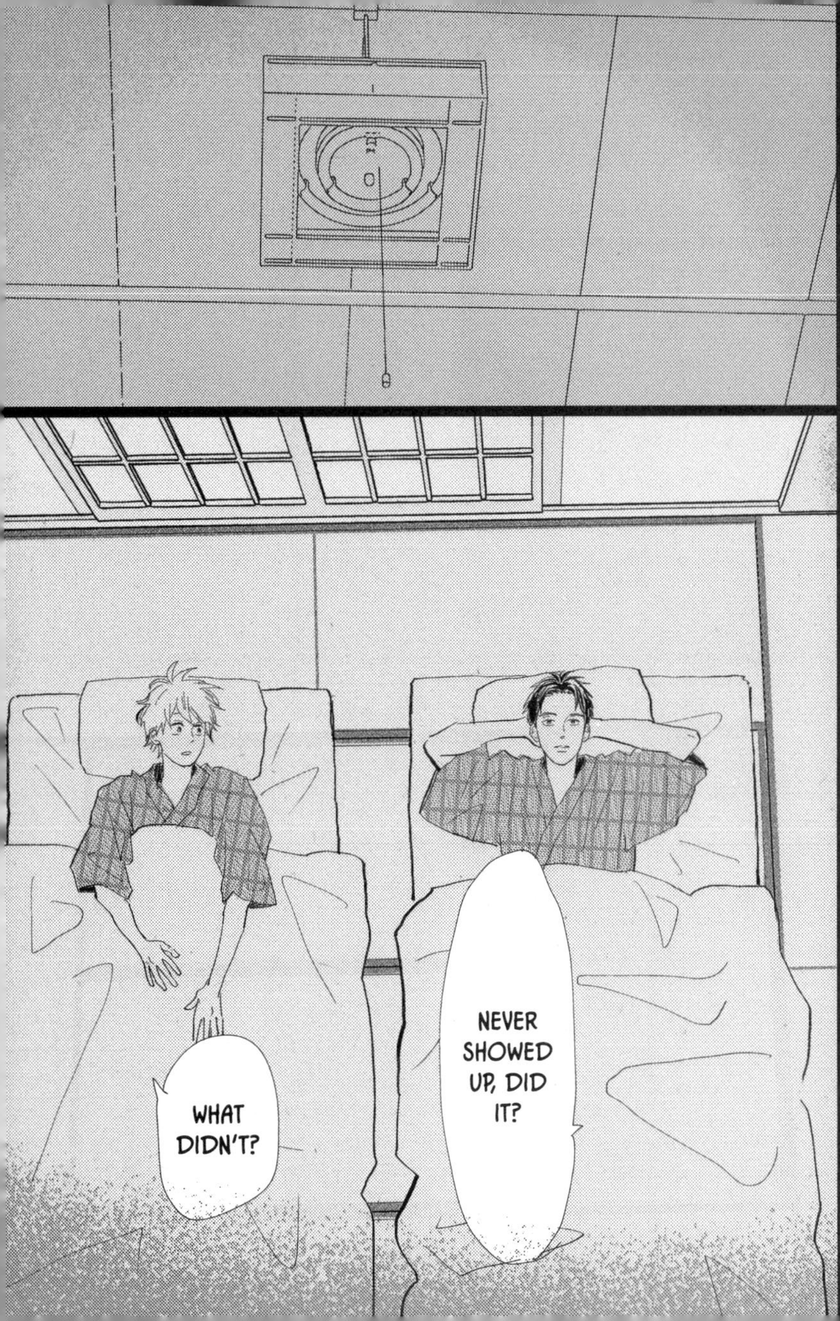
NEVER SHOWED UP, DID IT?
WHAT DIDN'T?

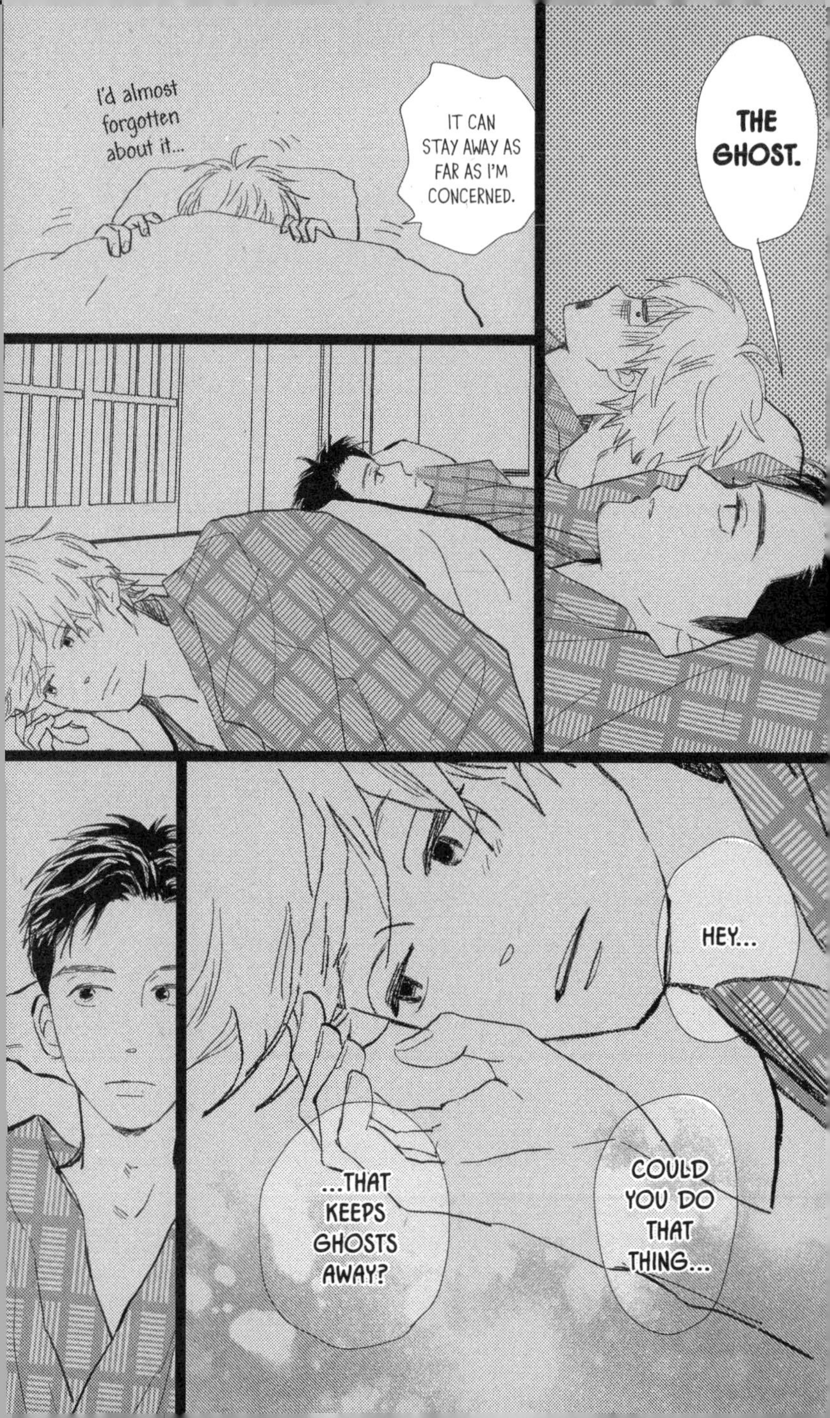
THE GHOST.
IT CAN STAY AWAY AS FAR AS I'M CONCERNED.
I'd almost forgotten about it...
HEY...
COULD YOU DO THAT THING...
...THAT KEEPS GHOSTS AWAY?

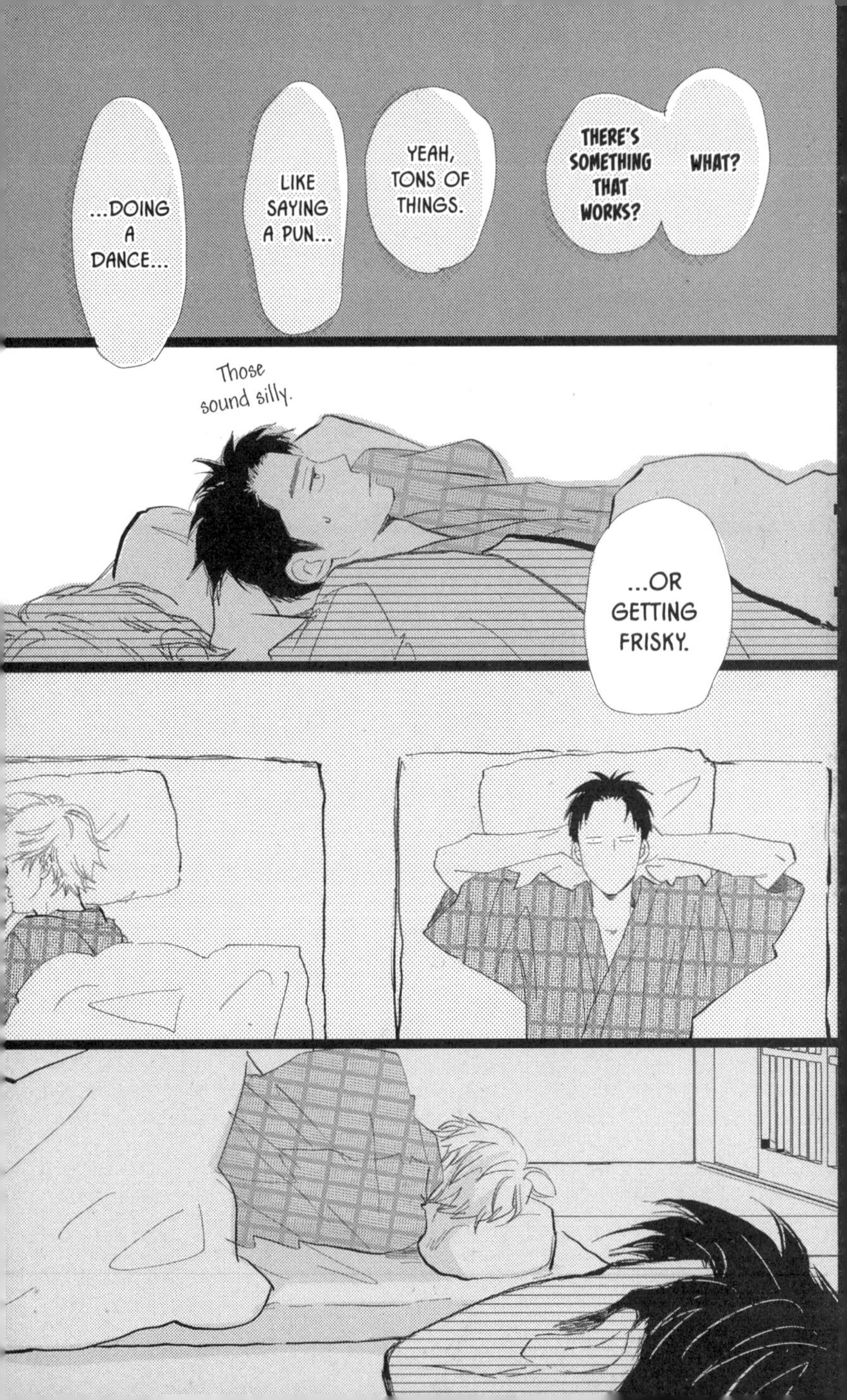
WHAT?
THERE'S SOMETHING THAT WORKS?
YEAH, TONS OF THINGS.
LIKE SAYING A PUN...
...DOING A DANCE...
...OR GETTING FRISKY.
Those sound silly.

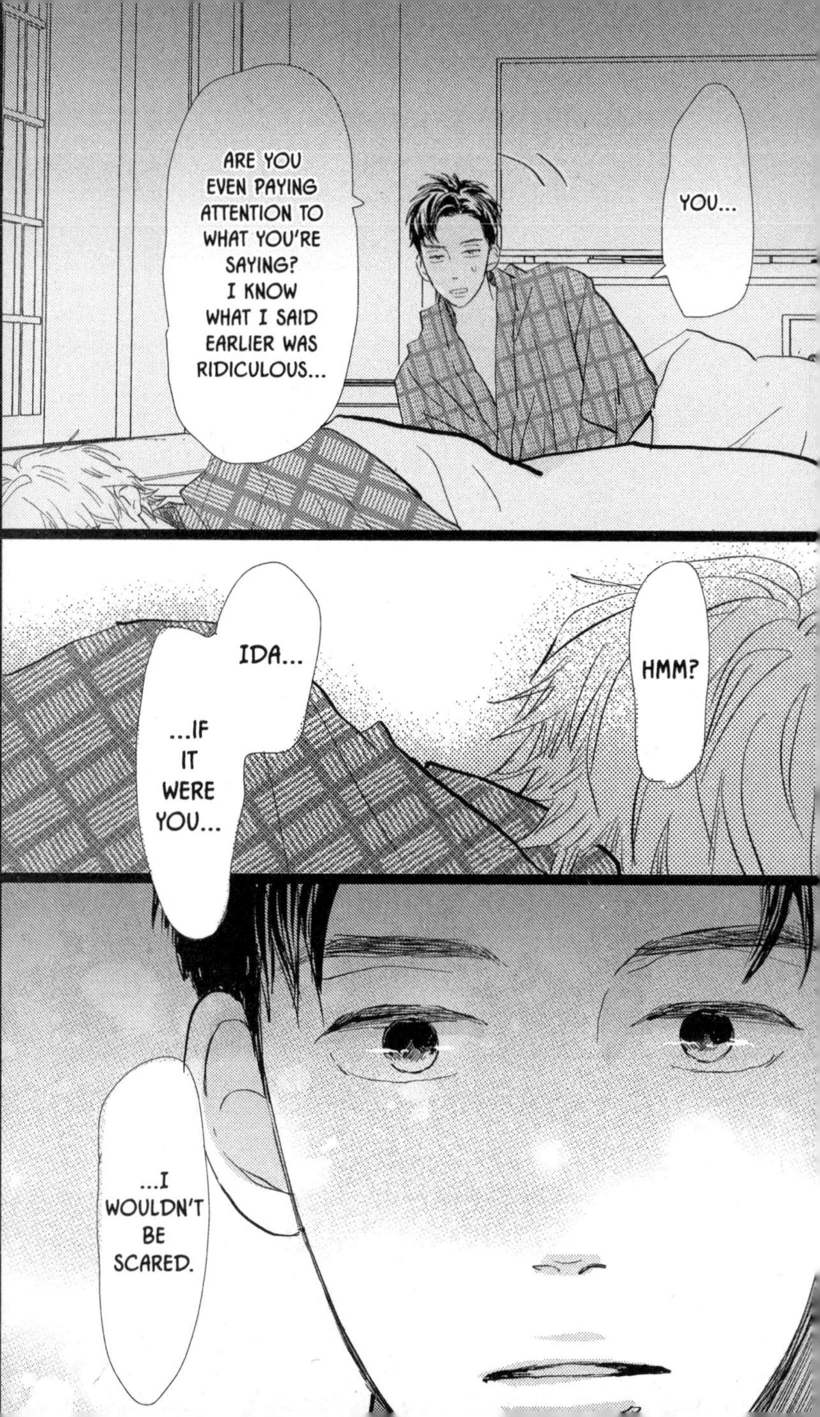
YOU...
ARE YOU EVEN PAYING ATTENTION TO WHAT YOU'RE SAYING? I KNOW WHAT I SAID EARLIER WAS RIDICULOUS...
HMM?
IDA...
...IF IT WERE YOU...
...I WOULDN'T BE SCARED.

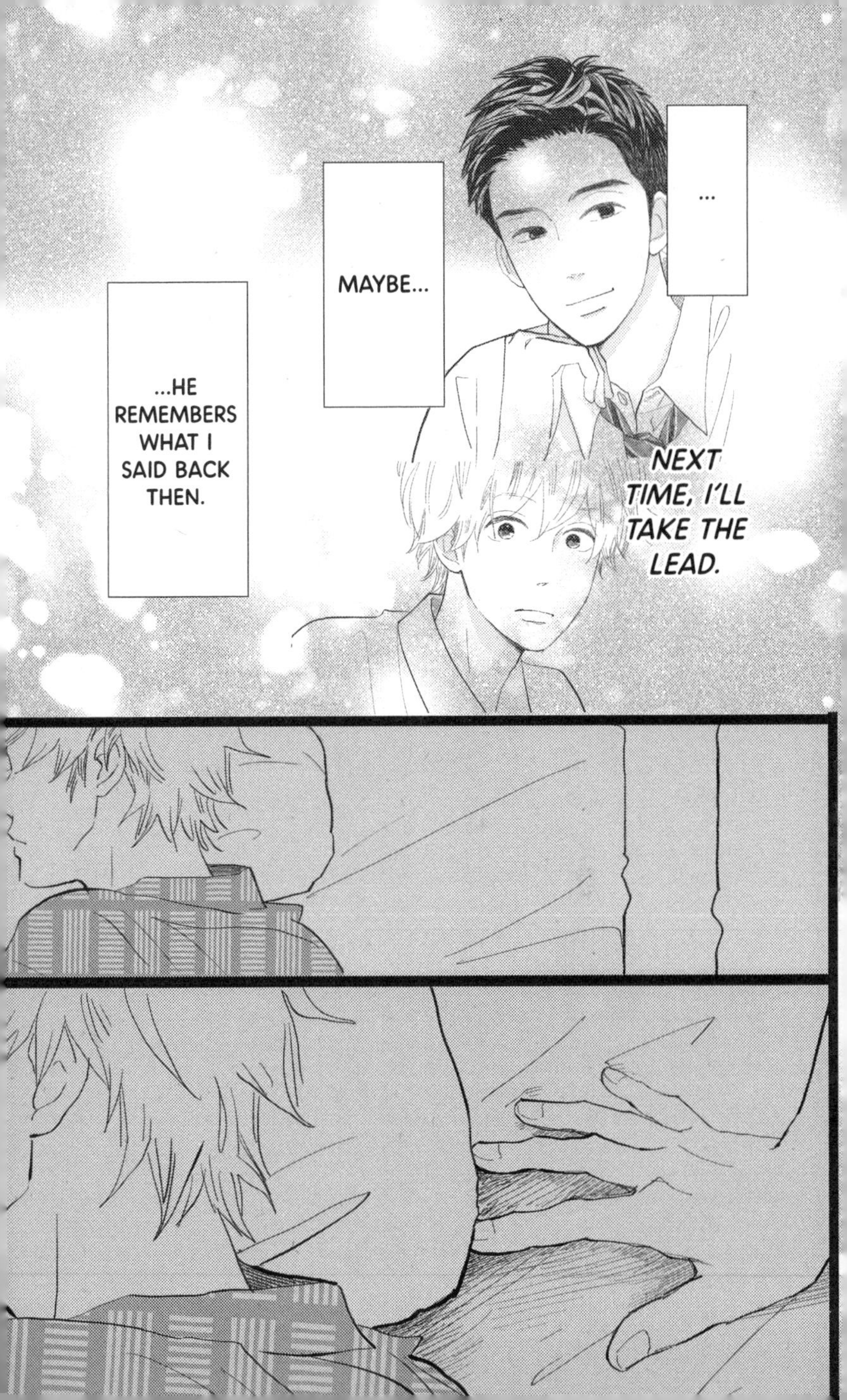
...
MAYBE...
...HE REMEMBERS WHAT I SAID BACK THEN.
NEXT TIME, I'LL TAKE THE LEAD.

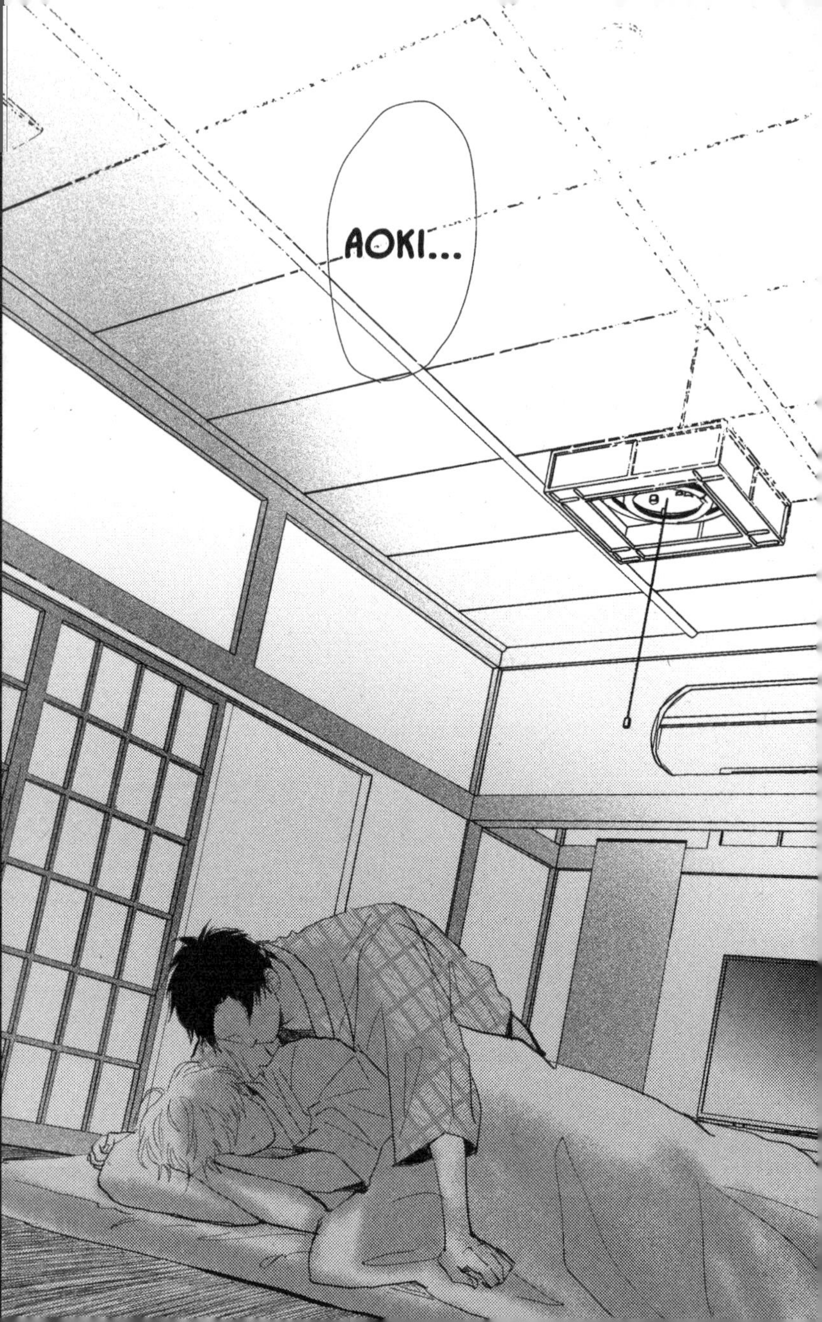
AOKI...

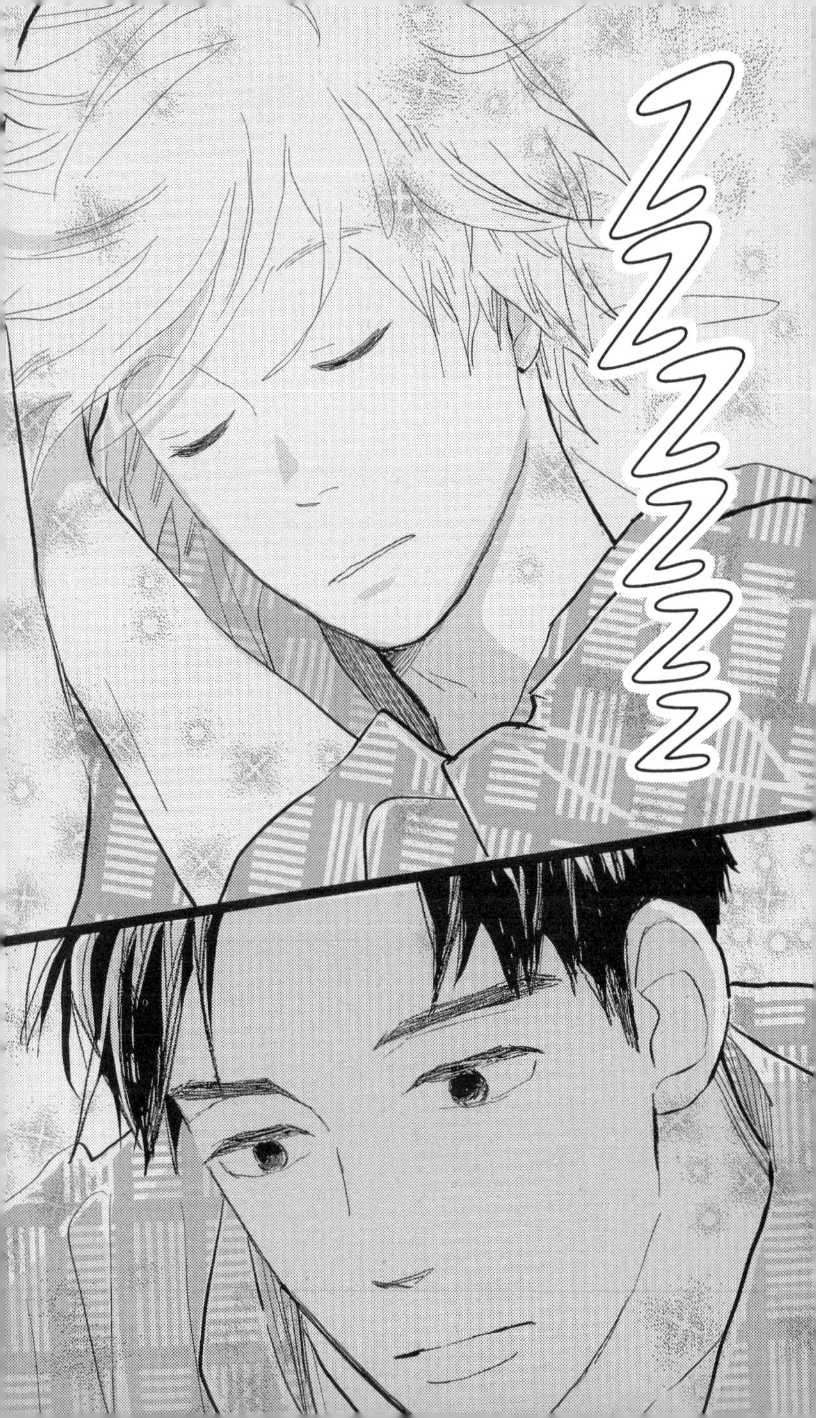
ZZZZZZZZ

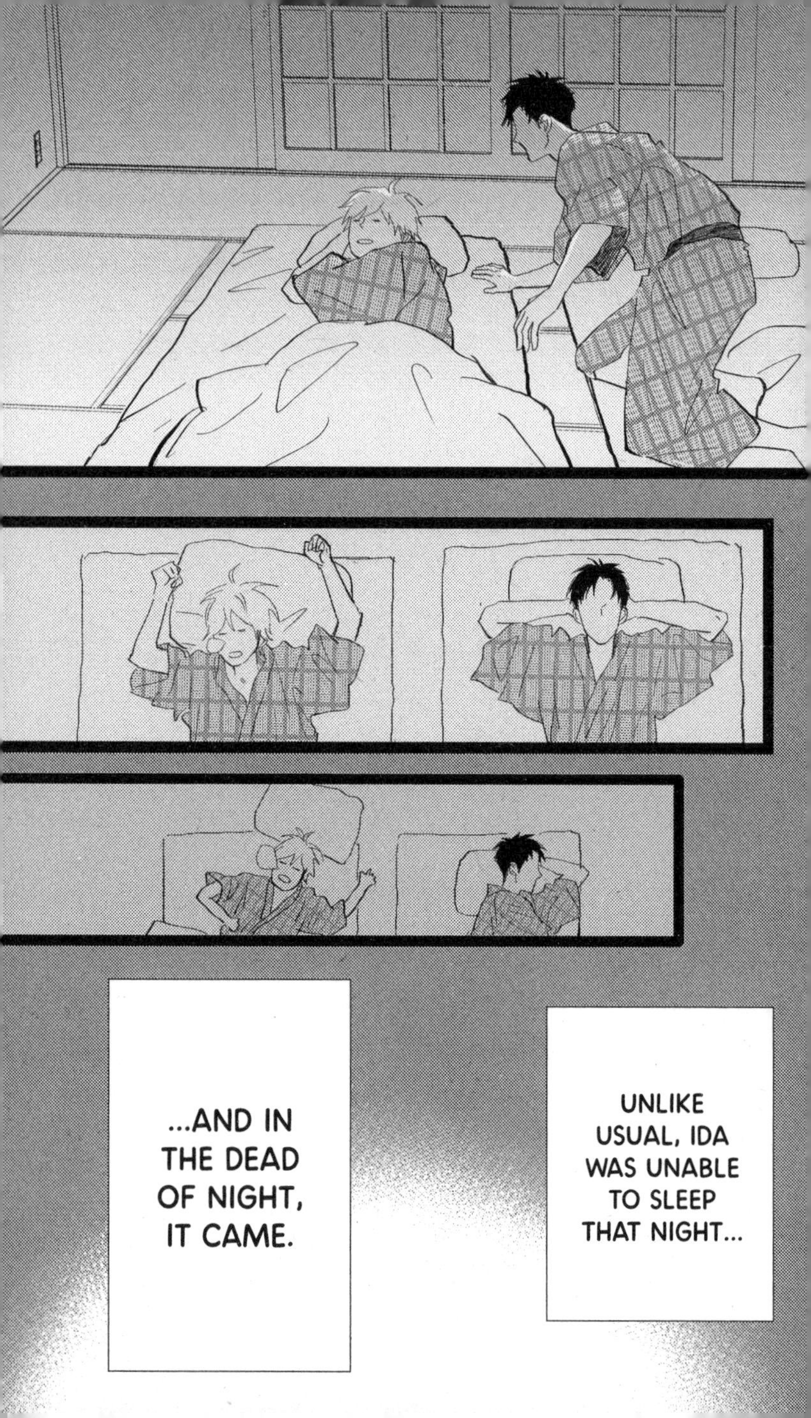
UNLIKE USUAL, IDA WAS UNABLE TO SLEEP THAT NIGHT...
...AND IN THE DEAD OF NIGHT, IT CAME.

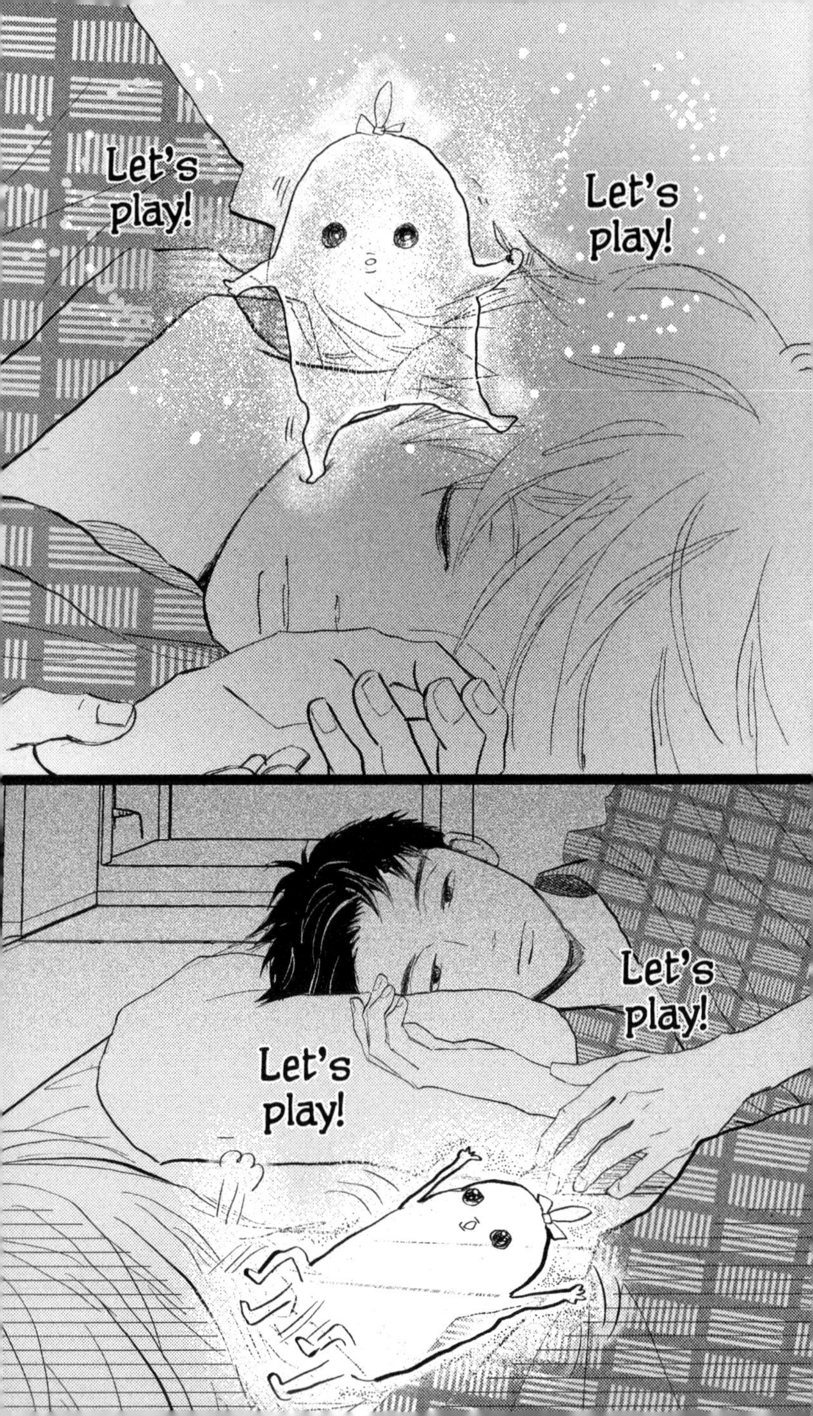
Let's play!
Let's play!
Let's play!
Let's play!

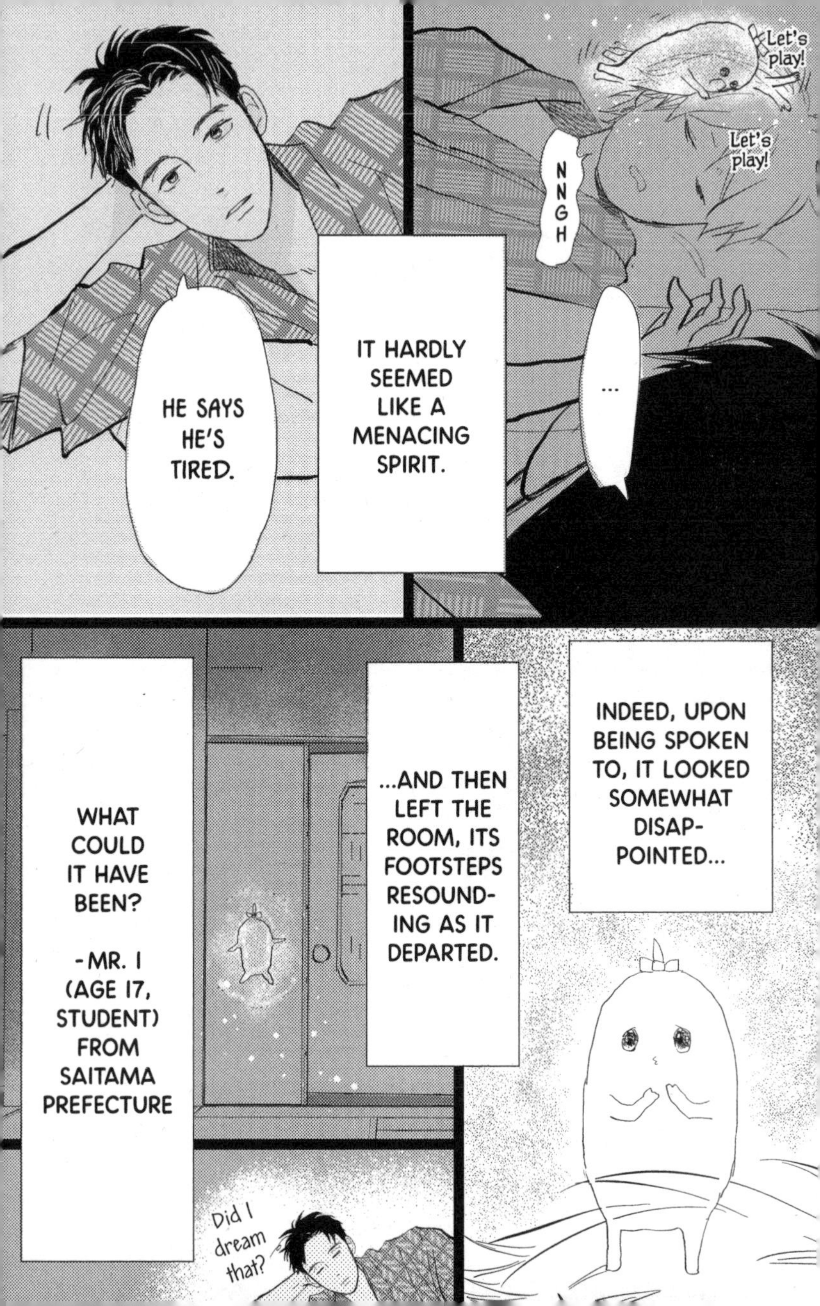
Let's play!
Let's play!
NNGH
...
IT HARDLY SEEMED LIKE A MENACING SPIRIT.
HE SAYS HE'S TIRED.
INDEED, UPON BEING SPOKEN TO, IT LOOKED SOMEWHAT DISAP-POINTED...
...AND THEN LEFT THE ROOM, ITS FOOTSTEPS RESOUND-ING AS IT DEPARTED.
WHAT COULD IT HAVE BEEN?
-MR. I (AGE 17, STUDENT) FROM SAITAMA PREFECTURE
Did I dream that?

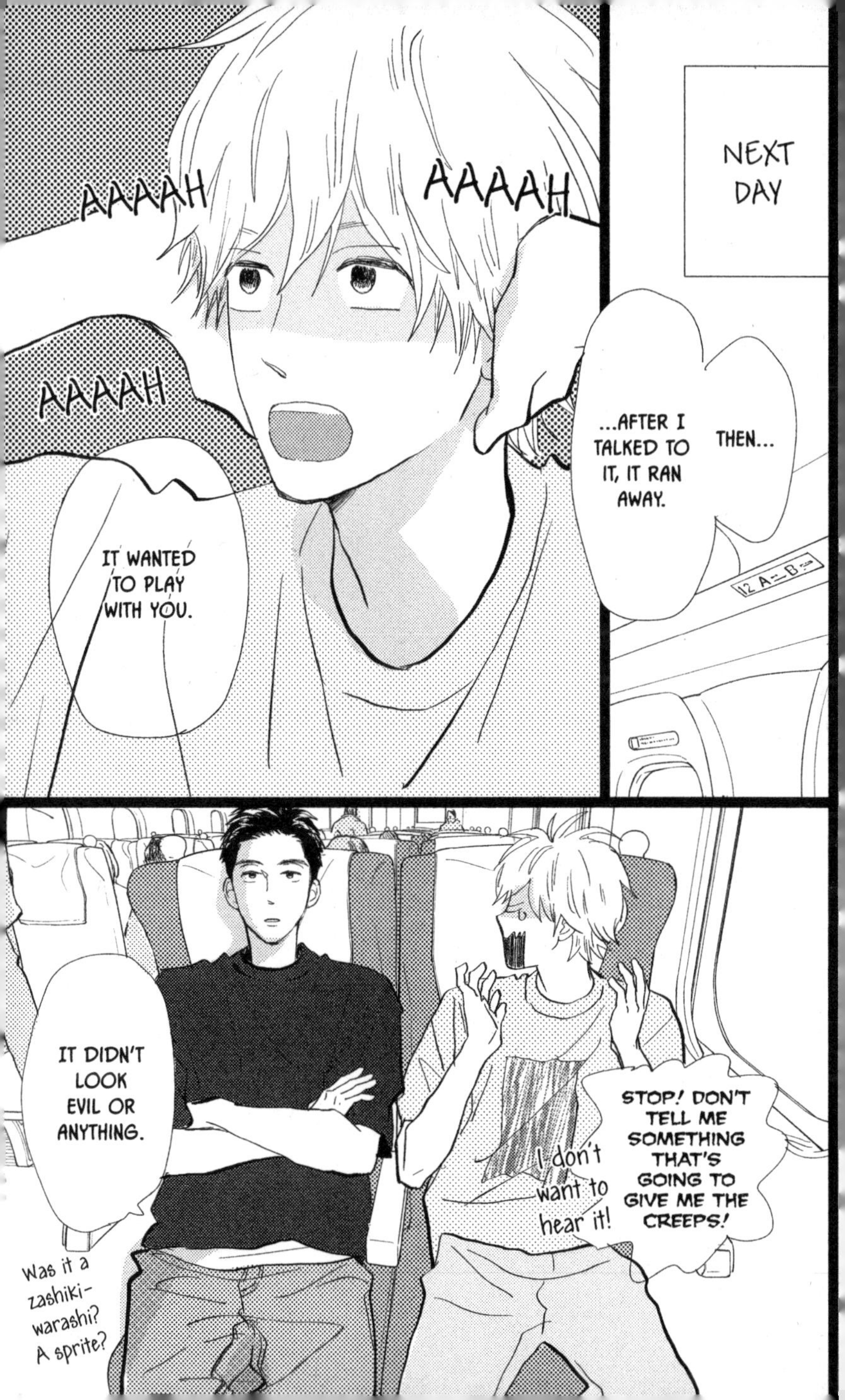
NEXT DAY
THEN... ...AFTER I TALKED TO IT, IT RAN AWAY.
AAAAH
AAAAH
AAAAH
IT WANTED TO PLAY WITH YOU.
STOP! DON'T TELL ME SOMETHING THAT'S GOING TO GIVE ME THE CREEPS!
I don't want to hear it!
IT DIDN'T LOOK EVIL OR ANYTHING.
Was it a zashiki-warashi? A sprite?

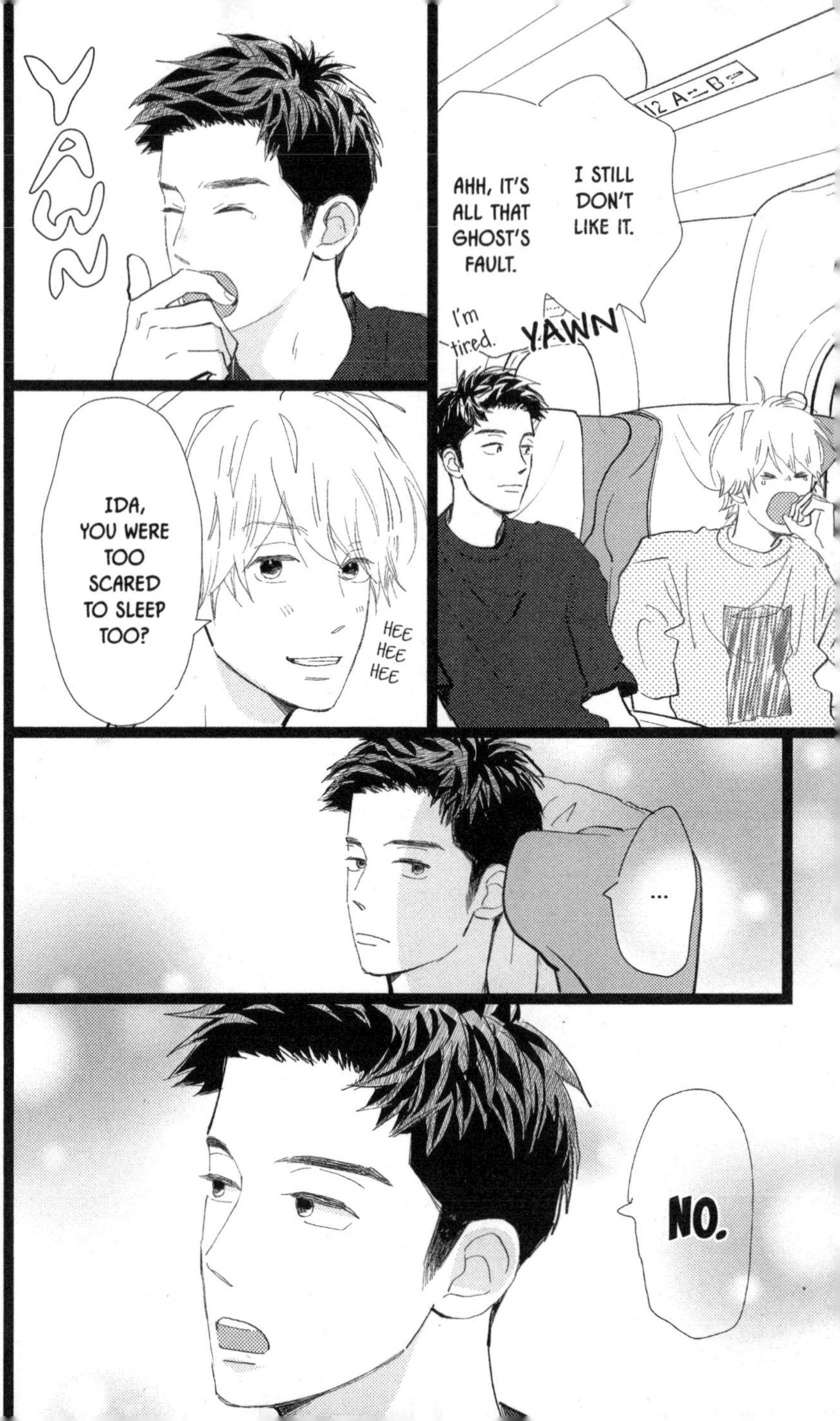
AHH, IT'S ALL THAT GHOST'S FAULT.
I STILL DON'T LIKE IT.
I'm tired.
YAWN
YAWN
IDA, YOU WERE TOO SCARED TO SLEEP TOO?
HEE HEE HEE
...
NO.

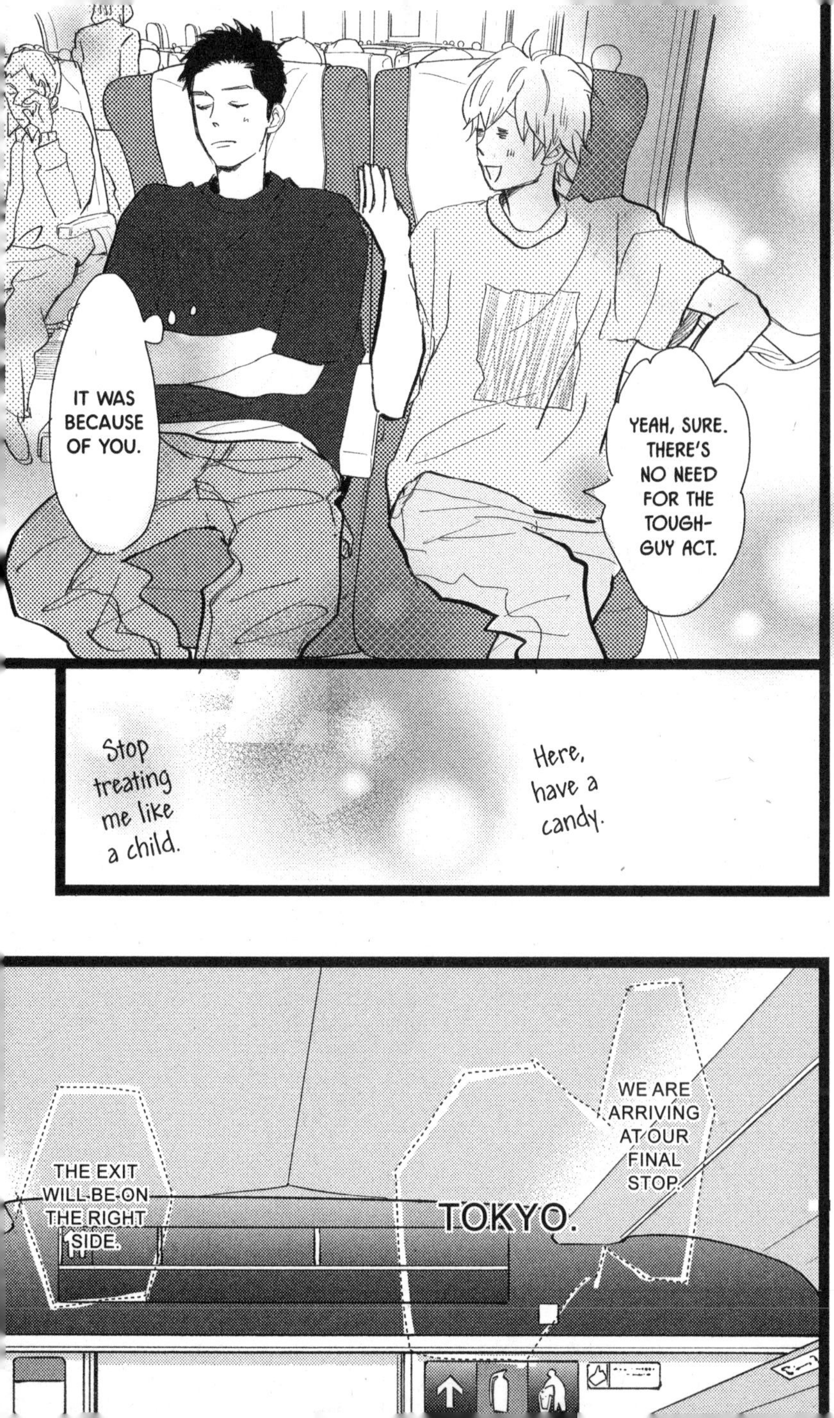
YEAH, SURE. THERE'S NO NEED FOR THE TOUGH-GUY ACT.
IT WAS BECAUSE OF YOU.
Here, have a candy.
Stop treating me like a child.
WE ARE ARRIVING AT OUR FINAL STOP,
TOKYO.
THE EXIT WILL BE ON THE RIGHT SIDE.

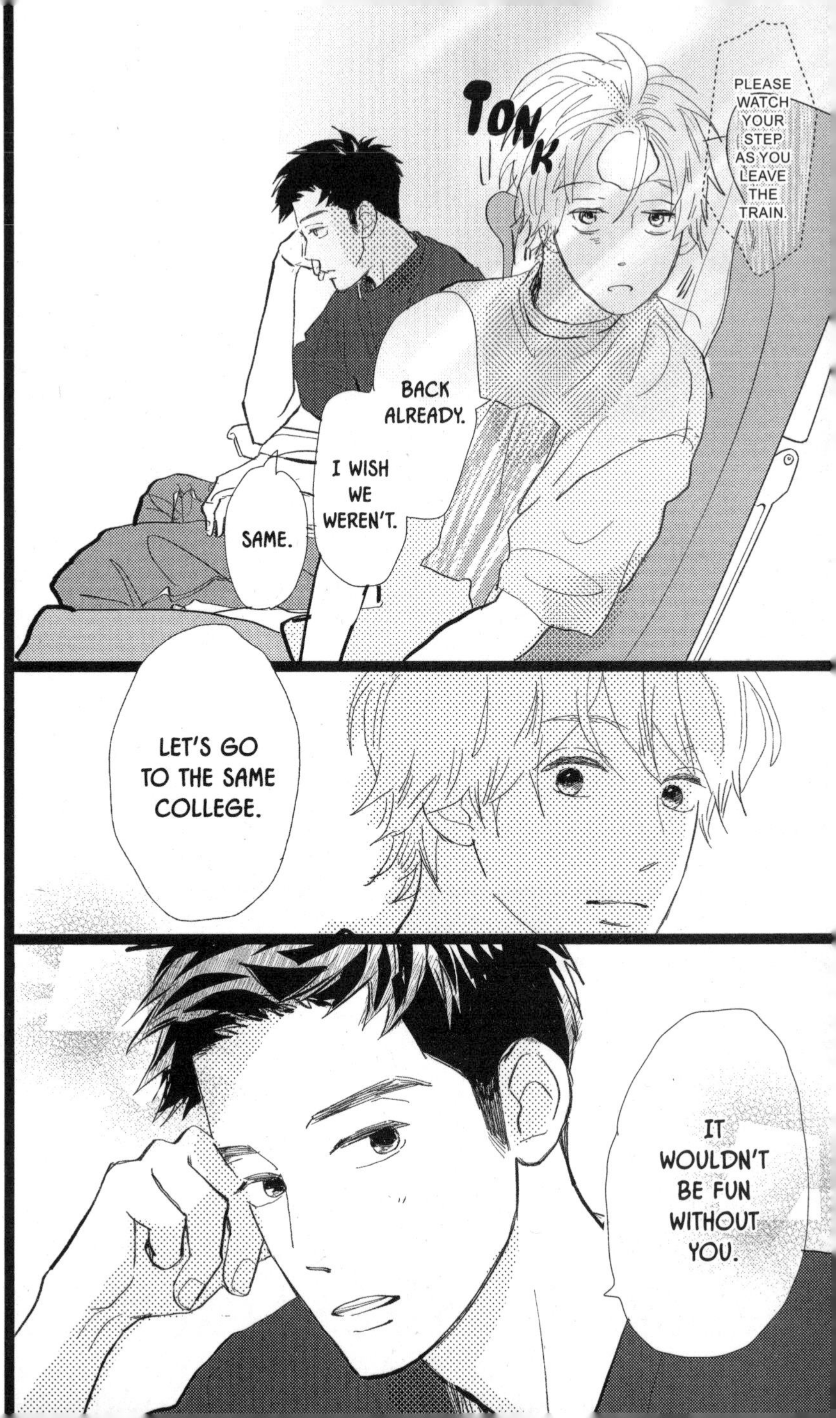
PLEASE WATCH YOUR STEP AS YOU LEAVE THE TRAIN.
TONK
BACK ALREADY.
I WISH WE WEREN'T.
SAME.
LET'S GO TO THE SAME COLLEGE.
IT WOULDN'T BE FUN WITHOUT YOU.

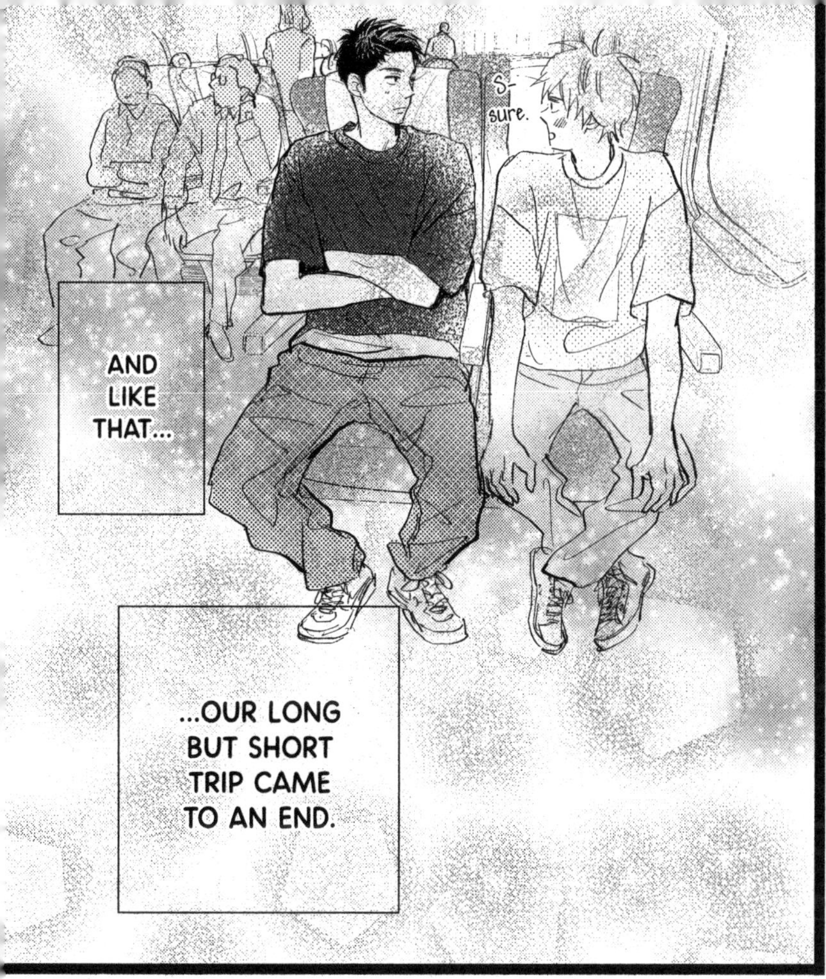
S-
sure.
AND LIKE THAT...
...OUR LONG BUT SHORT TRIP CAME TO AN END.
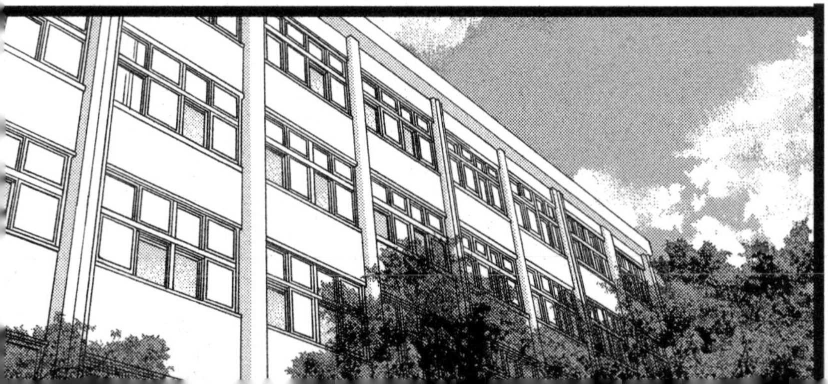

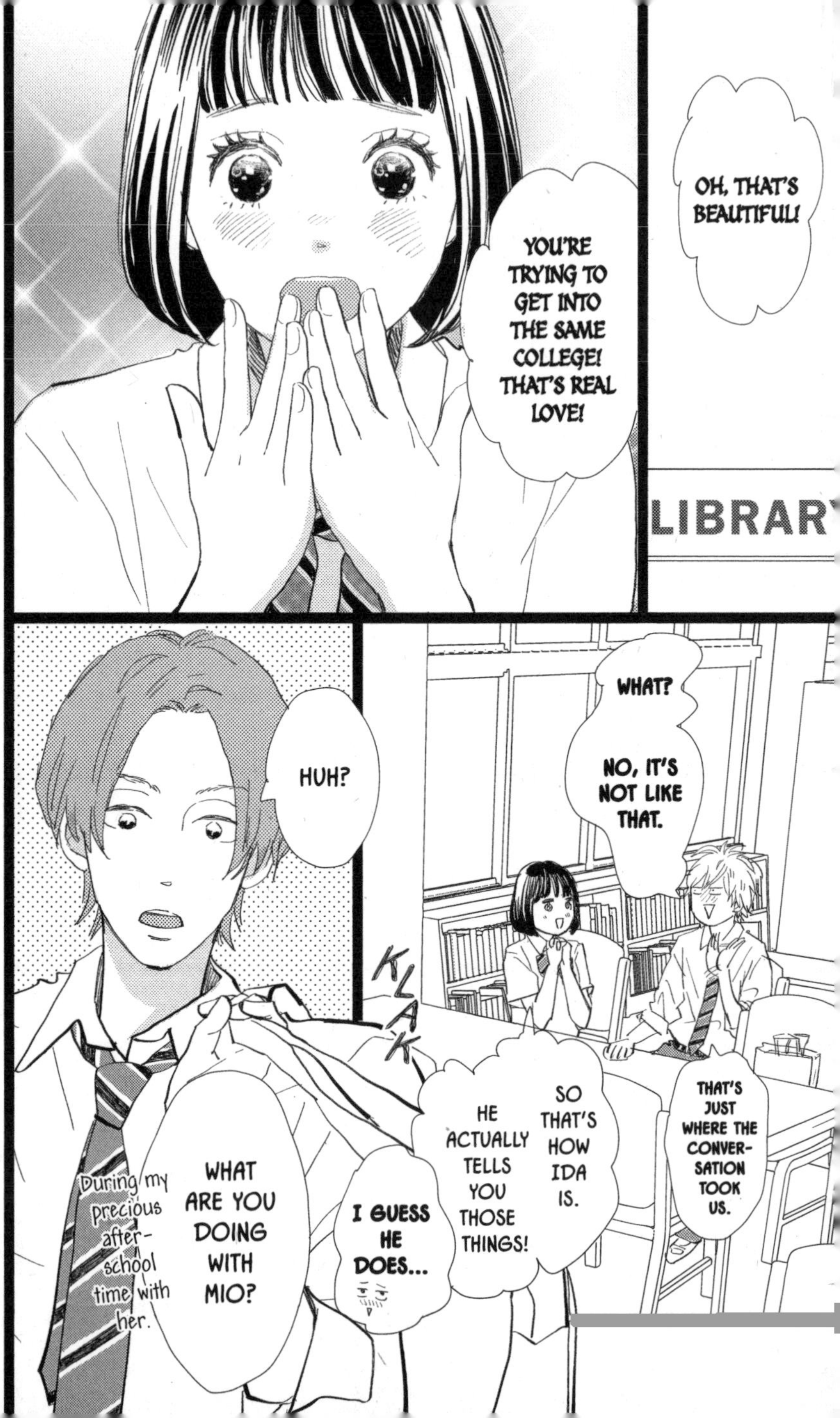
OH, THAT'S BEAUTIFUL!
LIBRARY
YOU'RE TRYING TO GET INTO THE SAME COLLEGE! THAT'S REAL LOVE!
WHAT?
NO, IT'S NOT LIKE THAT.
THAT'S JUST WHERE THE CONVERSATION TOOK US.
SO THAT'S HOW IDA IS.
HE ACTUALLY TELLS YOU THOSE THINGS!
I GUESS HE DOES...
KLAK
HUH?
WHAT ARE YOU DOING WITH MIO?
During my precious after-school time with her.

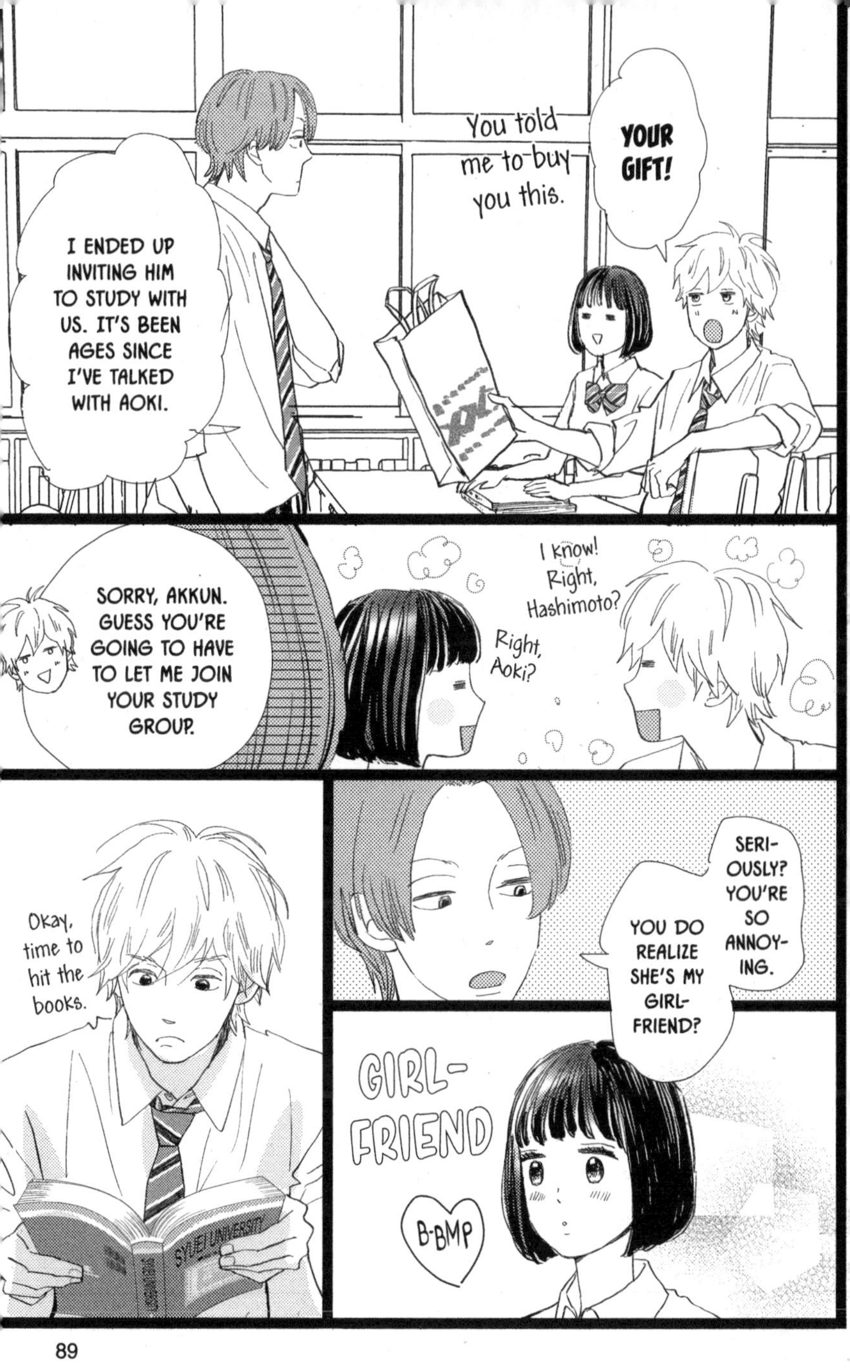
YOUR GIFT!
You told me to buy you this.
I ENDED UP INVITING HIM TO STUDY WITH US. IT'S BEEN AGES SINCE I'VE TALKED WITH AOKI.
I know! Right, Hashimoto?
Right, Aoki?
SORRY, AKKUN. GUESS YOU'RE GOING TO HAVE TO LET ME JOIN YOUR STUDY GROUP.
SERI-OUSLY? YOU'RE SO ANNOY-ING.
YOU DO REALIZE SHE'S MY GIRL-FRIEND?
GIRL-FRIEND
B-BMP
Okay, time to hit the books.
SYUEI UNIVERSITY

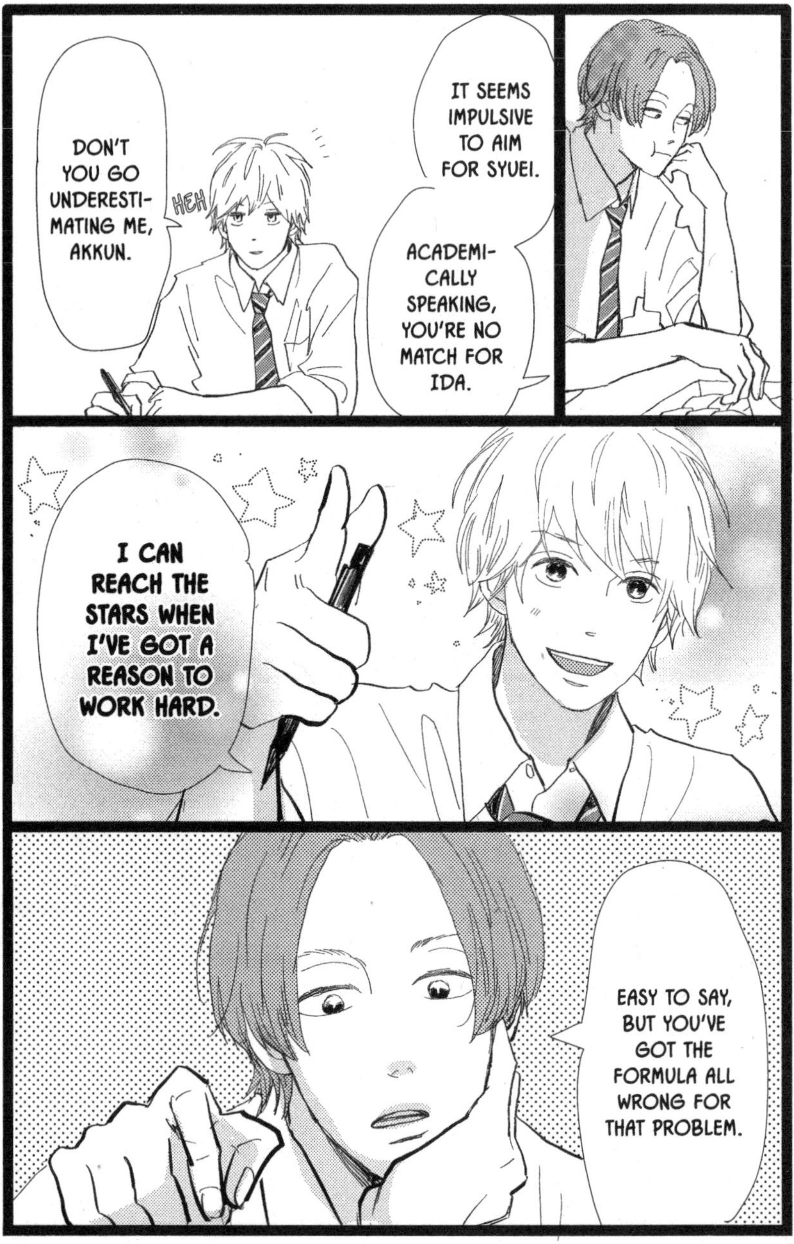
IT SEEMS IMPULSIVE TO AIM FOR SYUEI.
ACADEMI-CALLY SPEAKING, YOU'RE NO MATCH FOR IDA.
HEH
DON'T YOU GO UNDERESTI-MATING ME, AKKUN.
I CAN REACH THE STARS WHEN I'VE GOT A REASON TO WORK HARD.
EASY TO SAY, BUT YOU'VE GOT THE FORMULA ALL WRONG FOR THAT PROBLEM.

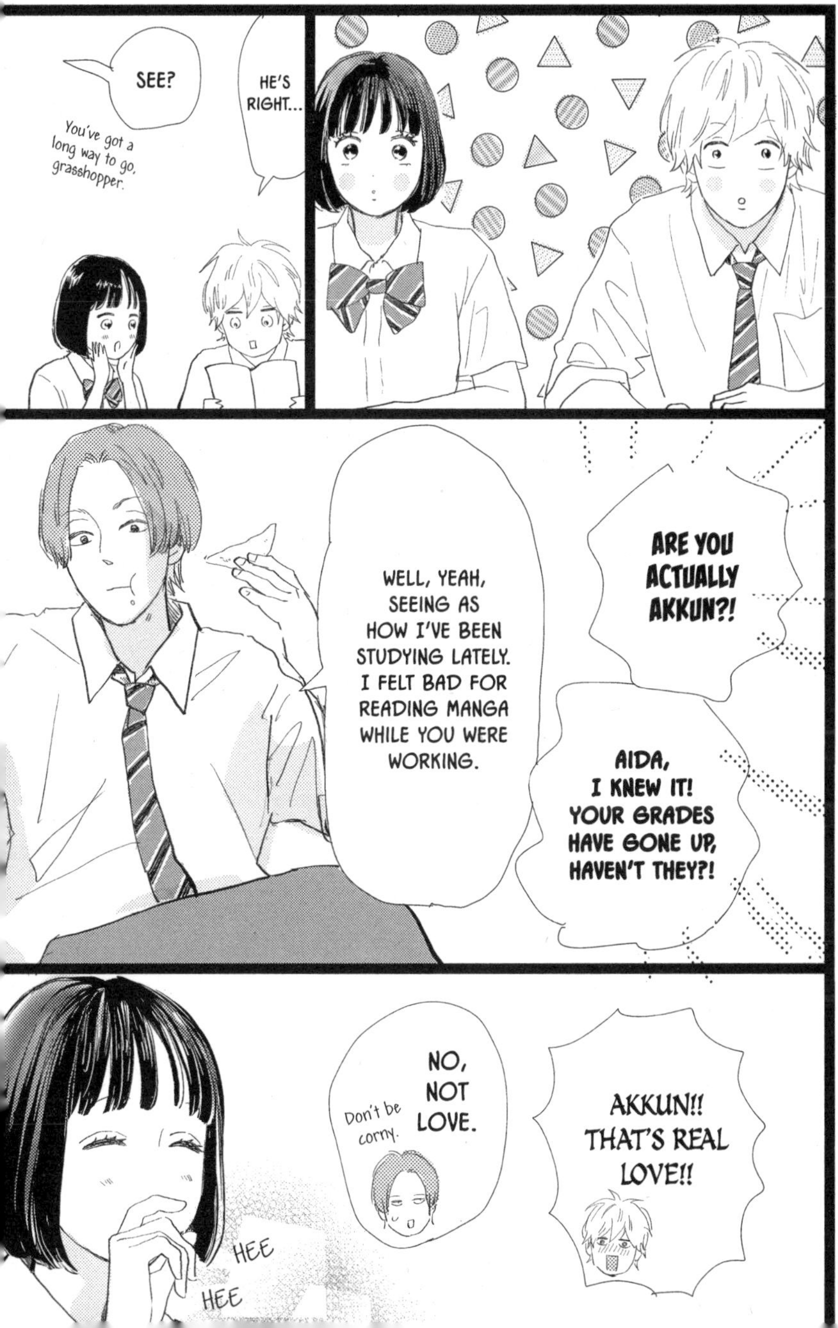
HE'S RIGHT...
SEE?
You've got a long way to go, grasshopper.
ARE YOU ACTUALLY AKKUN?!
AIDA, I KNEW IT! YOUR GRADES HAVE GONE UP, HAVEN'T THEY?!
WELL, YEAH, SEEING AS HOW I'VE BEEN STUDYING LATELY. I FELT BAD FOR READING MANGA WHILE YOU WERE WORKING.
AKKUN!! THAT'S REAL LOVE!!
NO, NOT LOVE.
Don't be corny.
HEE HEE

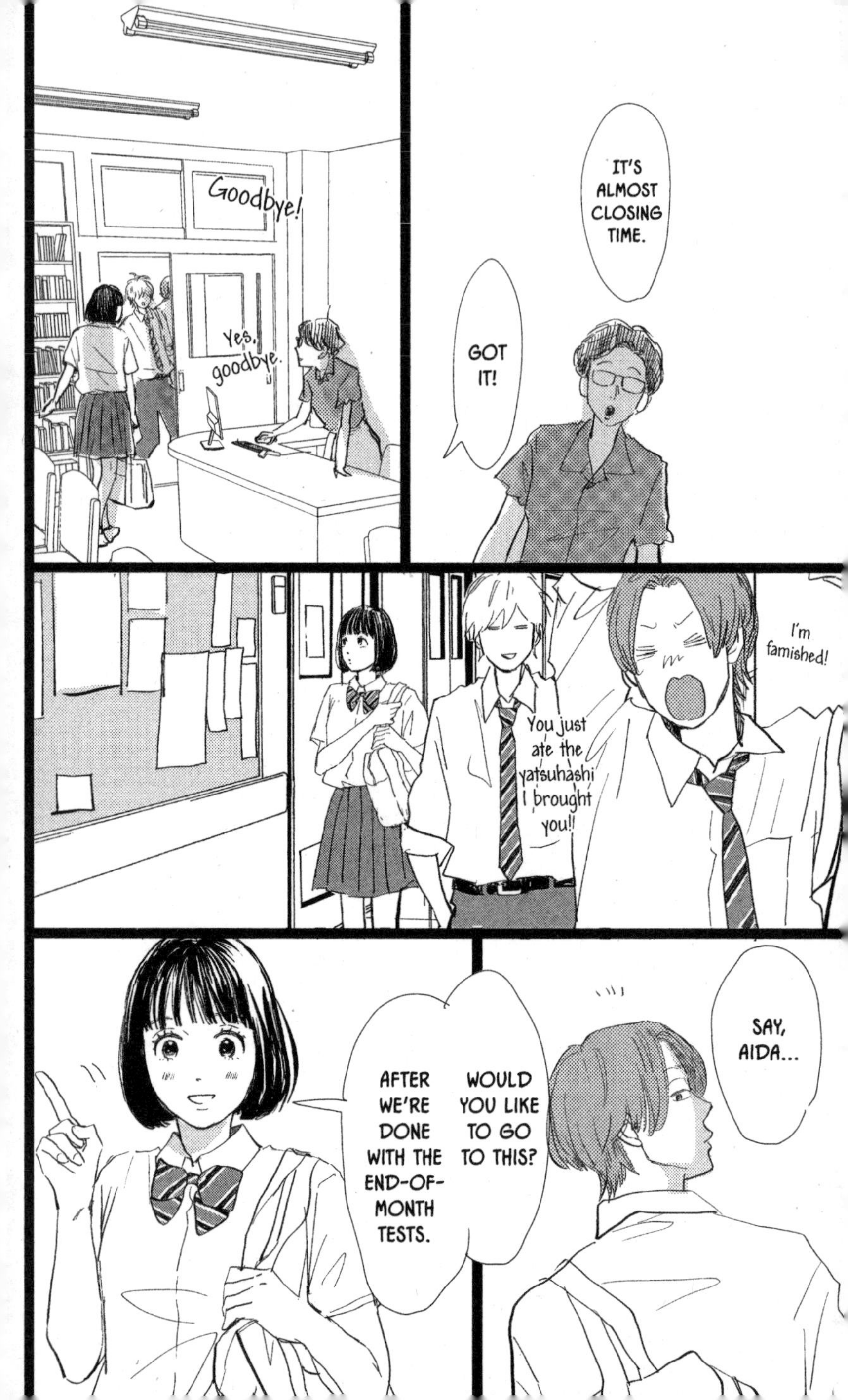
IT'S ALMOST CLOSING TIME.
GOT IT!
Goodbye!
Yes, goodbye.
I'm famished!
You just ate the yatsuhashi I brought you!!
SAY, AIDA...
WOULD YOU LIKE TO GO TO THIS?
AFTER WE'RE DONE WITH THE END-OF-MONTH TESTS.

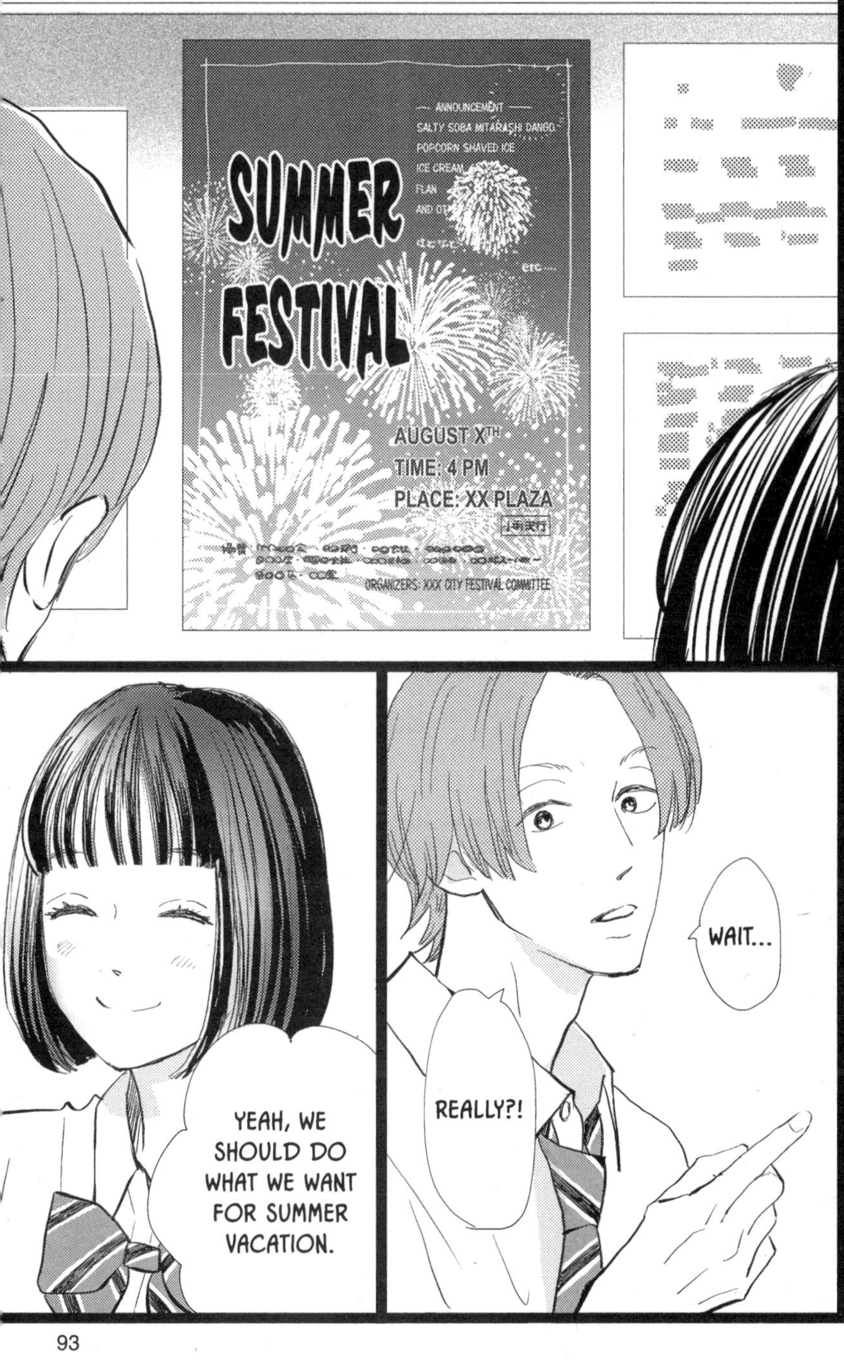
SUMMER FESTIVAL
— ANNOUNCEMENT —
SALTY SOBA MITARASHI DANGO
POPCORN SHAVED ICE
ICE CREAM
FLAN
etc...
AUGUST X^TH
TIME: 4 PM
PLACE: XX PLAZA
ORGANIZERS: XXX CITY FESTIVAL COMMITTEE
WAIT...
REALLY?!
YEAH, WE SHOULD DO WHAT WE WANT FOR SUMMER VACATION.

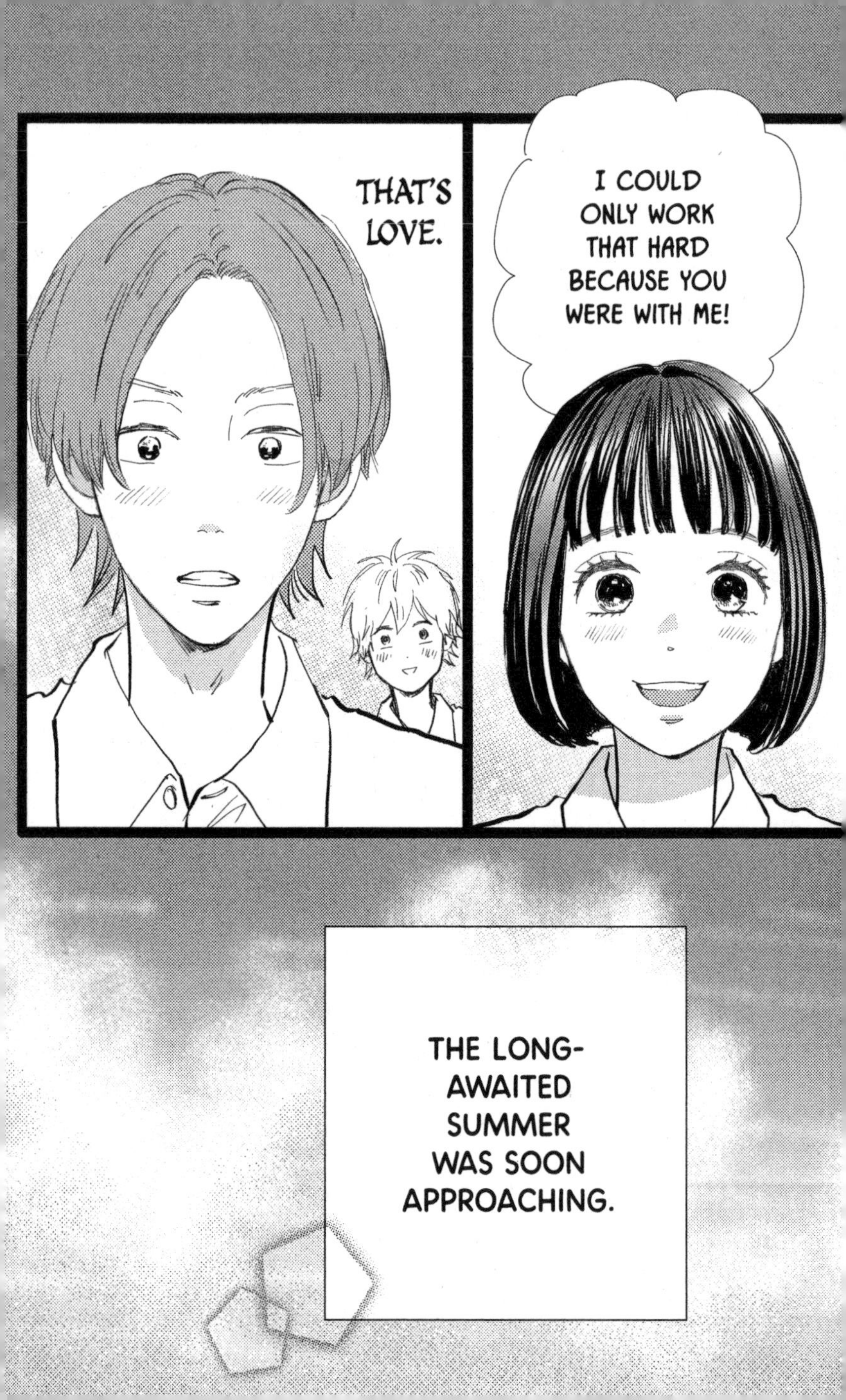
I COULD ONLY WORK THAT HARD BECAUSE YOU WERE WITH ME!
THAT'S LOVE.
THE LONG-AWAITED SUMMER WAS SOON APPROACHING.

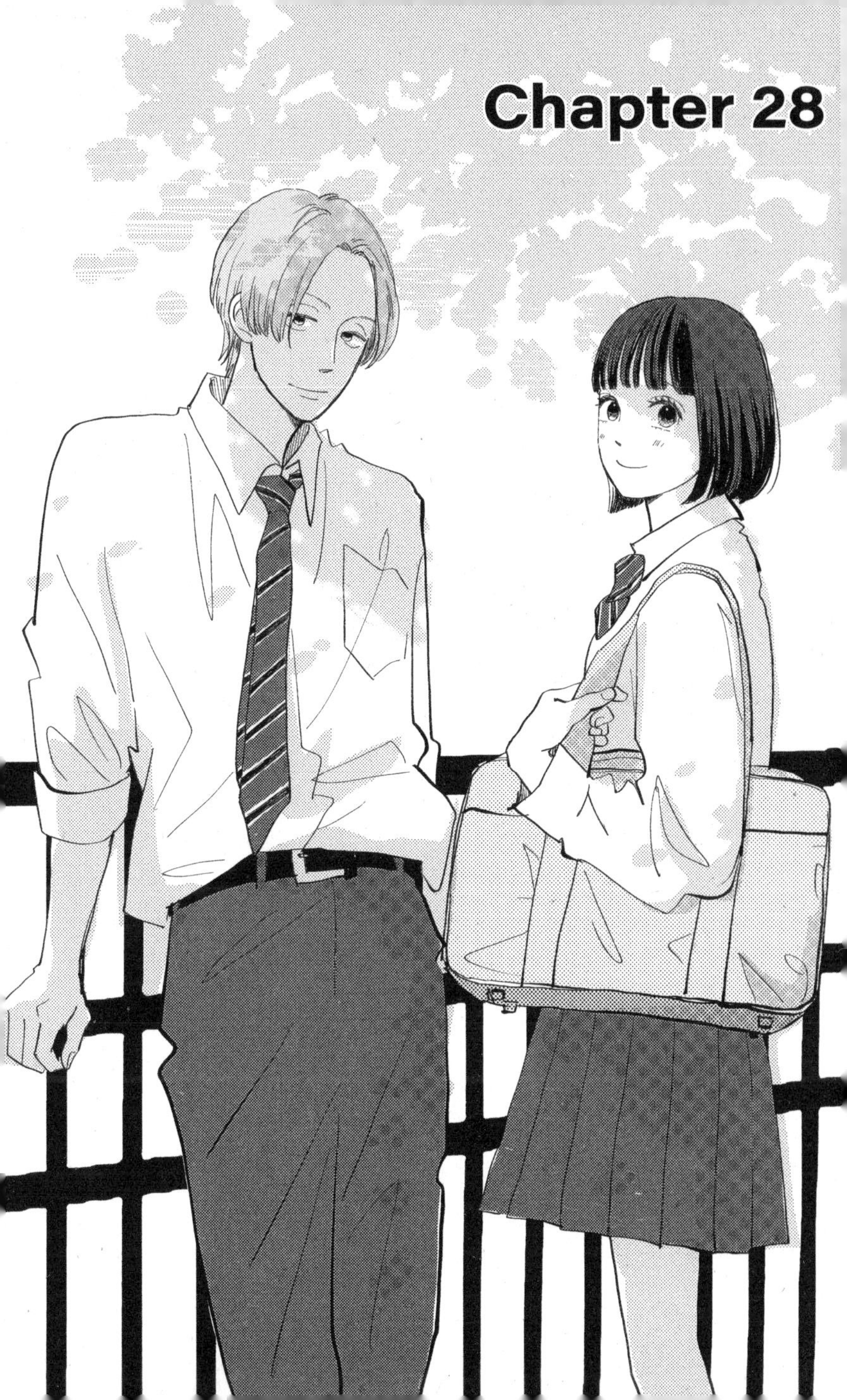
Chapter 28

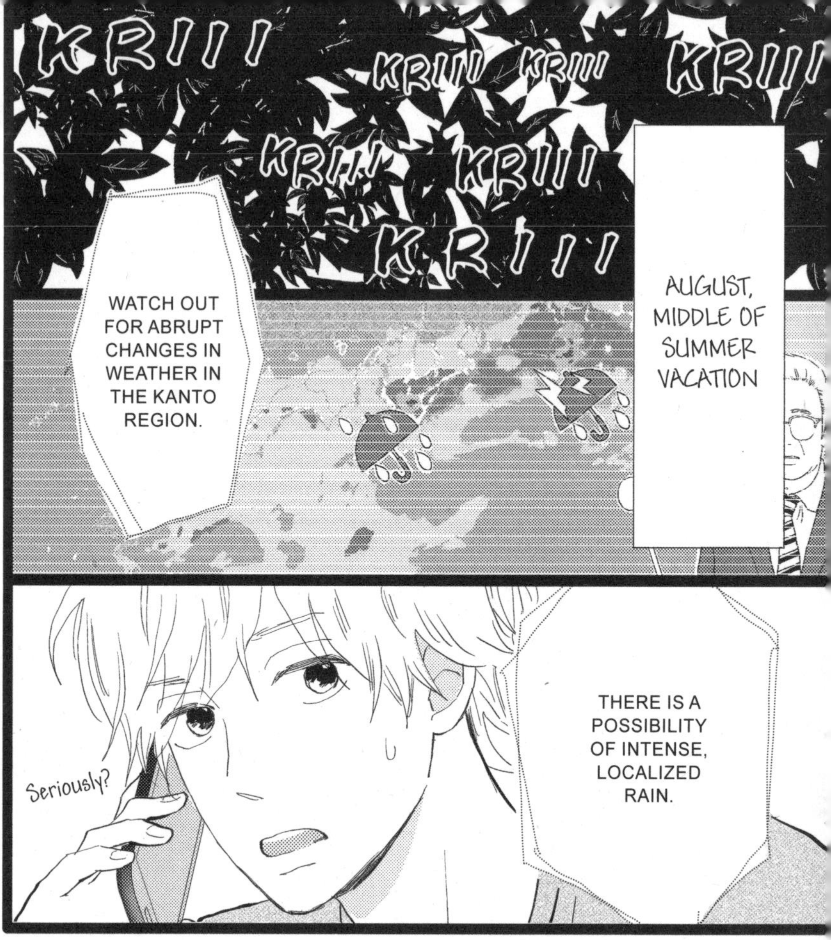
AUGUST, MIDDLE OF SUMMER VACATION
KRIII KRIII KRIII KRIII KRIII KRIII KRIII
WATCH OUT FOR ABRUPT CHANGES IN WEATHER IN THE KANTO REGION.
THERE IS A POSSIBILITY OF INTENSE, LOCALIZED RAIN.
Seriously?

My Love Mix-Up!

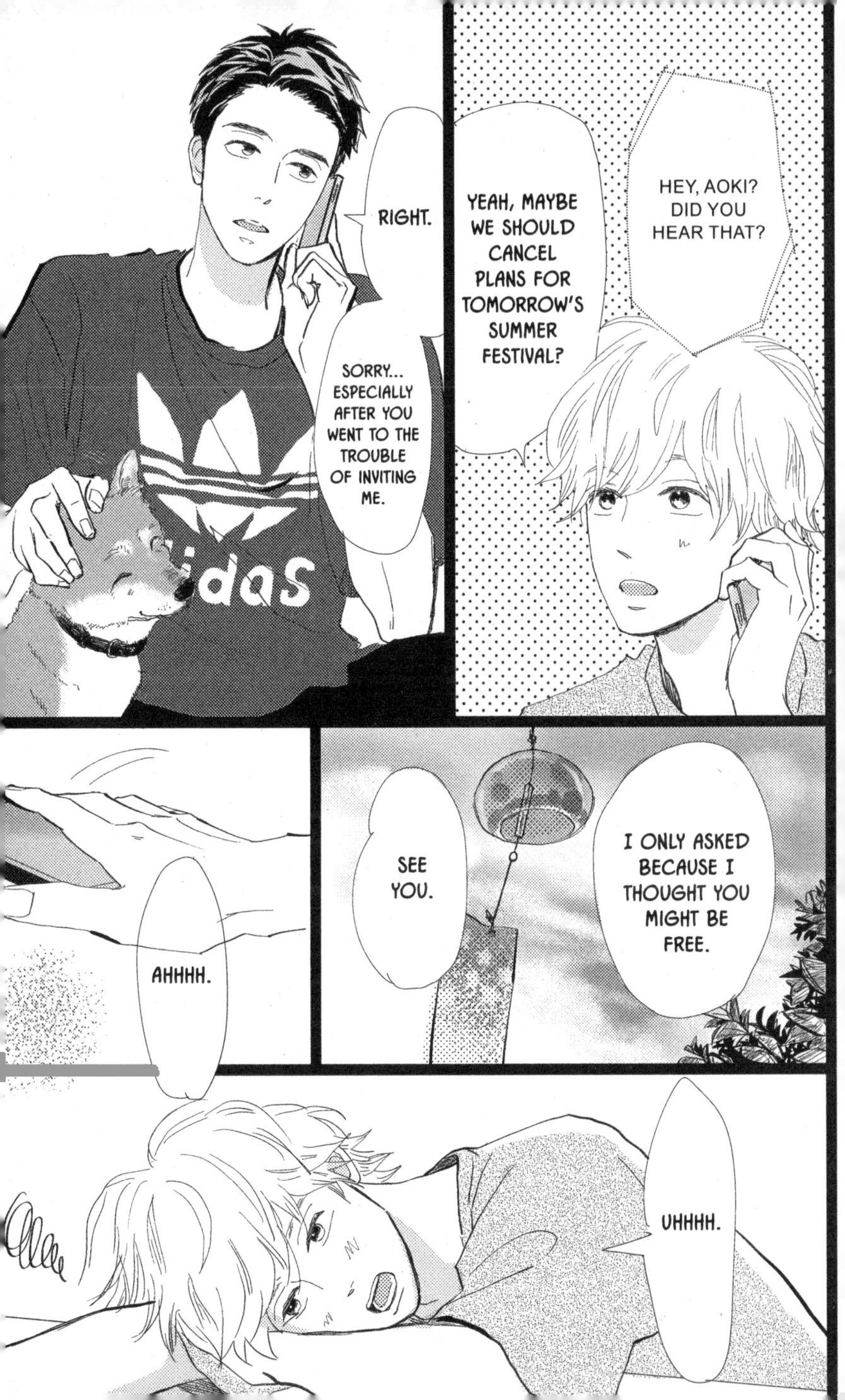
HEY, AOKI? DID YOU HEAR THAT?
YEAH, MAYBE WE SHOULD CANCEL PLANS FOR TOMORROW'S SUMMER FESTIVAL?
RIGHT.
SORRY... ESPECIALLY AFTER YOU WENT TO THE TROUBLE OF INVITING ME.
I ONLY ASKED BECAUSE I THOUGHT YOU MIGHT BE FREE.
SEE YOU.
AHHHH.
UHHHH.

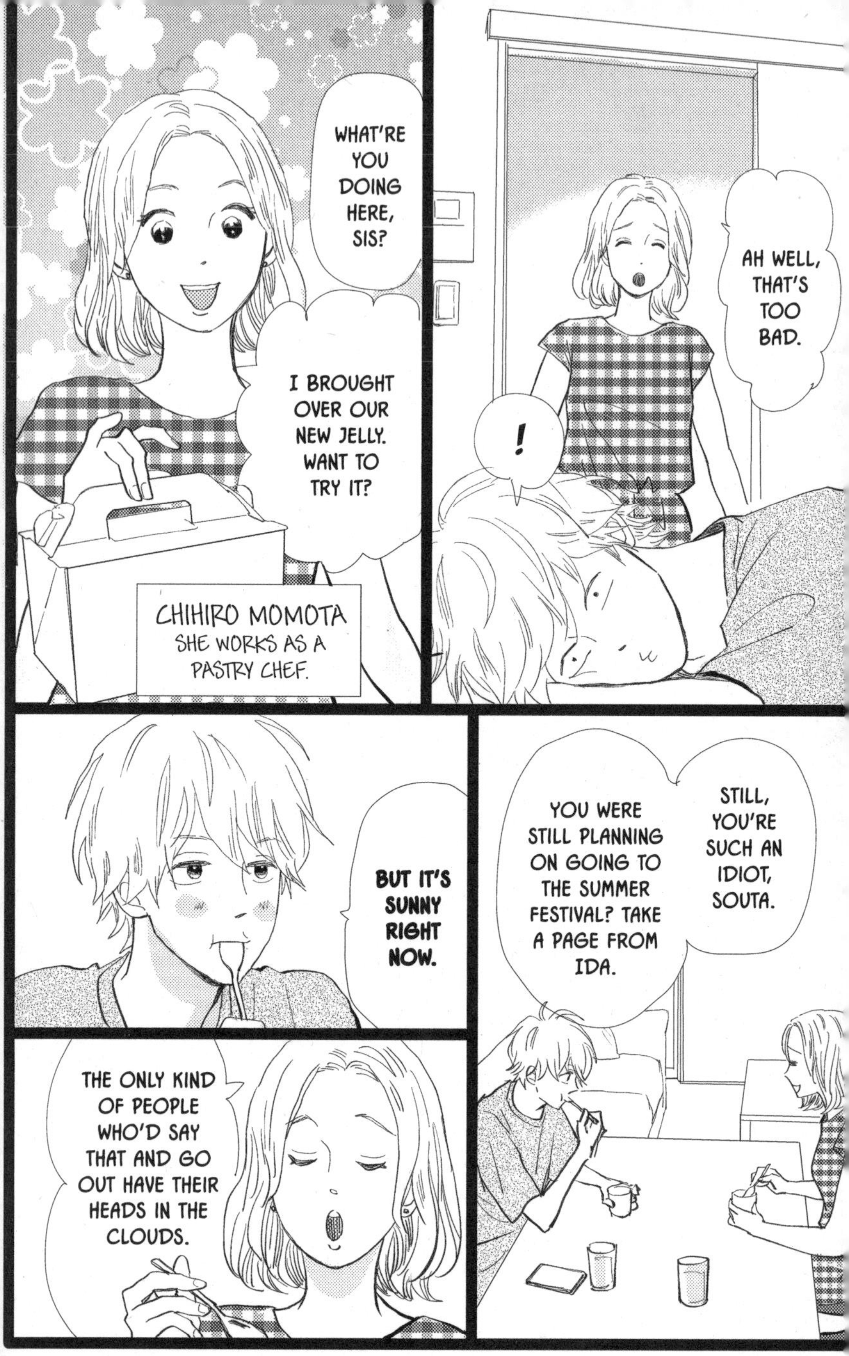
AH WELL, THAT'S TOO BAD.
!
WHAT'RE YOU DOING HERE, SIS?
I BROUGHT OVER OUR NEW JELLY. WANT TO TRY IT?
CHIHIRO MOMOTA SHE WORKS AS A PASTRY CHEF.
STILL, YOU'RE SUCH AN IDIOT, SOUTA.
YOU WERE STILL PLANNING ON GOING TO THE SUMMER FESTIVAL? TAKE A PAGE FROM IDA.
BUT IT'S SUNNY RIGHT NOW.
THE ONLY KIND OF PEOPLE WHO'D SAY THAT AND GO OUT HAVE THEIR HEADS IN THE CLOUDS.

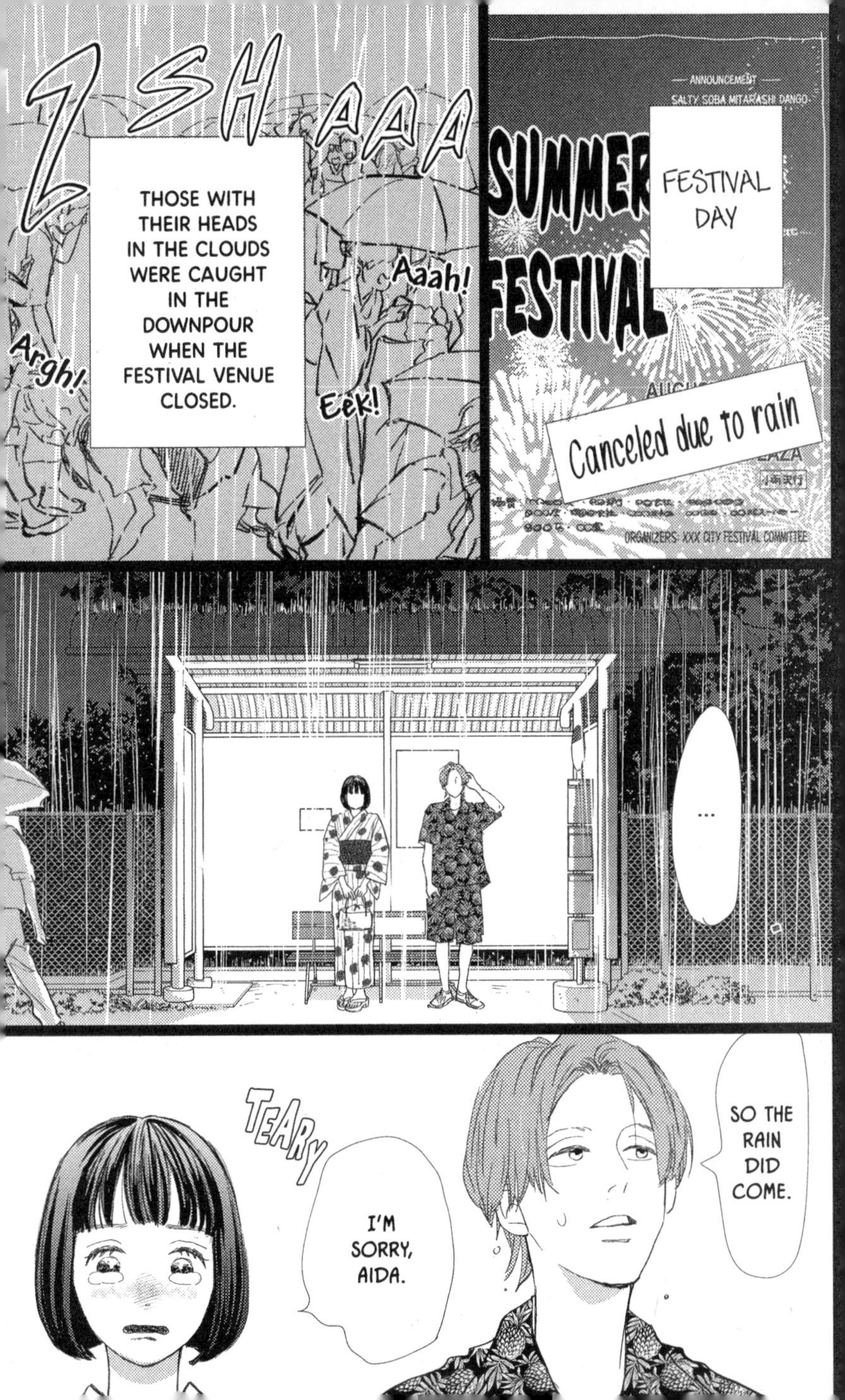
ANNOUNCEMENT
SALTY SOBA MITARASHI DANGO
SUMMER FESTIVAL
FESTIVAL DAY
Canceled due to rain
ORGANIZERS: XXX CITY FESTIVAL COMMITTEE
ZSHAAAA
THOSE WITH THEIR HEADS IN THE CLOUDS WERE CAUGHT IN THE DOWNPOUR WHEN THE FESTIVAL VENUE CLOSED.
Aaah!
Eek!
Argh!
...
SO THE RAIN DID COME.
TEARY
I'M SORRY, AIDA.

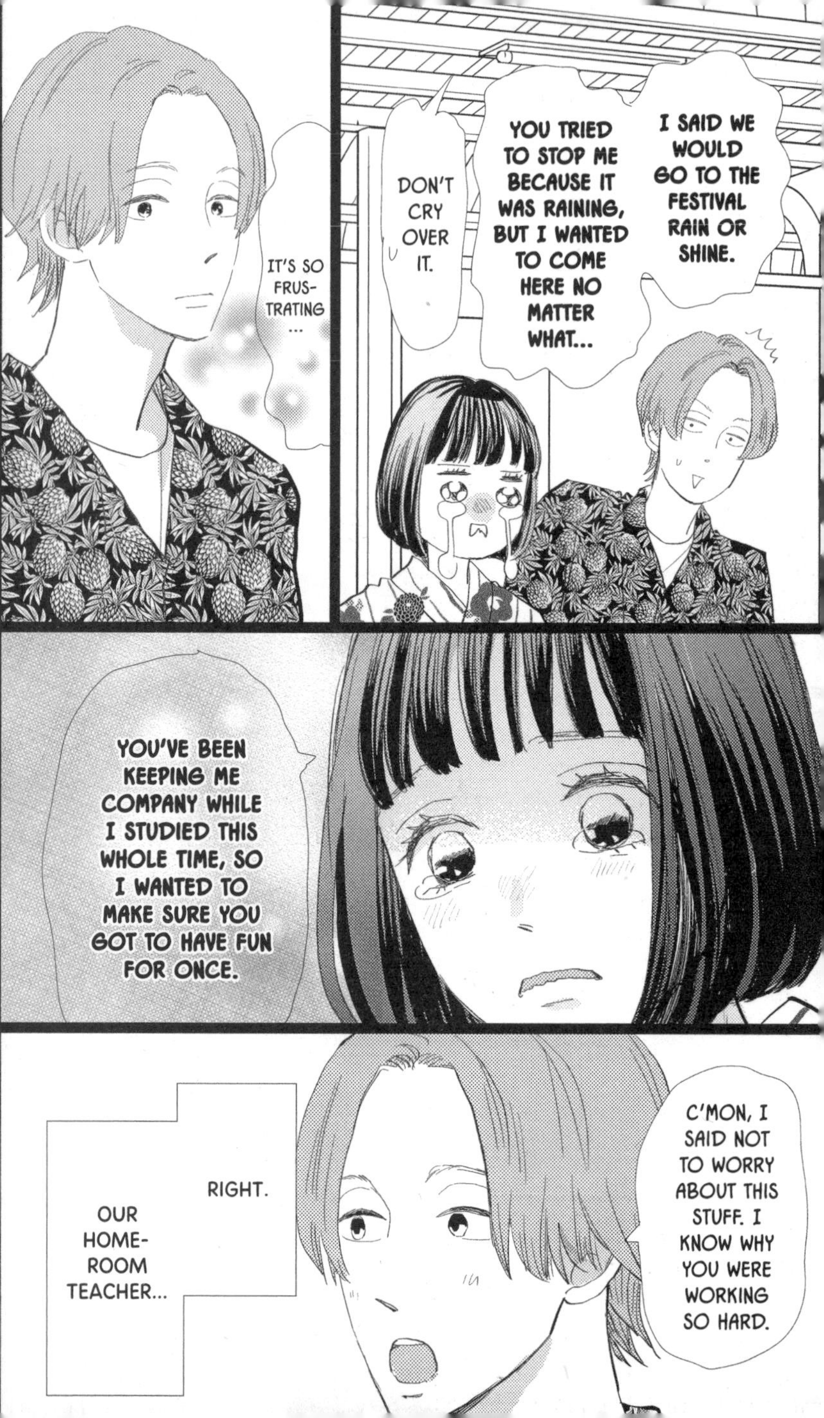
I SAID WE WOULD GO TO THE FESTIVAL RAIN OR SHINE.
YOU TRIED TO STOP ME BECAUSE IT WAS RAINING, BUT I WANTED TO COME HERE NO MATTER WHAT...
DON'T CRY OVER IT.
IT'S SO FRUS-TRATING...
YOU'VE BEEN KEEPING ME COMPANY WHILE I STUDIED THIS WHOLE TIME, SO I WANTED TO MAKE SURE YOU GOT TO HAVE FUN FOR ONCE.
C'MON, I SAID NOT TO WORRY ABOUT THIS STUFF. I KNOW WHY YOU WERE WORKING SO HARD.
RIGHT.
OUR HOME-ROOM TEACHER...

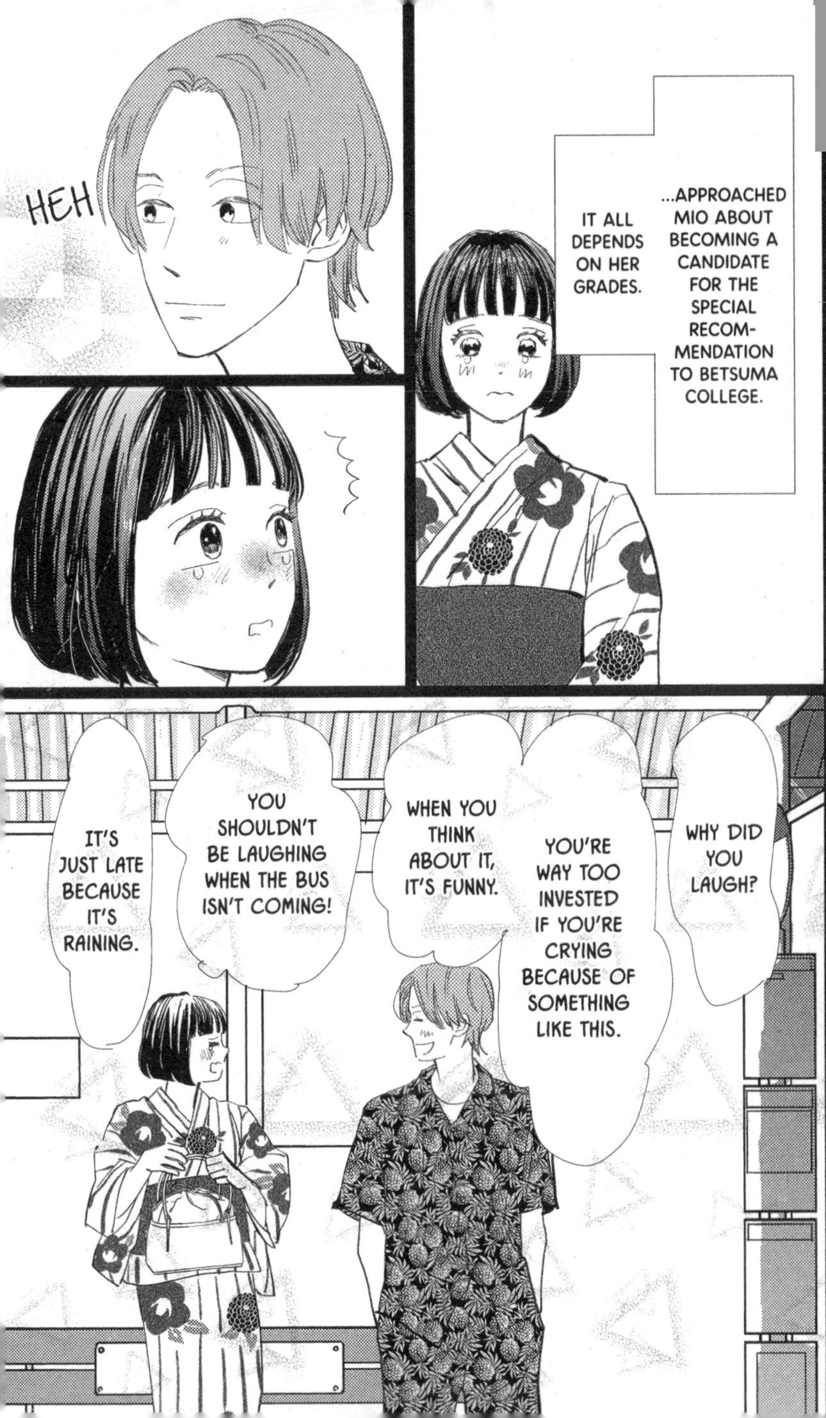
...APPROACHED MIO ABOUT BECOMING A CANDIDATE FOR THE SPECIAL RECOM-MENDATION TO BETSUMA COLLEGE.
IT ALL DEPENDS ON HER GRADES.
HEH
WHY DID YOU LAUGH?
YOU'RE WAY TOO INVESTED IF YOU'RE CRYING BECAUSE OF SOMETHING LIKE THIS.
WHEN YOU THINK ABOUT IT, IT'S FUNNY.
YOU SHOULDN'T BE LAUGHING WHEN THE BUS ISN'T COMING!
IT'S JUST LATE BECAUSE IT'S RAINING.

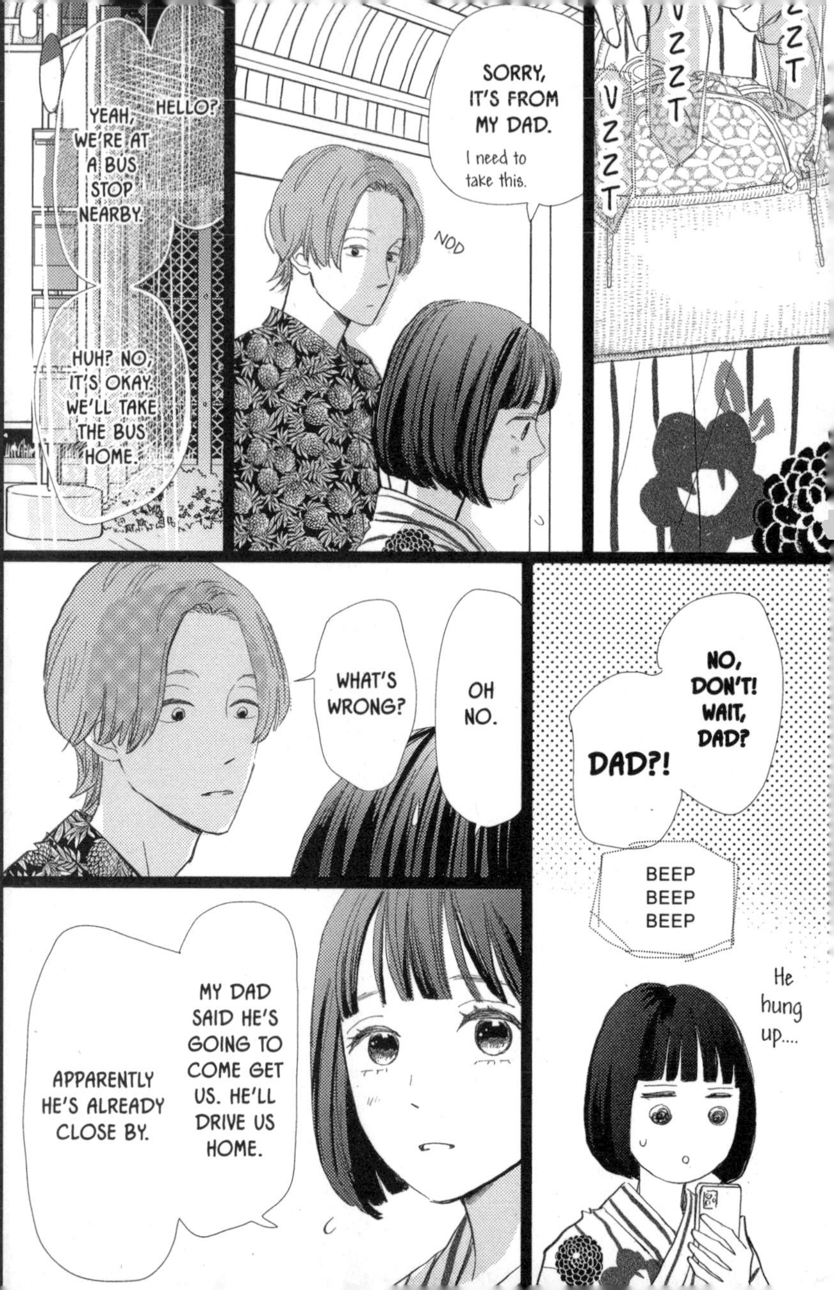
VZZT
VZZT
VZZT
SORRY, IT'S FROM MY DAD.
I need to take this.
NOD
HELLO?
YEAH, WE'RE AT A BUS STOP NEARBY.
HUH? NO, IT'S OKAY. WE'LL TAKE THE BUS HOME.
NO, DON'T! WAIT, DAD?
DAD?!
BEEP BEEP BEEP
He hung up....
OH NO.
WHAT'S WRONG?
MY DAD SAID HE'S GOING TO COME GET US. HE'LL DRIVE US HOME.
APPARENTLY HE'S ALREADY CLOSE BY.

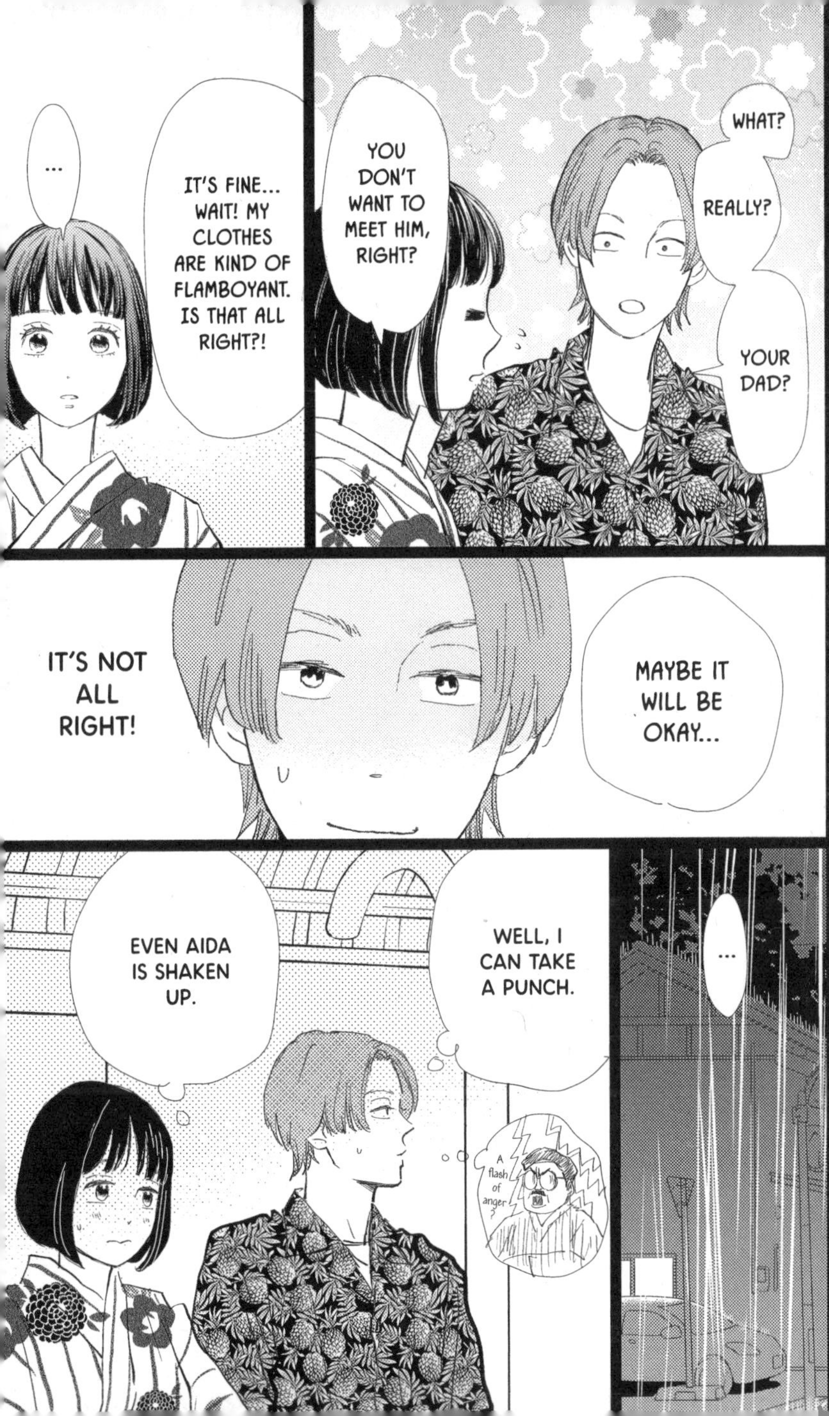
WHAT?
REALLY?
YOUR DAD?
YOU DON'T WANT TO MEET HIM, RIGHT?
IT'S FINE... WAIT! MY CLOTHES ARE KIND OF FLAMBOYANT. IS THAT ALL RIGHT?!
...
MAYBE IT WILL BE OKAY...
IT'S NOT ALL RIGHT!
...
WELL, I CAN TAKE A PUNCH.
EVEN AIDA IS SHAKEN UP.
A flash of anger?

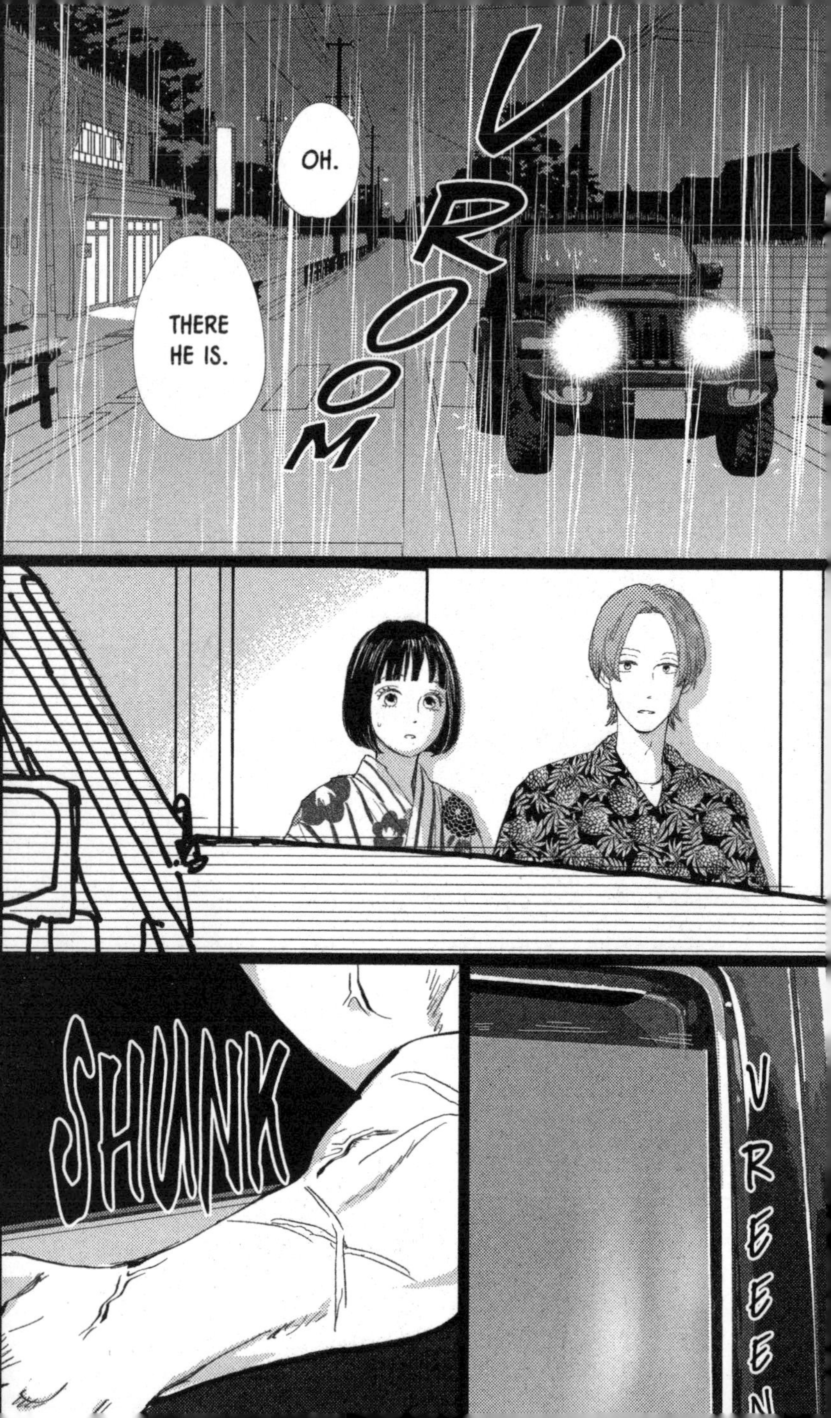
VROOM
OH.
THERE HE IS.
VREEN
SHUNK

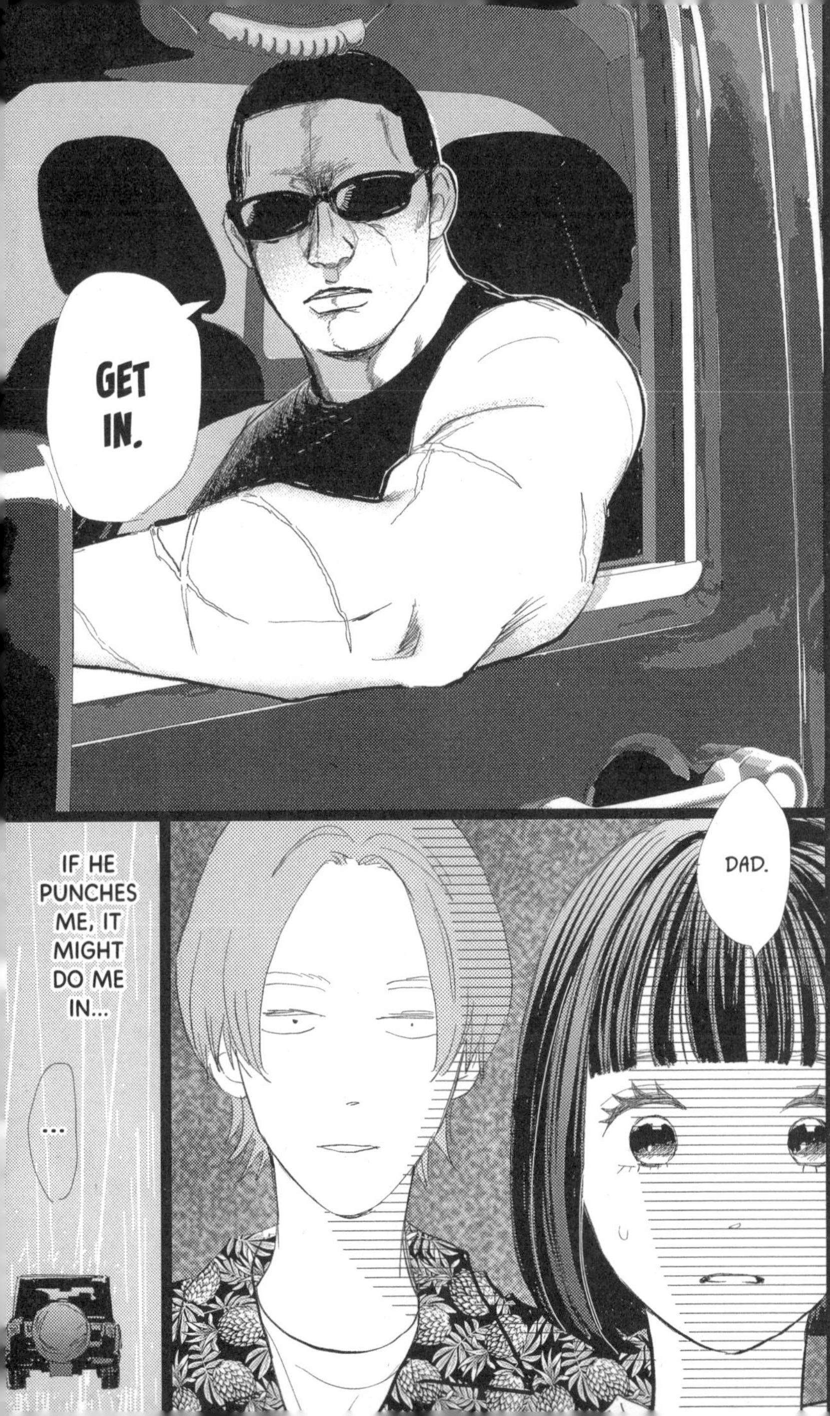
GET IN.
DAD.
IF HE PUNCHES ME, IT MIGHT DO ME IN...
...

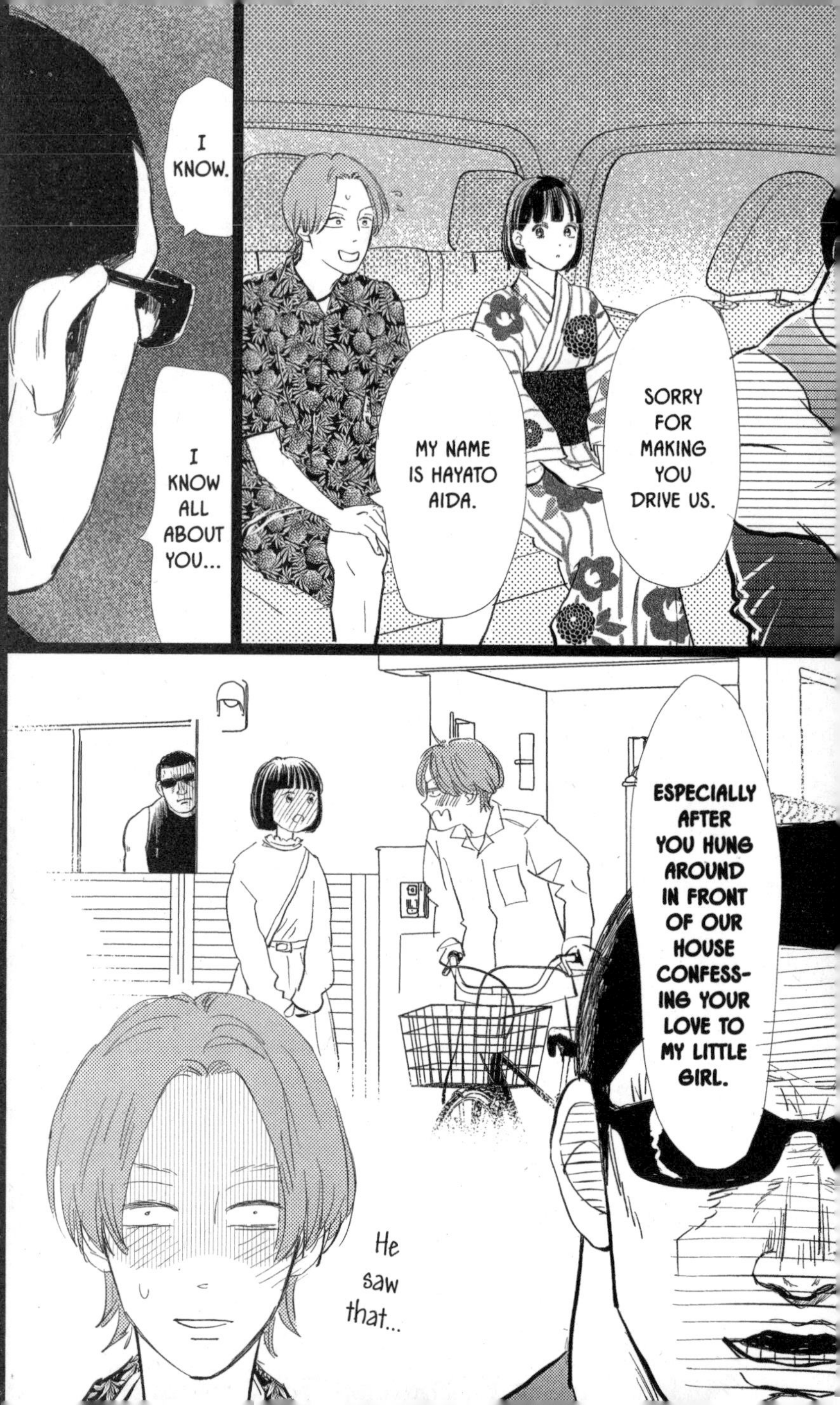
SORRY FOR MAKING YOU DRIVE US.
MY NAME IS HAYATO AIDA.
I KNOW.
I KNOW ALL ABOUT YOU...
ESPECIALLY AFTER YOU HUNG AROUND IN FRONT OF OUR HOUSE CONFESSING YOUR LOVE TO MY LITTLE GIRL.
He saw that...

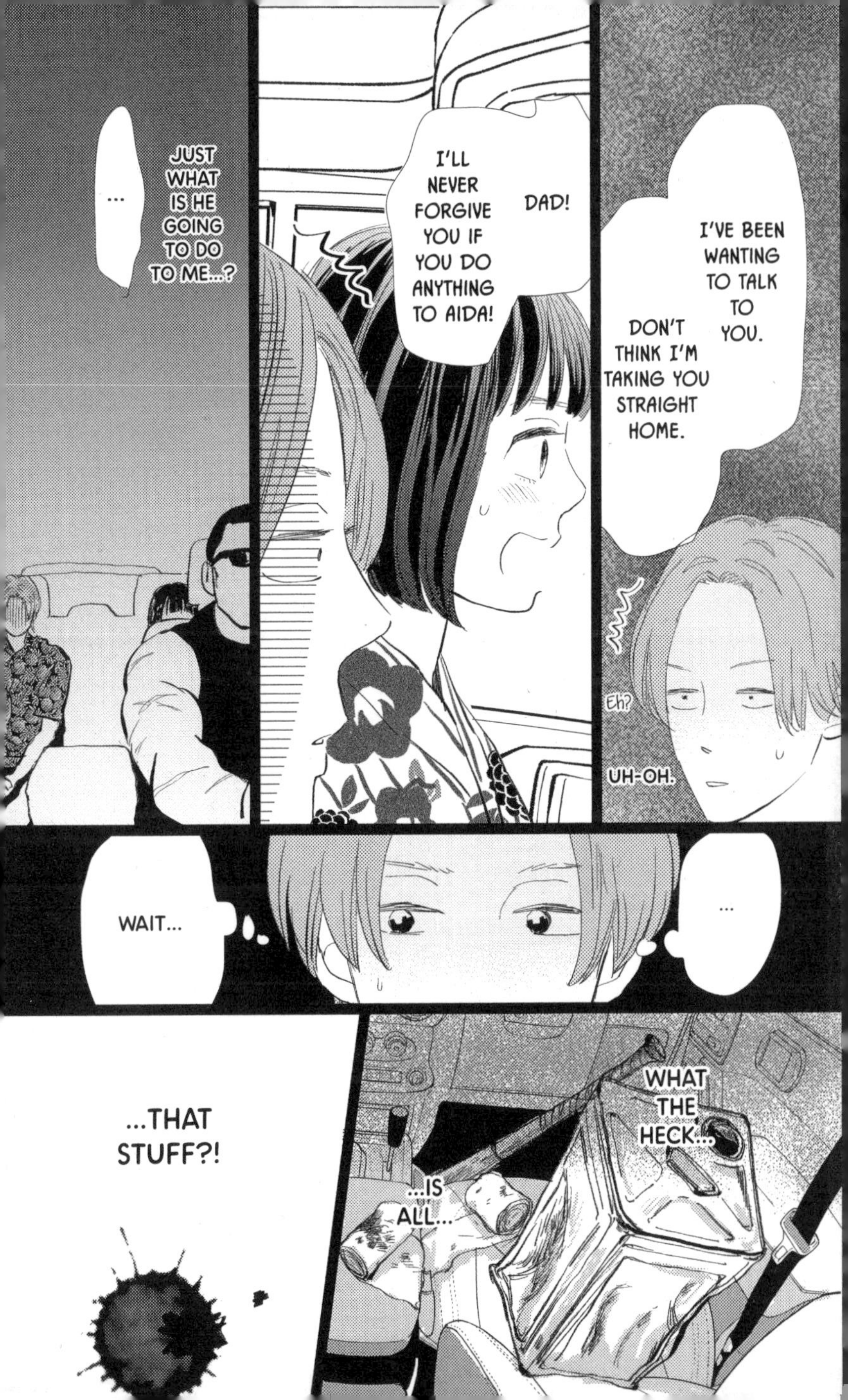
I'VE BEEN WANTING TO TALK TO YOU.
DON'T THINK I'M TAKING YOU STRAIGHT HOME.
Eh?
UH-OH.
DAD!
I'LL NEVER FORGIVE YOU IF YOU DO ANYTHING TO AIDA!
JUST WHAT IS HE GOING TO DO TO ME...?
...
...
WAIT...
WHAT THE HECK...
...IS ALL...
...THAT STUFF?!

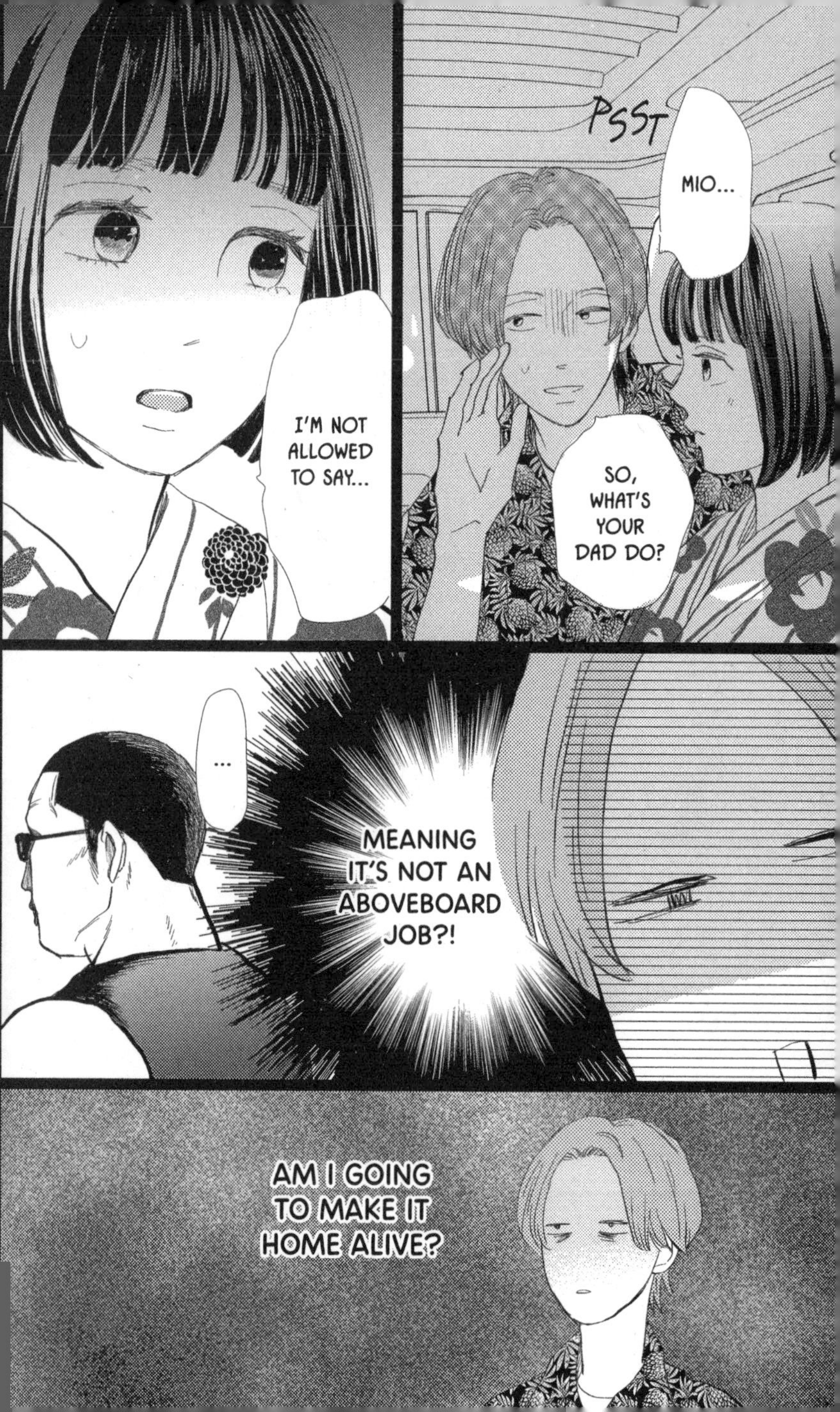
PSST
MIO...
SO, WHAT'S YOUR DAD DO?
I'M NOT ALLOWED TO SAY...
MEANING IT'S NOT AN ABOVEBOARD JOB?!
...
AM I GOING TO MAKE IT HOME ALIVE?

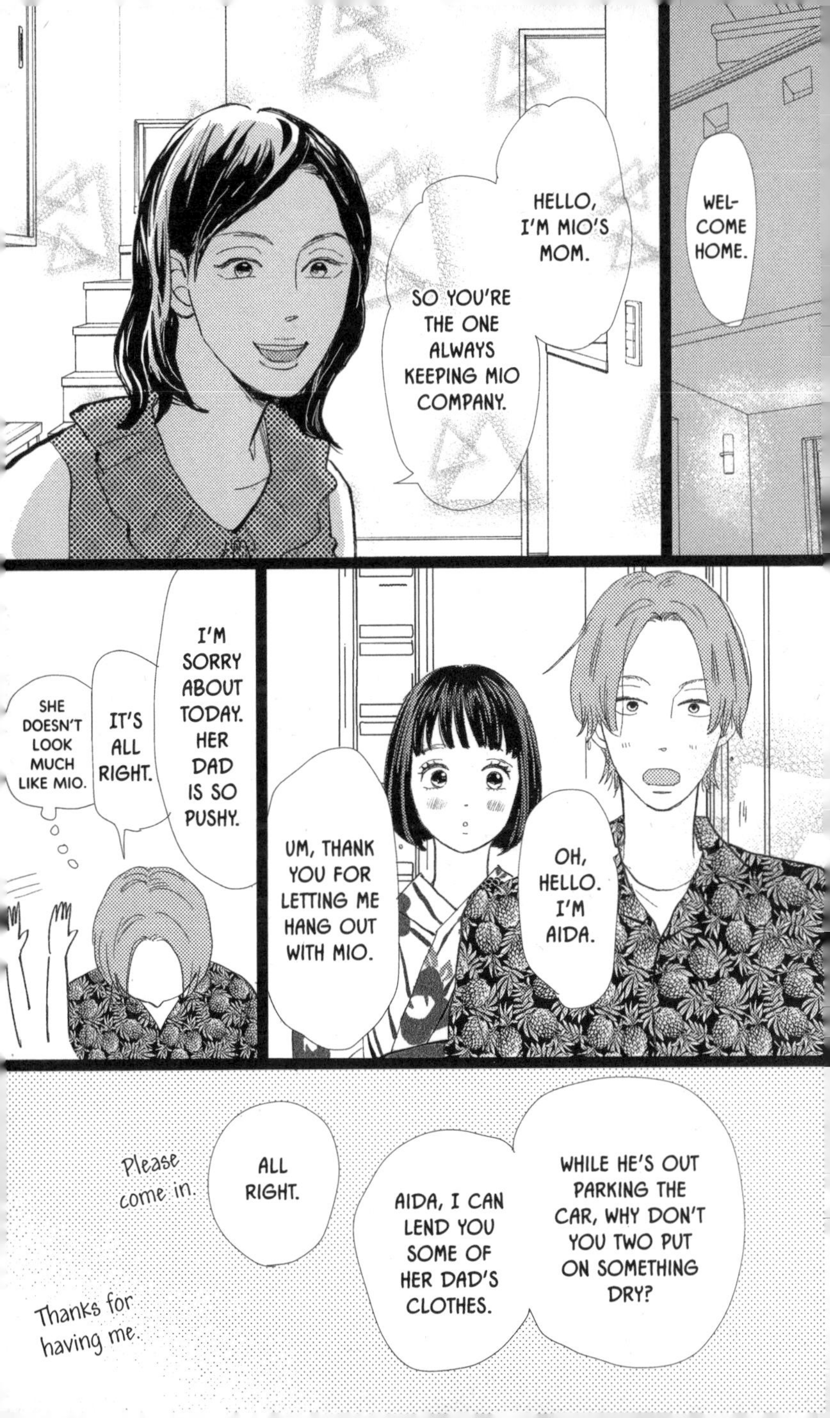
WEL-COME HOME.
HELLO, I'M MIO'S MOM.
SO YOU'RE THE ONE ALWAYS KEEPING MIO COMPANY.
OH, HELLO. I'M AIDA.
UM, THANK YOU FOR LETTING ME HANG OUT WITH MIO.
I'M SORRY ABOUT TODAY. HER DAD IS SO PUSHY.
IT'S ALL RIGHT.
SHE DOESN'T LOOK MUCH LIKE MIO.
WHILE HE'S OUT PARKING THE CAR, WHY DON'T YOU TWO PUT ON SOMETHING DRY?
AIDA, I CAN LEND YOU SOME OF HER DAD'S CLOTHES.
ALL RIGHT.
Please come in.
Thanks for having me.

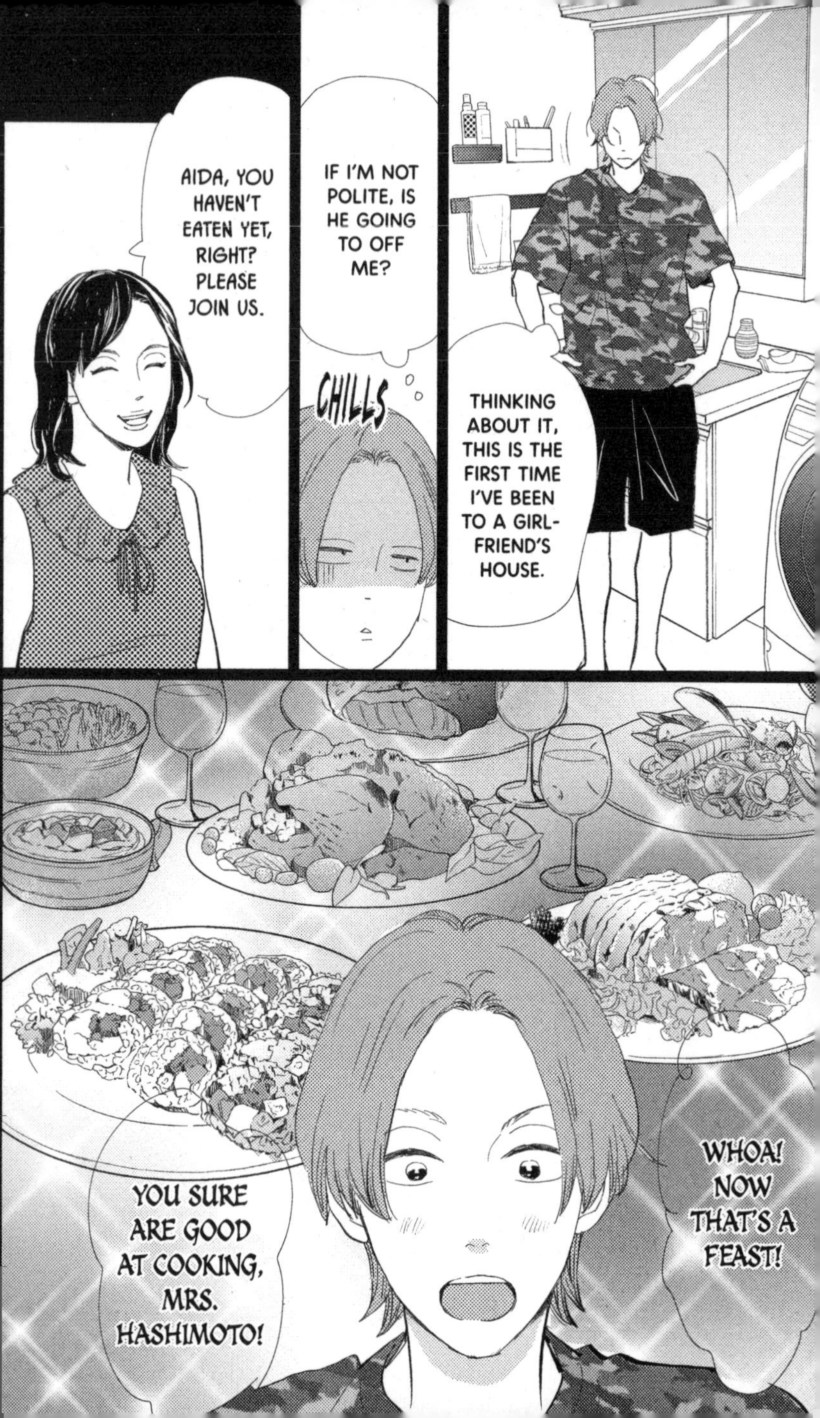
THINKING ABOUT IT, THIS IS THE FIRST TIME I'VE BEEN TO A GIRL-FRIEND'S HOUSE.
IF I'M NOT POLITE, IS HE GOING TO OFF ME?
CHILLS
AIDA, YOU HAVEN'T EATEN YET, RIGHT? PLEASE JOIN US.
WHOA! NOW THAT'S A FEAST!
YOU SURE ARE GOOD AT COOKING, MRS. HASHIMOTO!

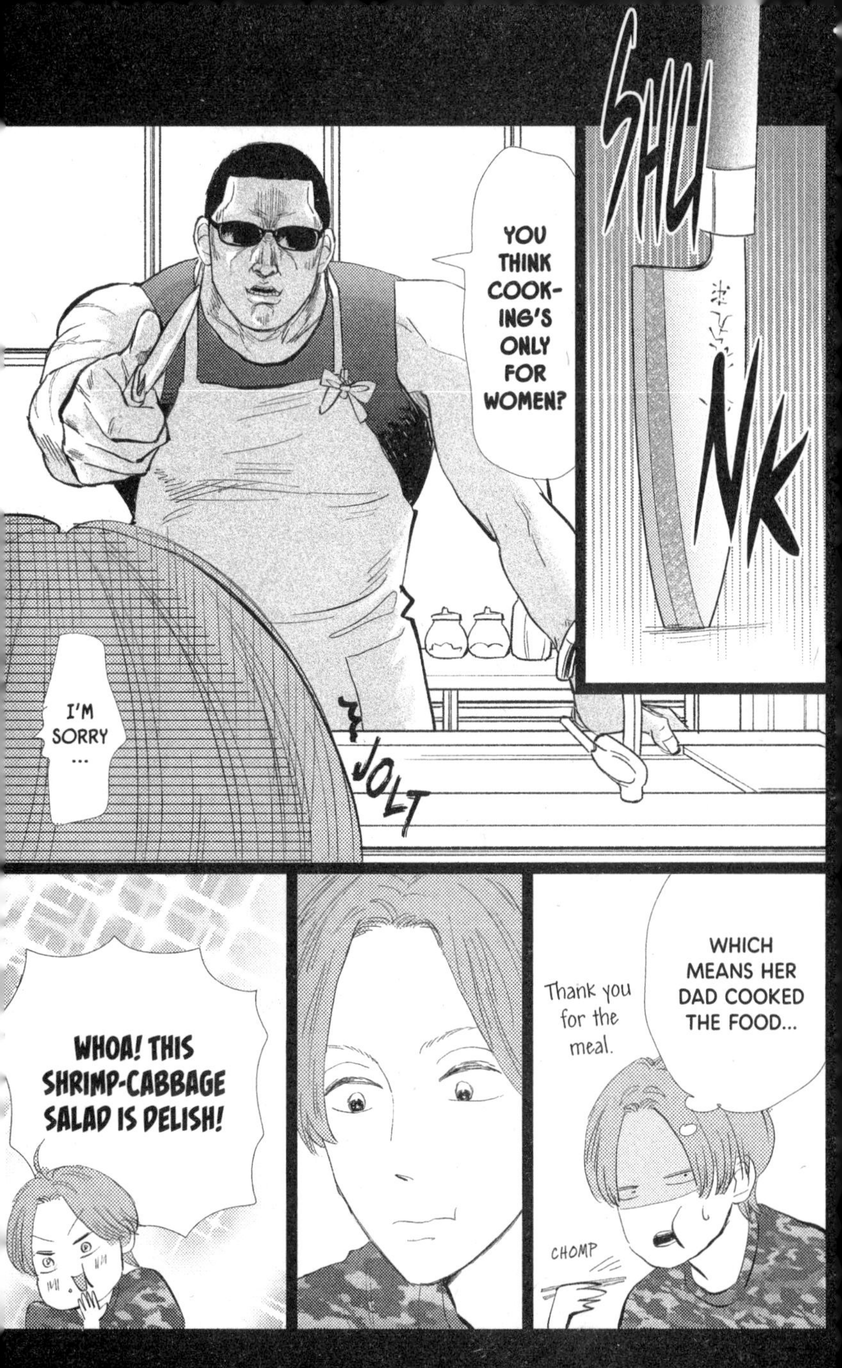
SHUNK
YOU THINK COOKING'S ONLY FOR WOMEN?
JOLT
I'M SORRY...
WHICH MEANS HER DAD COOKED THE FOOD...
Thank you for the meal.
CHOMP
WHOA! THIS SHRIMP-CABBAGE SALAD IS DELISH!

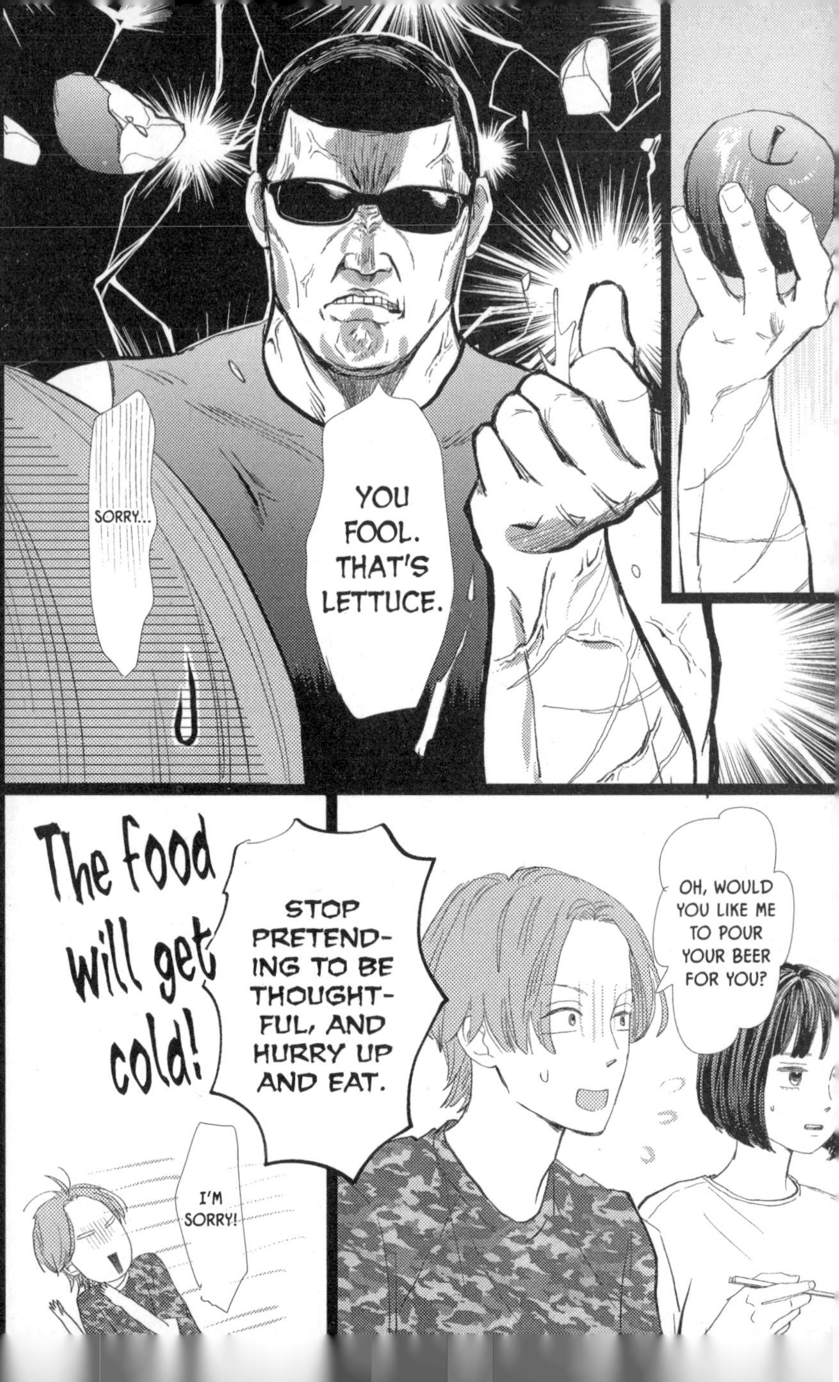
YOU FOOL. THAT'S LETTUCE.
SORRY...
OH, WOULD YOU LIKE ME TO POUR YOUR BEER FOR YOU?
STOP PRETENDING TO BE THOUGHTFUL, AND HURRY UP AND EAT.
The food will get cold!
I'M SORRY!

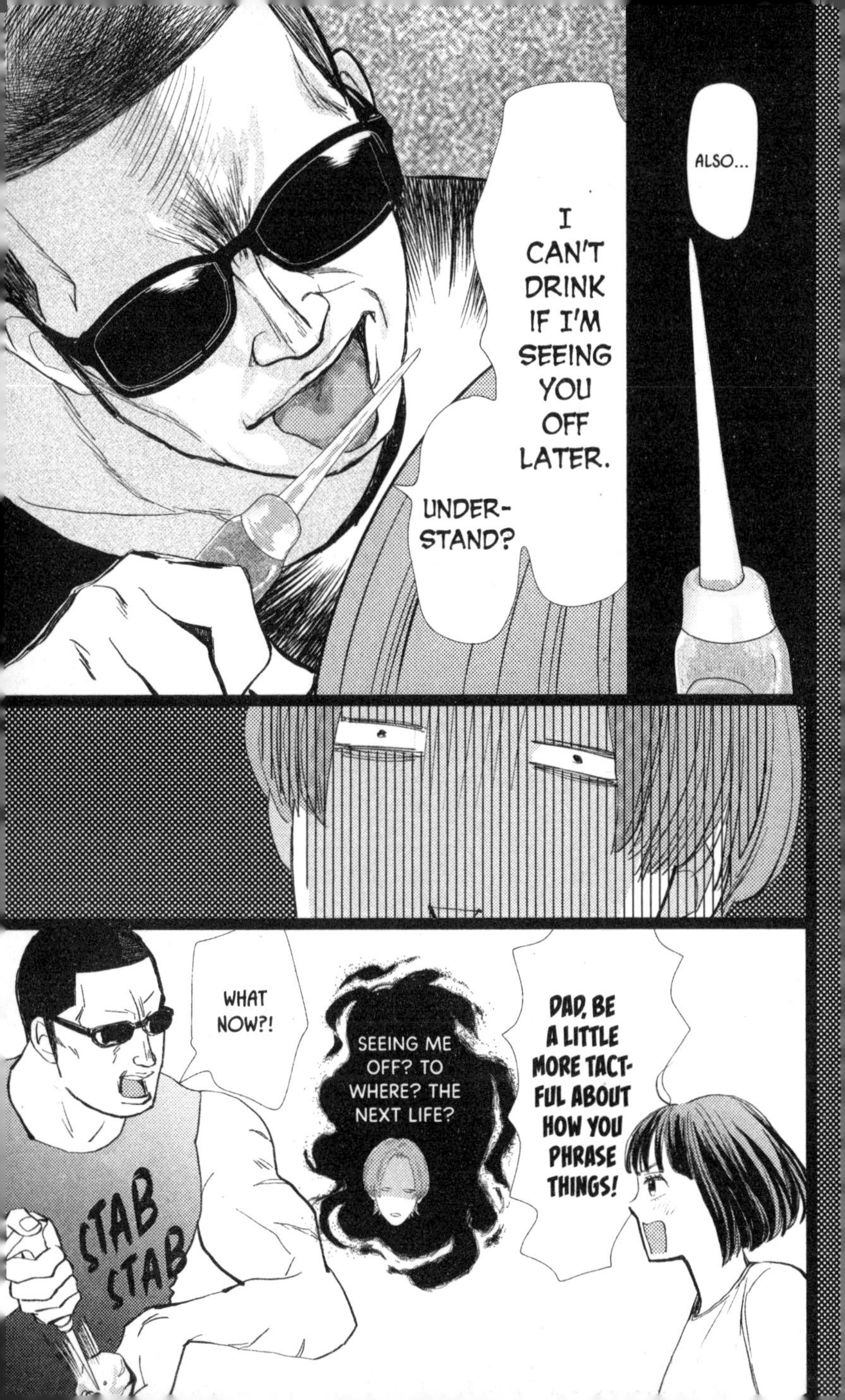
ALSO...
I CAN'T DRINK IF I'M SEEING YOU OFF LATER.
UNDER-STAND?
DAD, BE A LITTLE MORE TACT-FUL ABOUT HOW YOU PHRASE THINGS!
SEEING ME OFF? TO WHERE? THE NEXT LIFE?
WHAT NOW?!
STAB STAB

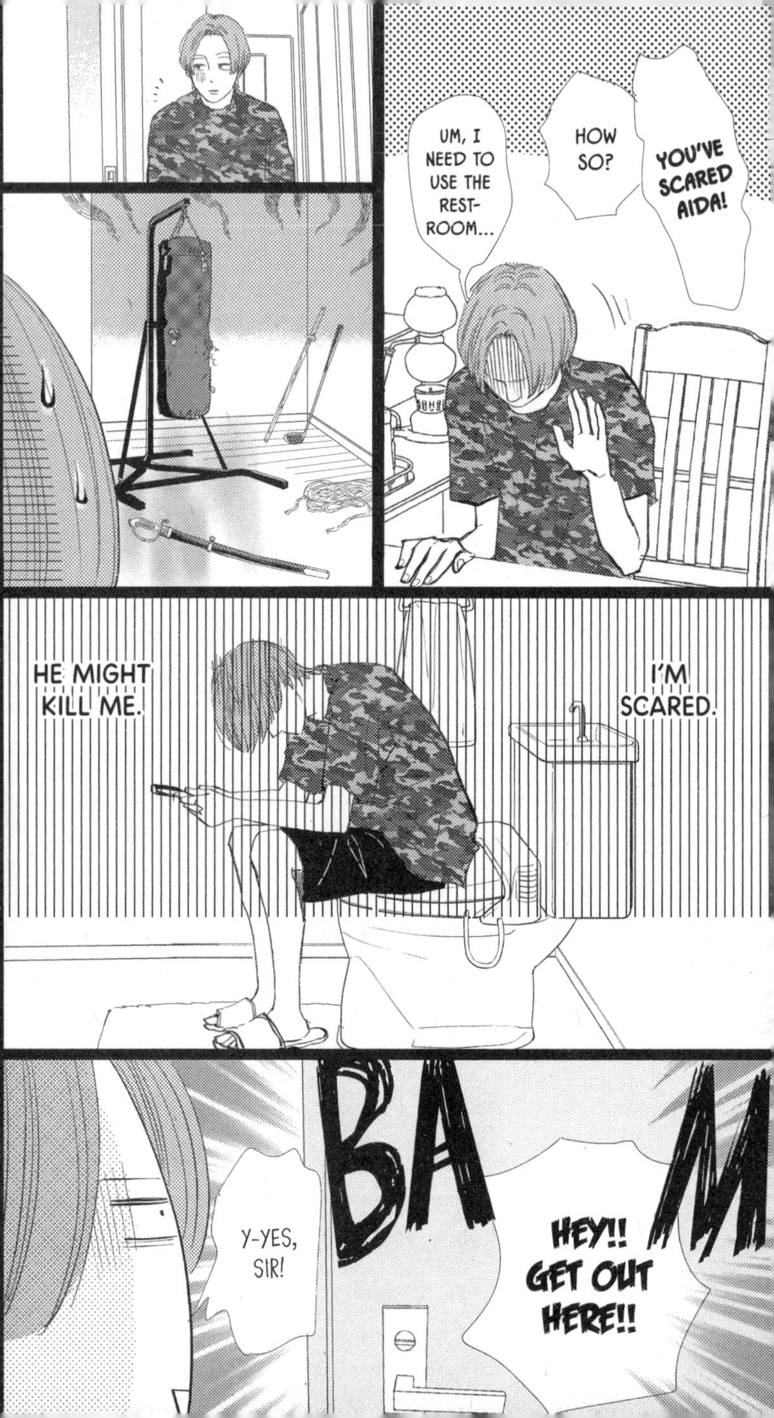
YOU'VE SCARED AIDA!
HOW SO?
UM, I NEED TO USE THE REST-ROOM...
I'M SCARED.
HE MIGHT KILL ME.
BAM
HEY!! GET OUT HERE!!
Y-YES, SIR!

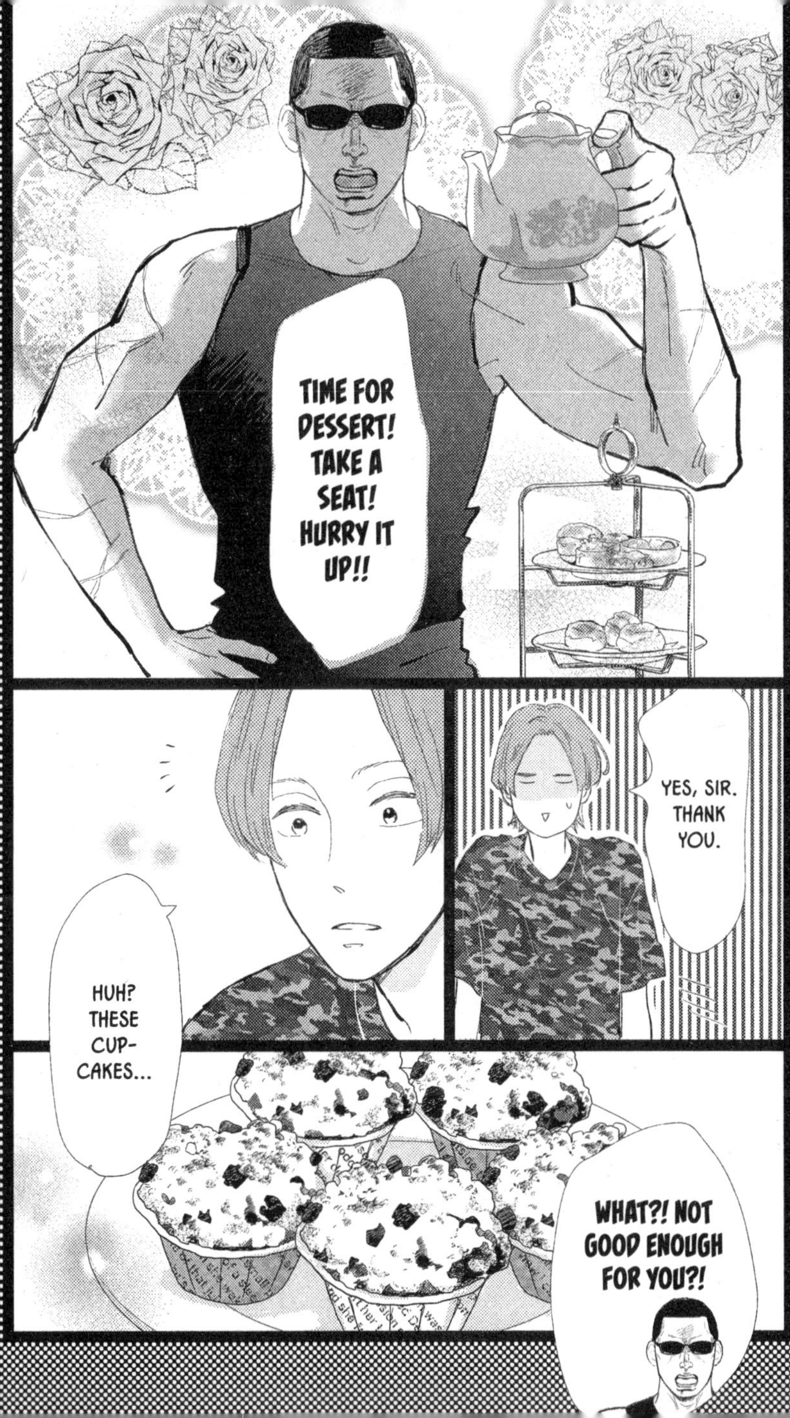
TIME FOR DESSERT! TAKE A SEAT! HURRY IT UP!!
YES, SIR. THANK YOU.
HUH? THESE CUP-CAKES...
WHAT?! NOT GOOD ENOUGH FOR YOU?!

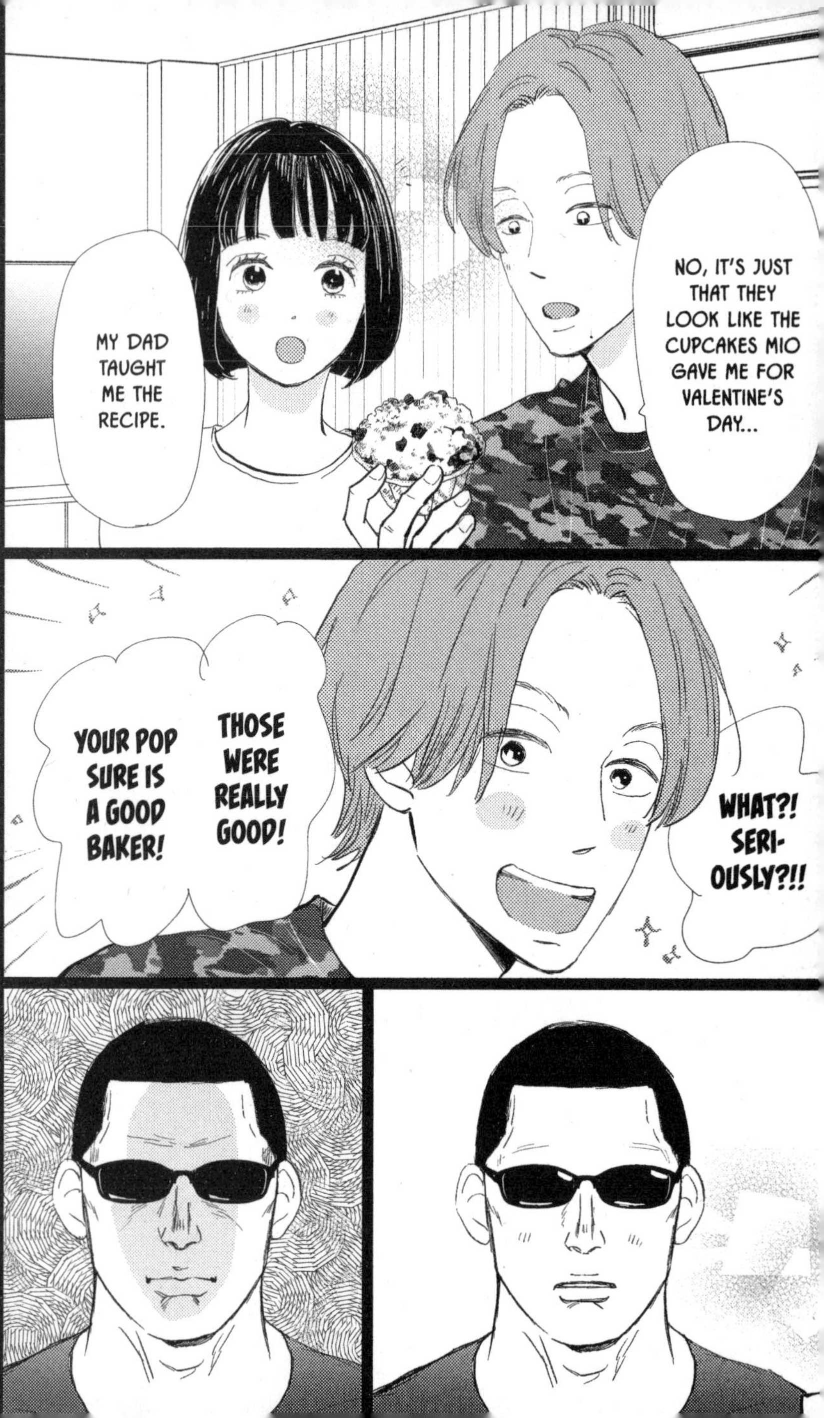
NO, IT'S JUST THAT THEY LOOK LIKE THE CUPCAKES MIO GAVE ME FOR VALENTINE'S DAY...
MY DAD TAUGHT ME THE RECIPE.
WHAT?! SERI-OUSLY?!!
THOSE WERE REALLY GOOD!
YOUR POP SURE IS A GOOD BAKER!

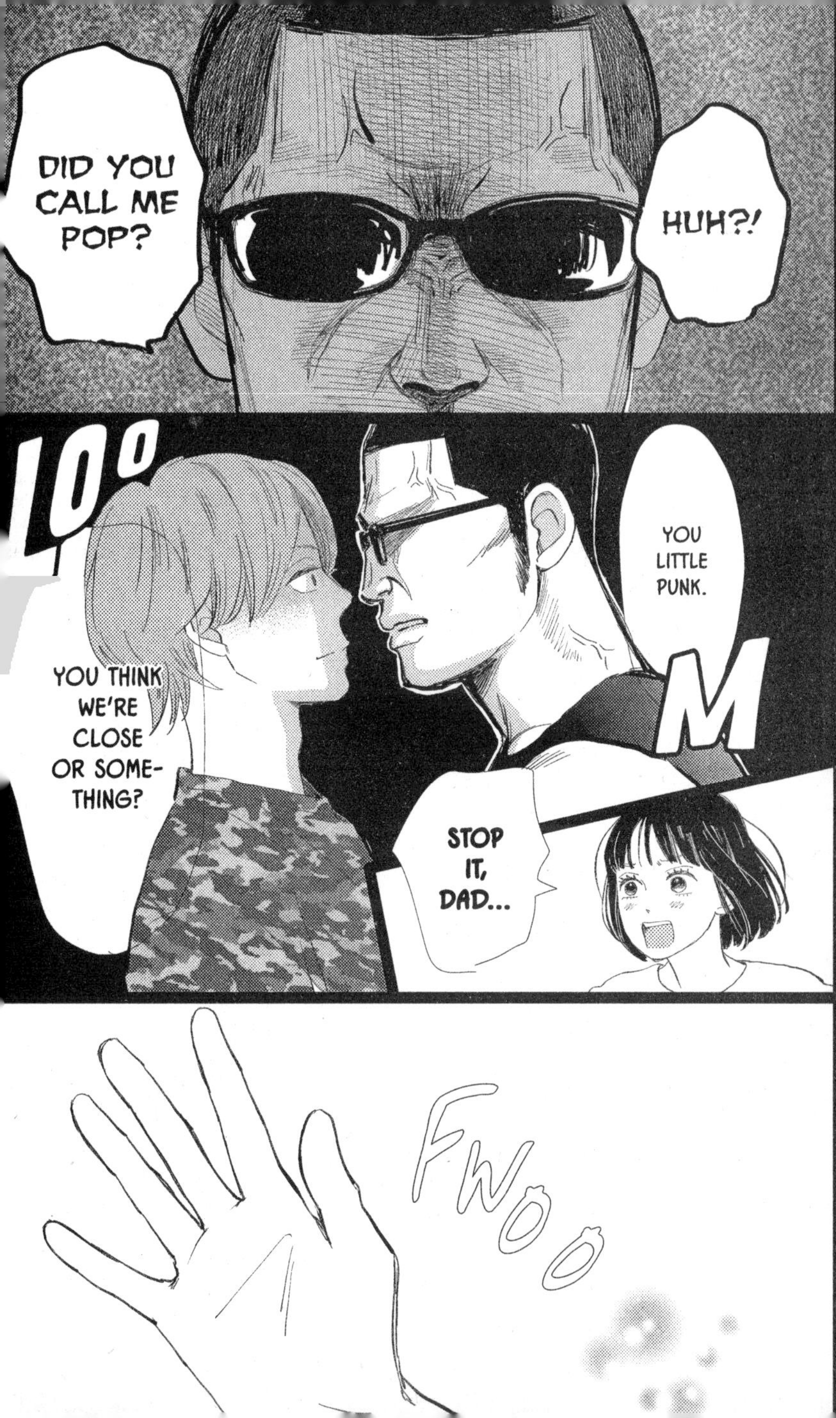
HUH?!
DID YOU CALL ME POP?
YOU LITTLE PUNK.
M
LOO
YOU THINK WE'RE CLOSE OR SOME-THING?
STOP IT, DAD...
FWOO

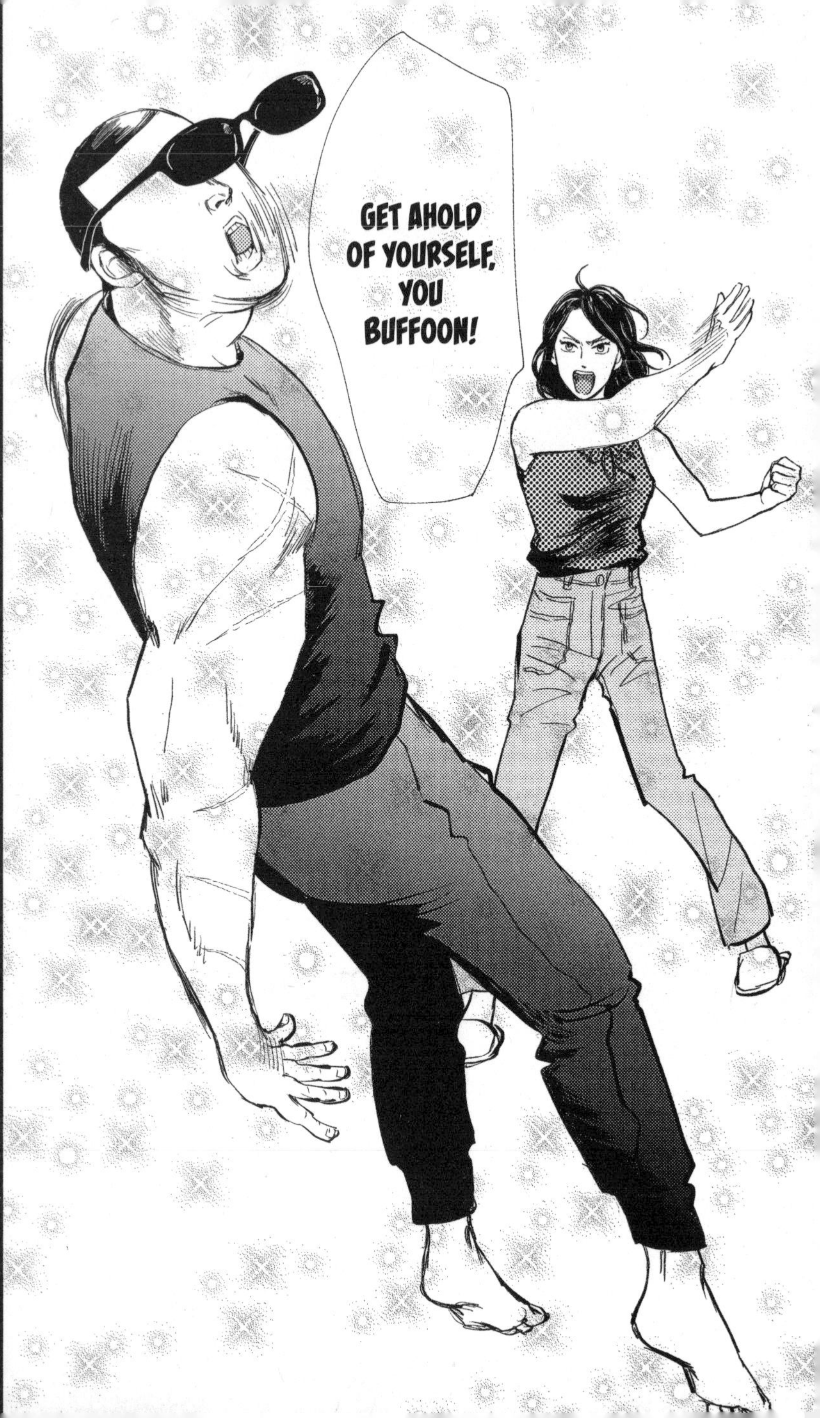
GET AHOLD OF YOURSELF, YOU BUFFOON!

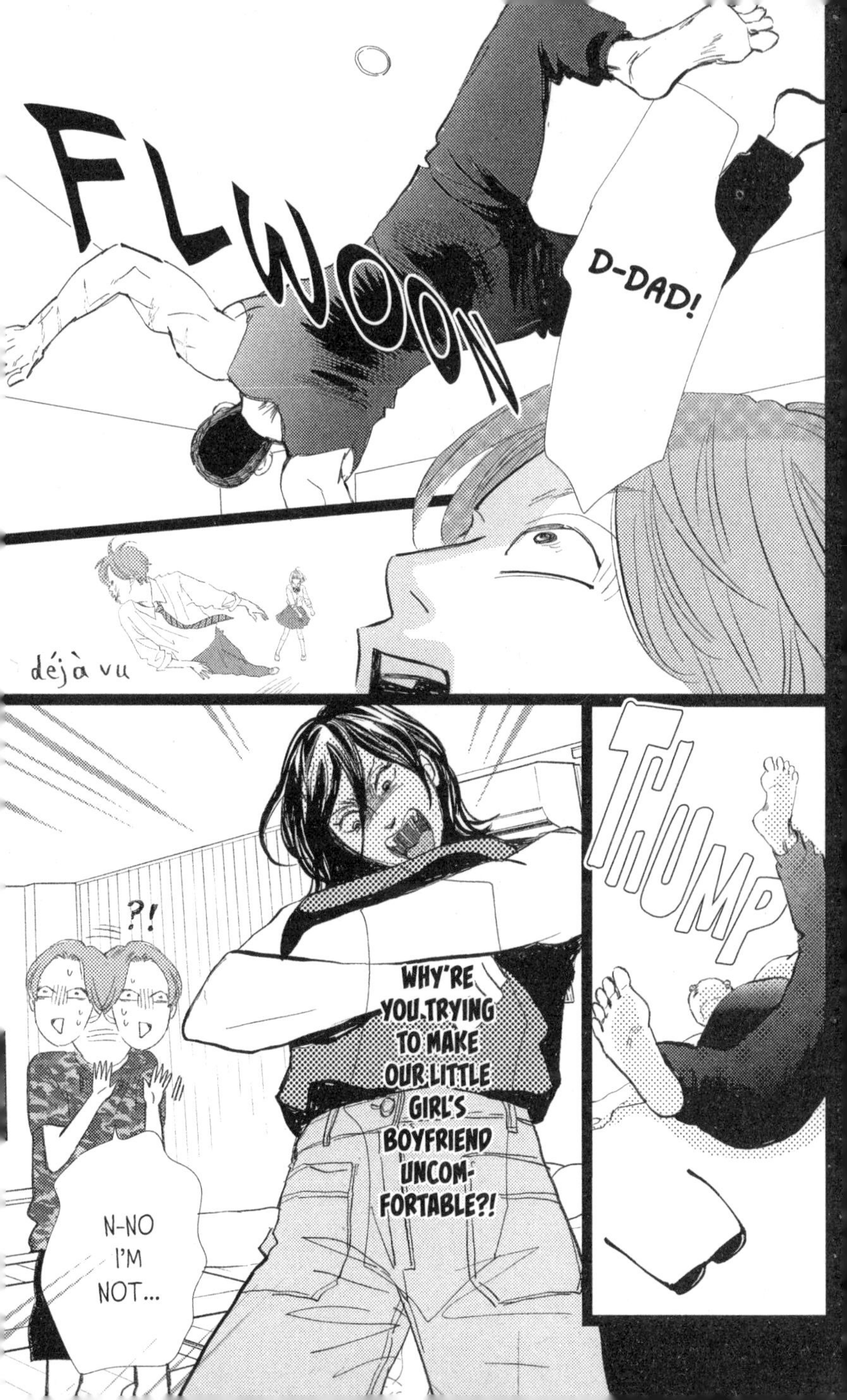
FLWOOOM
D-DAD!
déjà vu
THUMP
WHY'RE YOU TRYING TO MAKE OUR LITTLE GIRL'S BOYFRIEND UNCOM-FORTABLE?!
?!
N-NO I'M NOT...

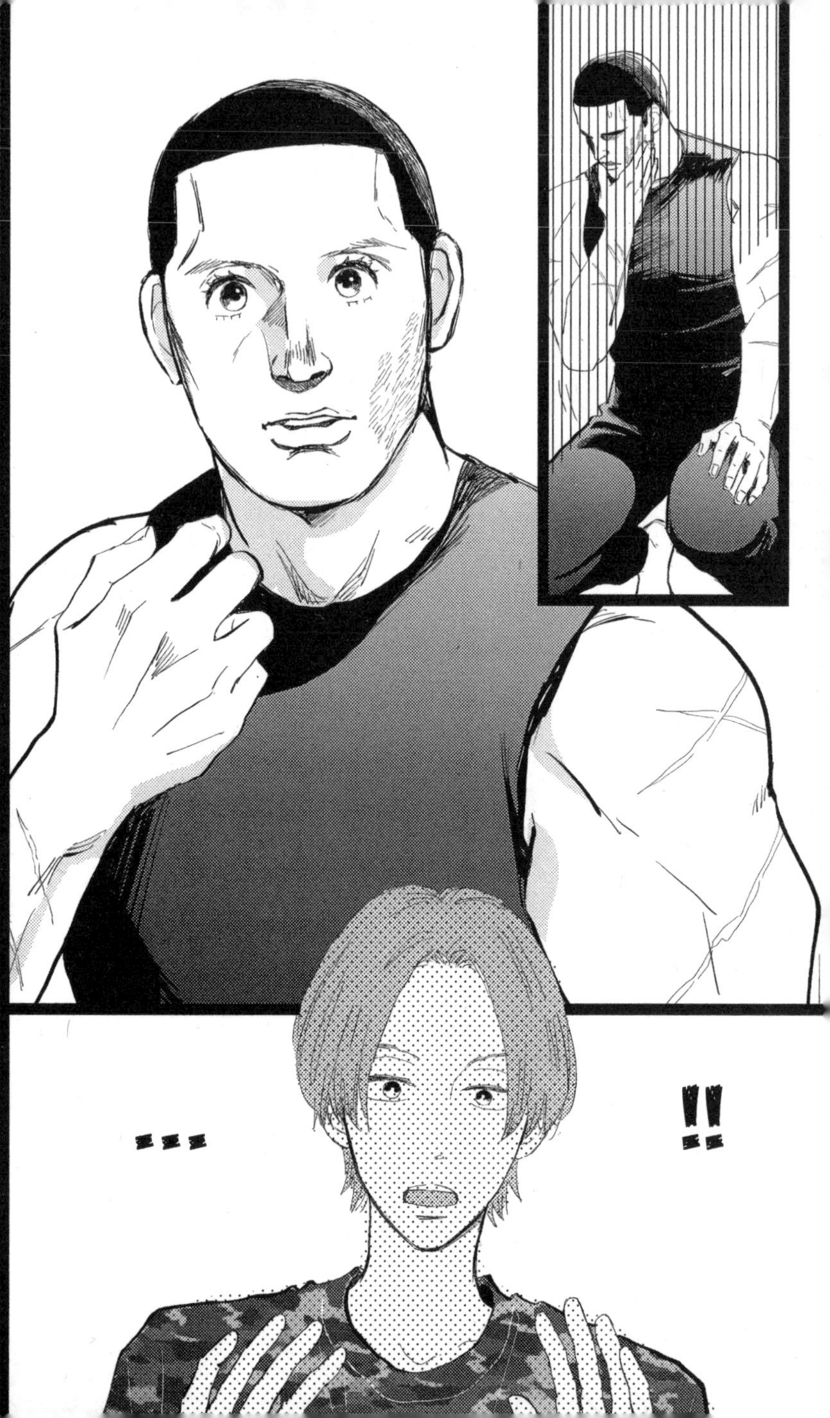
!!
…

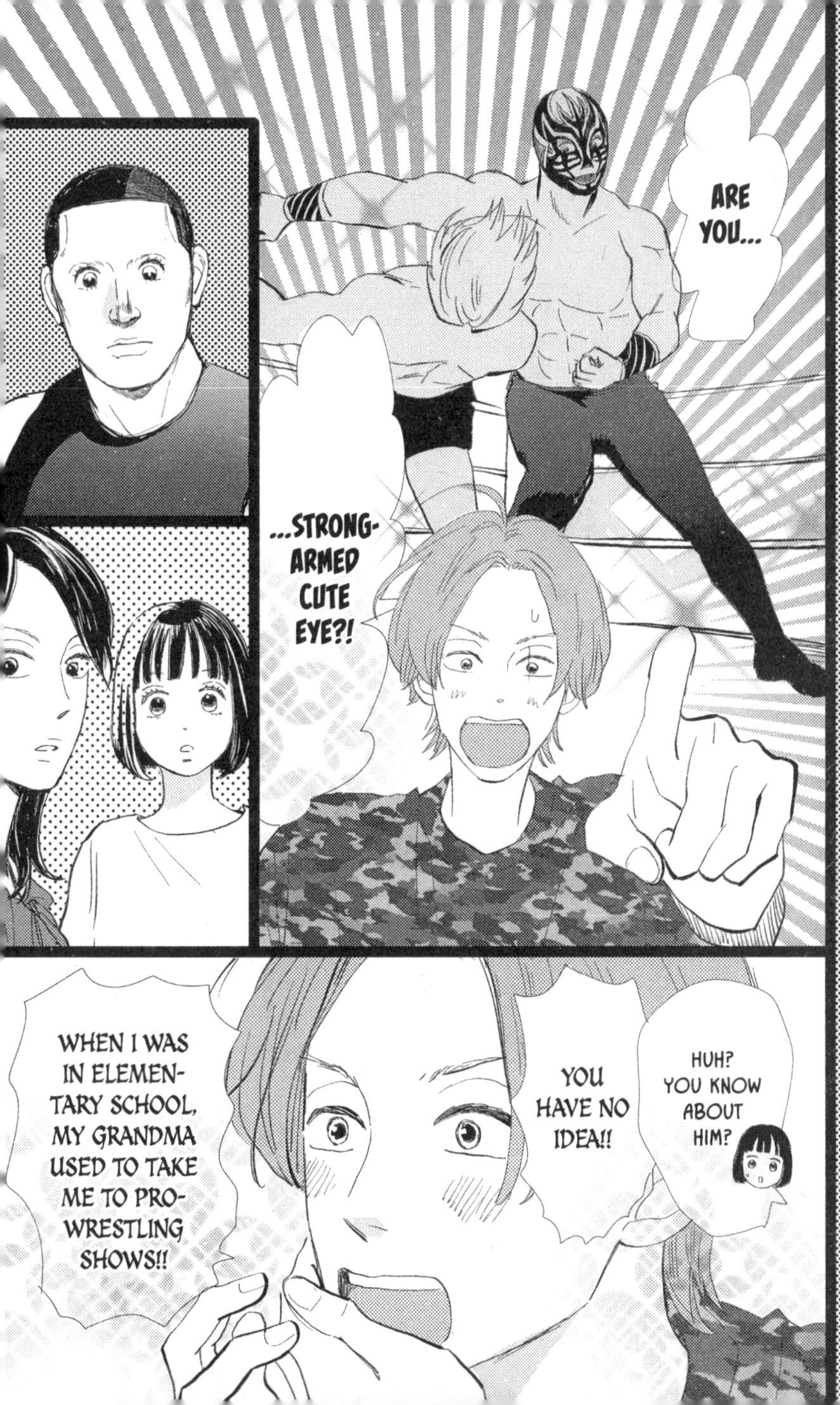
ARE YOU...
...STRONG-ARMED CUTE EYE?!
HUH? YOU KNOW ABOUT HIM?
YOU HAVE NO IDEA!!
WHEN I WAS IN ELEMENTARY SCHOOL, MY GRANDMA USED TO TAKE ME TO PRO-WRESTLING SHOWS!!

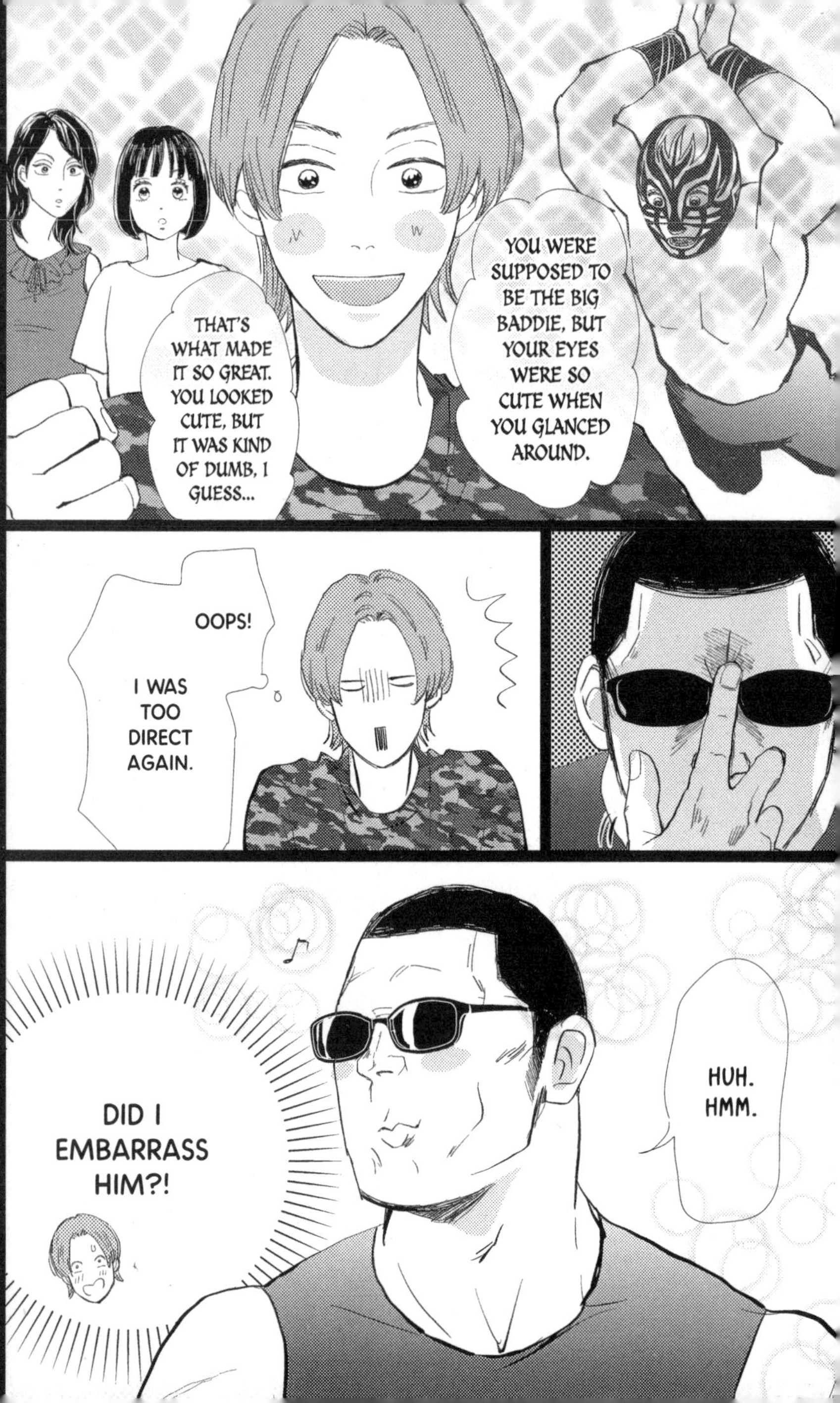
YOU WERE SUPPOSED TO BE THE BIG BADDIE, BUT YOUR EYES WERE SO CUTE WHEN YOU GLANCED AROUND.
THAT'S WHAT MADE IT SO GREAT. YOU LOOKED CUTE, BUT IT WAS KIND OF DUMB, I GUESS...
OOPS!
I WAS TOO DIRECT AGAIN.
HUH. HMM.
DID I EMBARRASS HIM?!

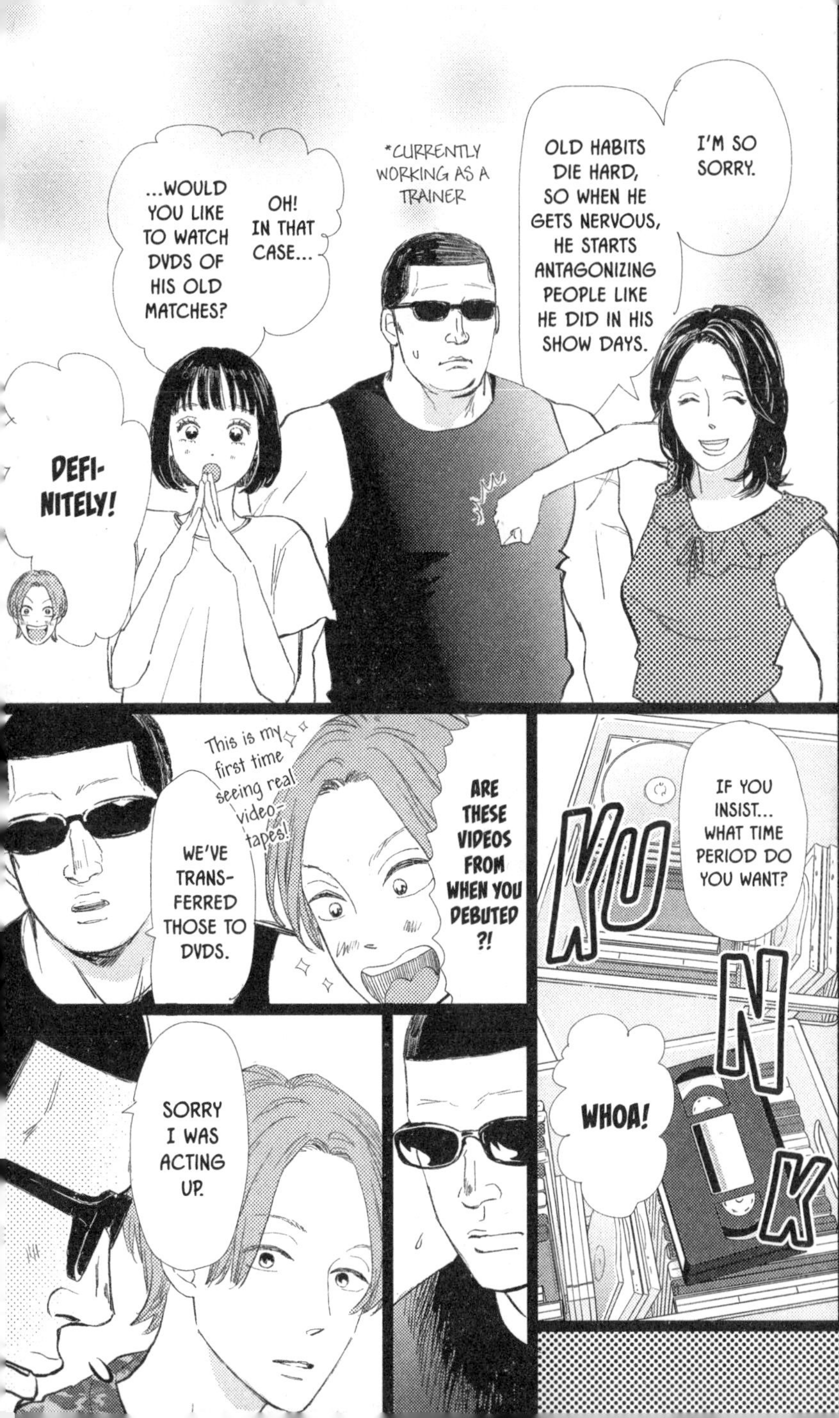
I'M SO SORRY.
OLD HABITS DIE HARD, SO WHEN HE GETS NERVOUS, HE STARTS ANTAGONIZING PEOPLE LIKE HE DID IN HIS SHOW DAYS.
*CURRENTLY WORKING AS A TRAINER
OH! IN THAT CASE...
...WOULD YOU LIKE TO WATCH DVDS OF HIS OLD MATCHES?
DEFI-NITELY!
IF YOU INSIST... WHAT TIME PERIOD DO YOU WANT?
KUNNK
WHOA!
ARE THESE VIDEOS FROM WHEN YOU DEBUTED?!
This is my first time seeing real video-tapes!
WE'VE TRANS-FERRED THOSE TO DVDS.
SORRY I WAS ACTING UP.

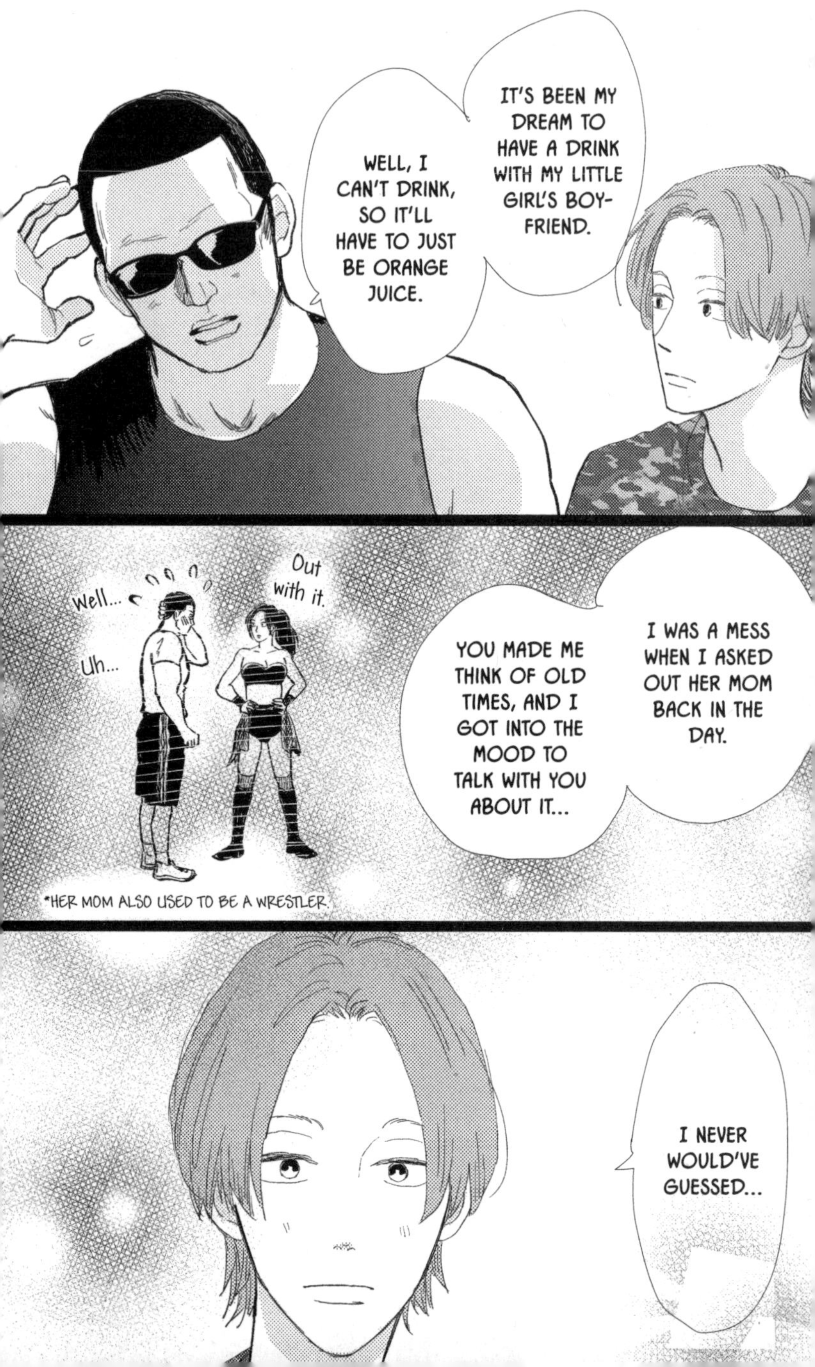
IT'S BEEN MY DREAM TO HAVE A DRINK WITH MY LITTLE GIRL'S BOY-FRIEND.
WELL, I CAN'T DRINK, SO IT'LL HAVE TO JUST BE ORANGE JUICE.
I WAS A MESS WHEN I ASKED OUT HER MOM BACK IN THE DAY.
YOU MADE ME THINK OF OLD TIMES, AND I GOT INTO THE MOOD TO TALK WITH YOU ABOUT IT...
Out with it.
Well...
Uh...
*HER MOM ALSO USED TO BE A WRESTLER.
I NEVER WOULD'VE GUESSED...

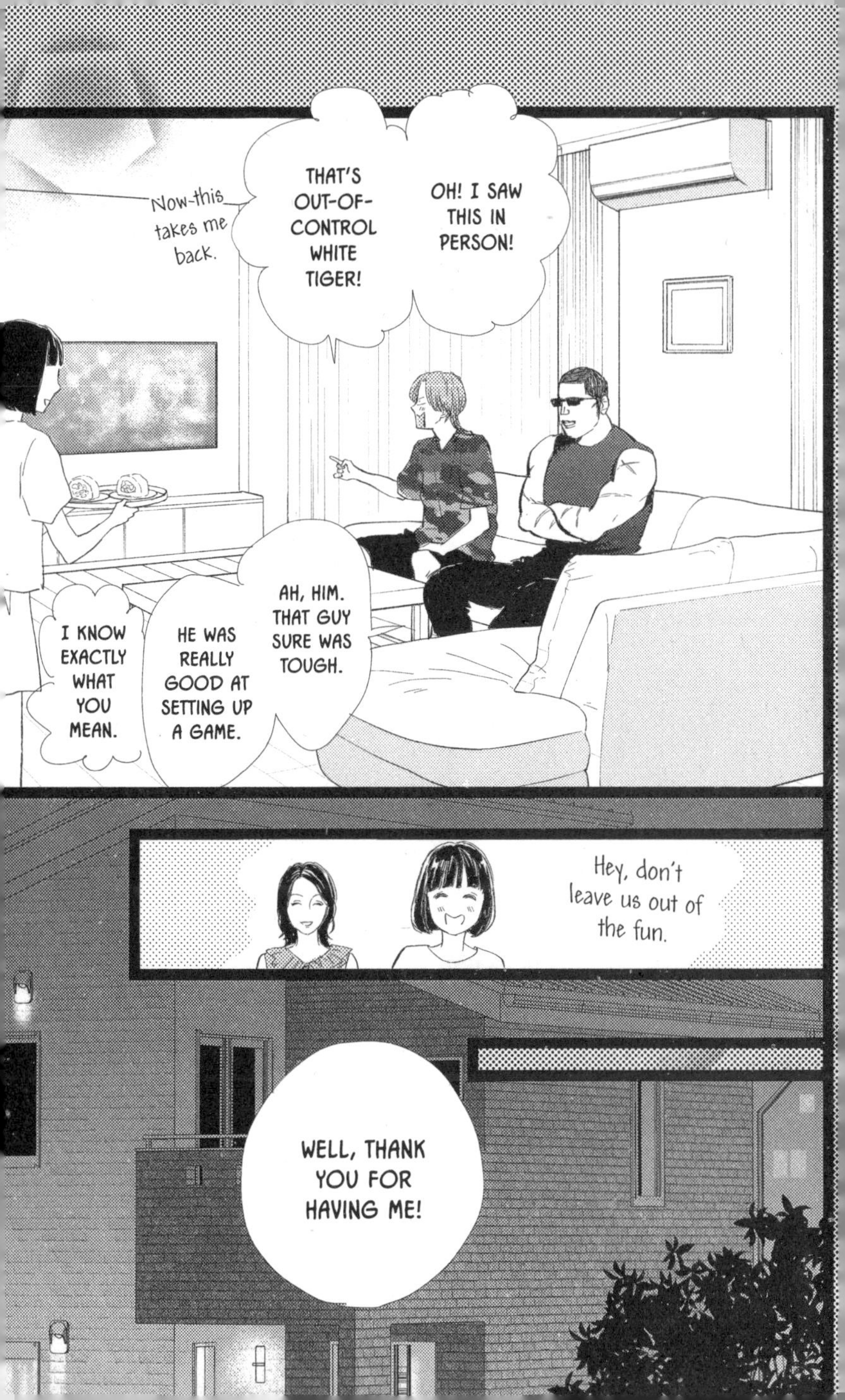
OH! I SAW THIS IN PERSON!
THAT'S OUT-OF-CONTROL WHITE TIGER!
Now-this takes me back.
AH, HIM. THAT GUY SURE WAS TOUGH.
HE WAS REALLY GOOD AT SETTING UP A GAME.
I KNOW EXACTLY WHAT YOU MEAN.
Hey, don't leave us out of the fun.
WELL, THANK YOU FOR HAVING ME!

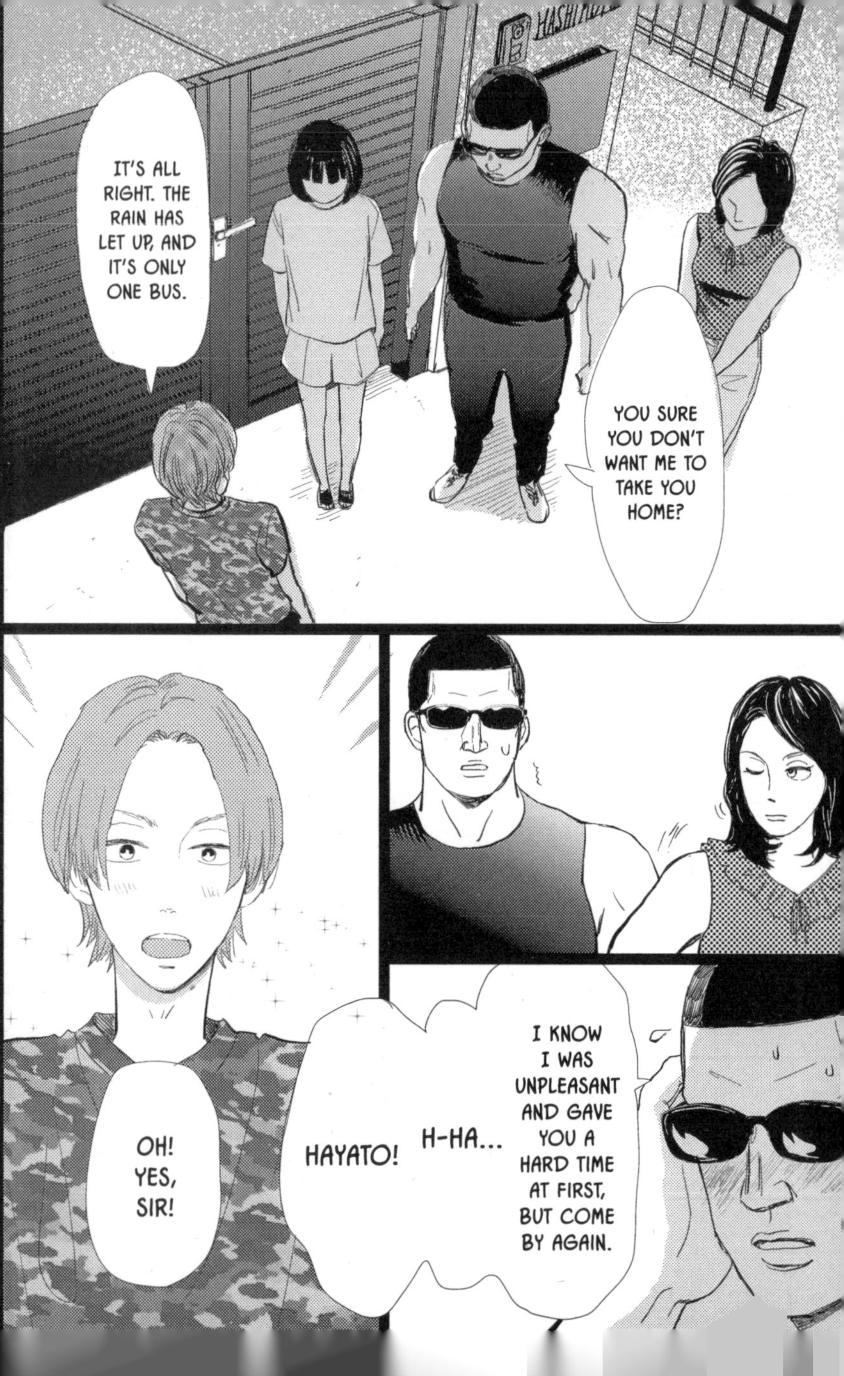
YOU SURE YOU DON'T WANT ME TO TAKE YOU HOME?
IT'S ALL RIGHT. THE RAIN HAS LET UP, AND IT'S ONLY ONE BUS.
I KNOW I WAS UNPLEASANT AND GAVE YOU A HARD TIME AT FIRST, BUT COME BY AGAIN.
H-HA...
HAYATO!
OH! YES, SIR!

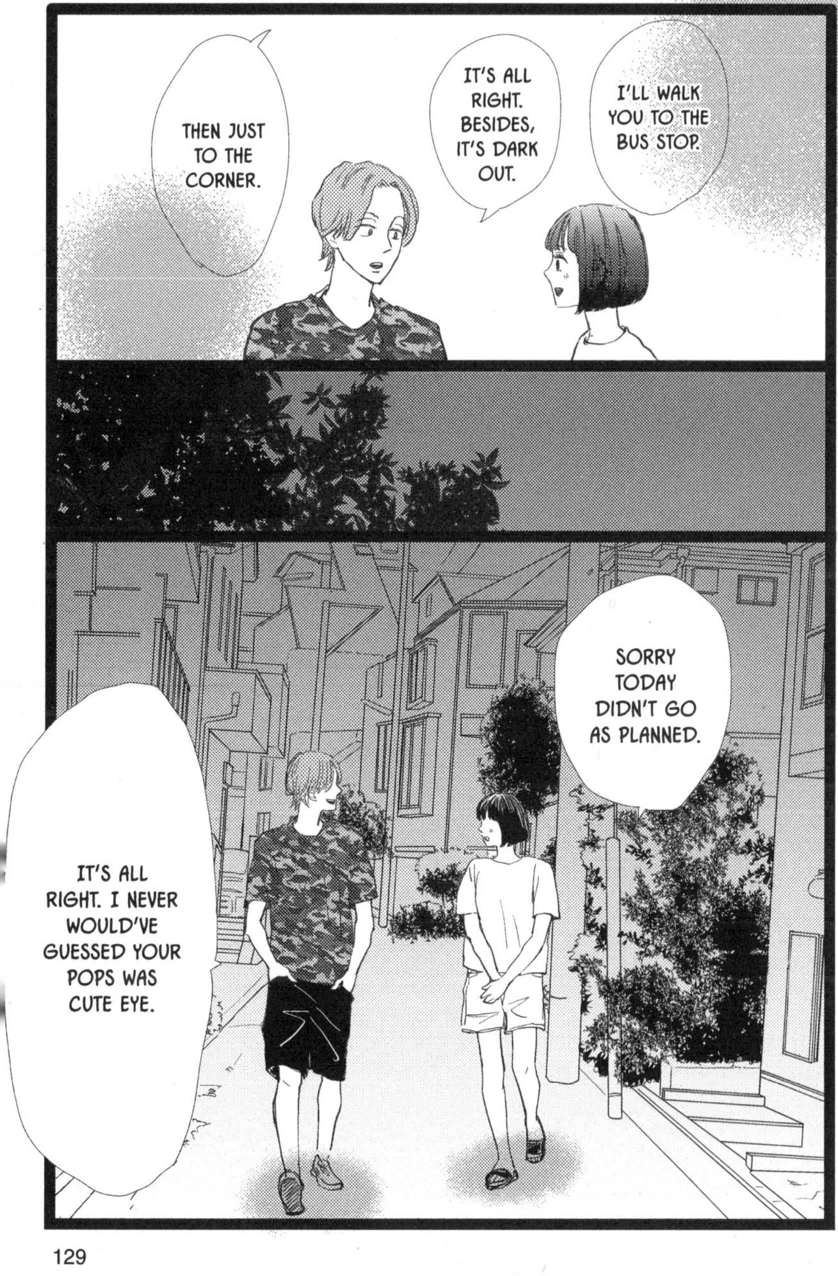
I'LL WALK YOU TO THE BUS STOP.
IT'S ALL RIGHT. BESIDES, IT'S DARK OUT.
THEN JUST TO THE CORNER.
SORRY TODAY DIDN'T GO AS PLANNED.
IT'S ALL RIGHT. I NEVER WOULD'VE GUESSED YOUR POPS WAS CUTE EYE.

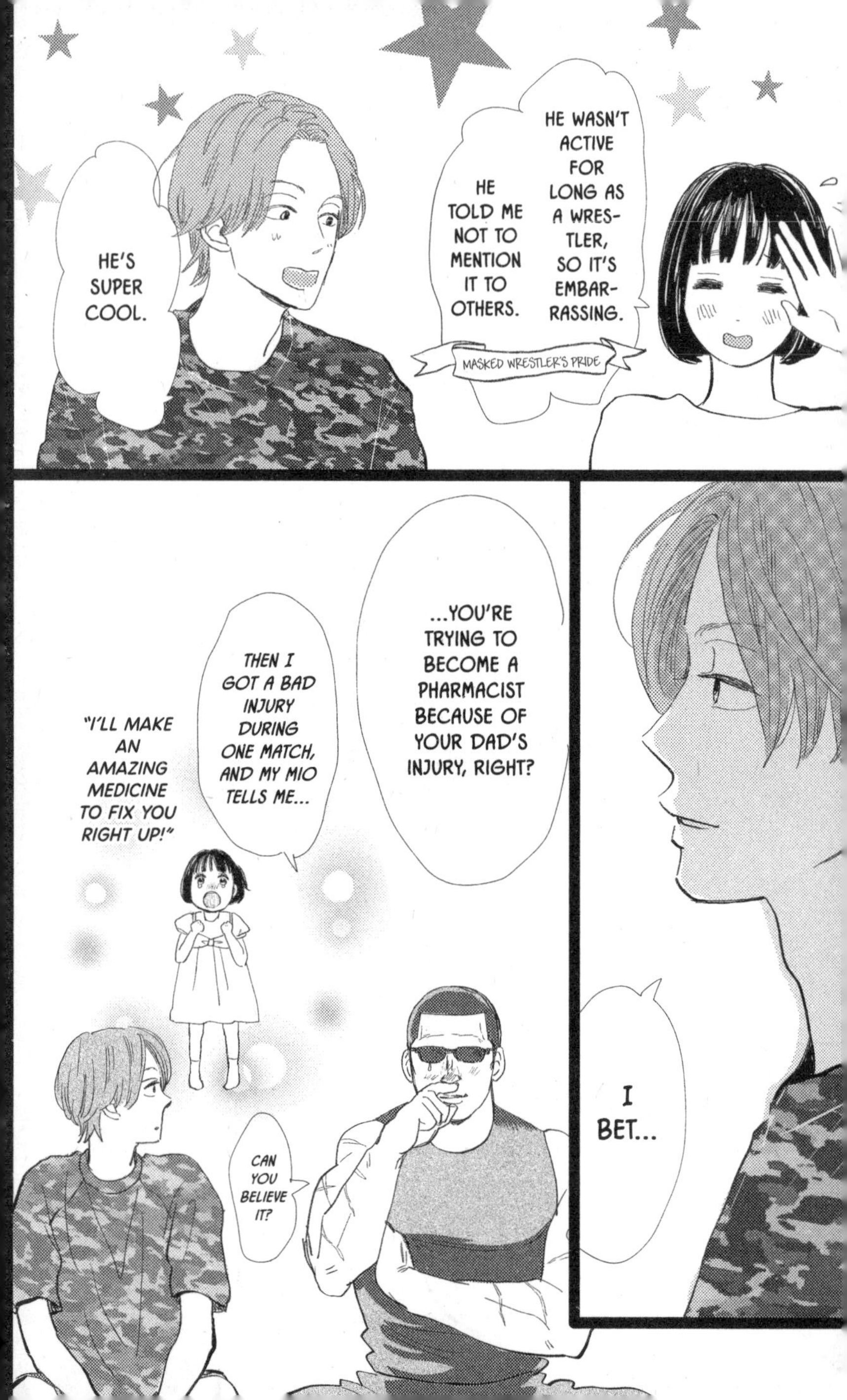
HE WASN'T ACTIVE FOR LONG AS A WRES-TLER, SO IT'S EMBAR-RASSING.
HE TOLD ME NOT TO MENTION IT TO OTHERS.
MASKED WRESTLER'S PRIDE
HE'S SUPER COOL.
I BET...
...YOU'RE TRYING TO BECOME A PHARMACIST BECAUSE OF YOUR DAD'S INJURY, RIGHT?
THEN I GOT A BAD INJURY DURING ONE MATCH, AND MY MIO TELLS ME...
"I'LL MAKE AN AMAZING MEDICINE TO FIX YOU RIGHT UP!"
CAN YOU BELIEVE IT?

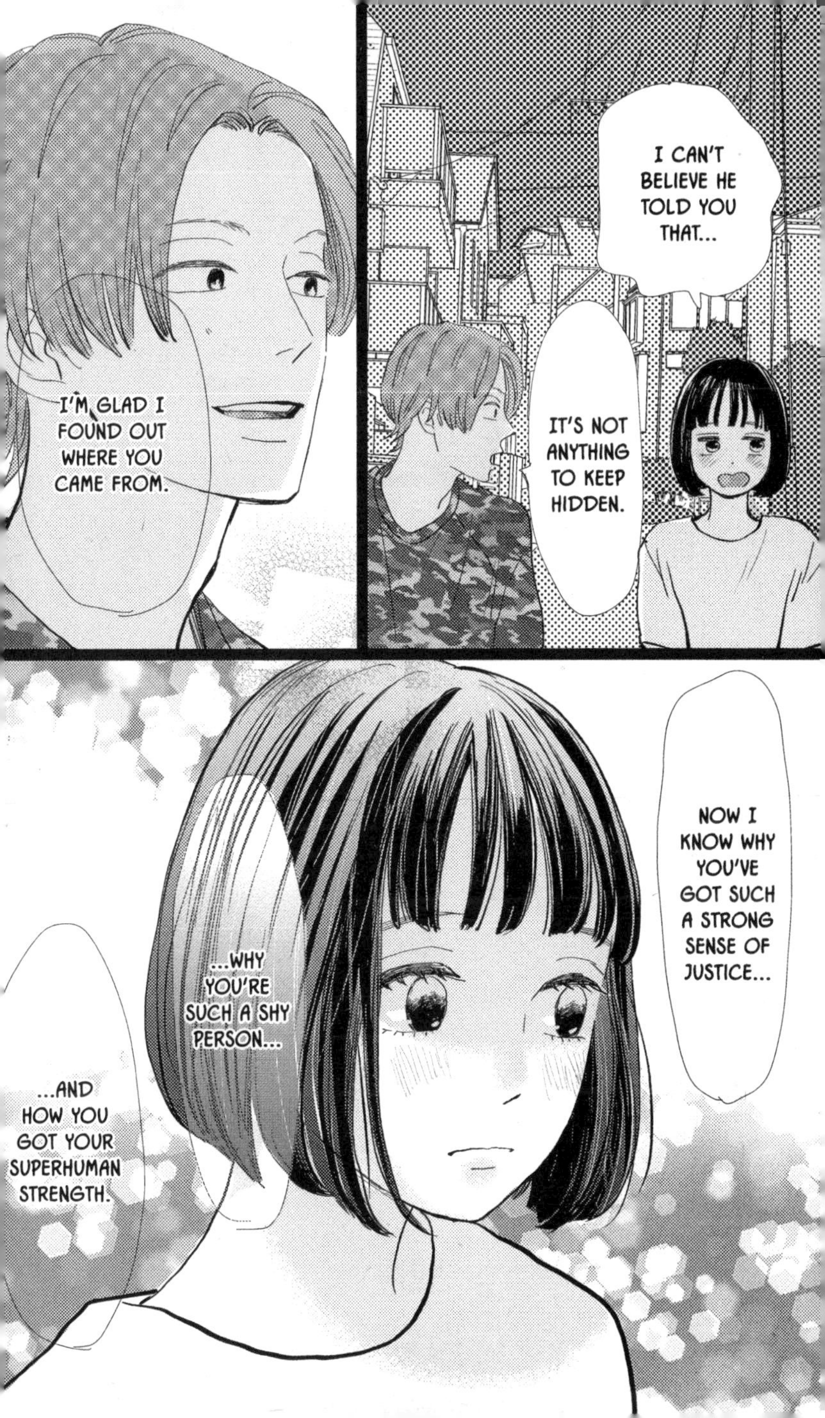
I CAN'T BELIEVE HE TOLD YOU THAT...
IT'S NOT ANYTHING TO KEEP HIDDEN.
I'M GLAD I FOUND OUT WHERE YOU CAME FROM.
NOW I KNOW WHY YOU'VE GOT SUCH A STRONG SENSE OF JUSTICE...
...WHY YOU'RE SUCH A SHY PERSON...
...AND HOW YOU GOT YOUR SUPERHUMAN STRENGTH.

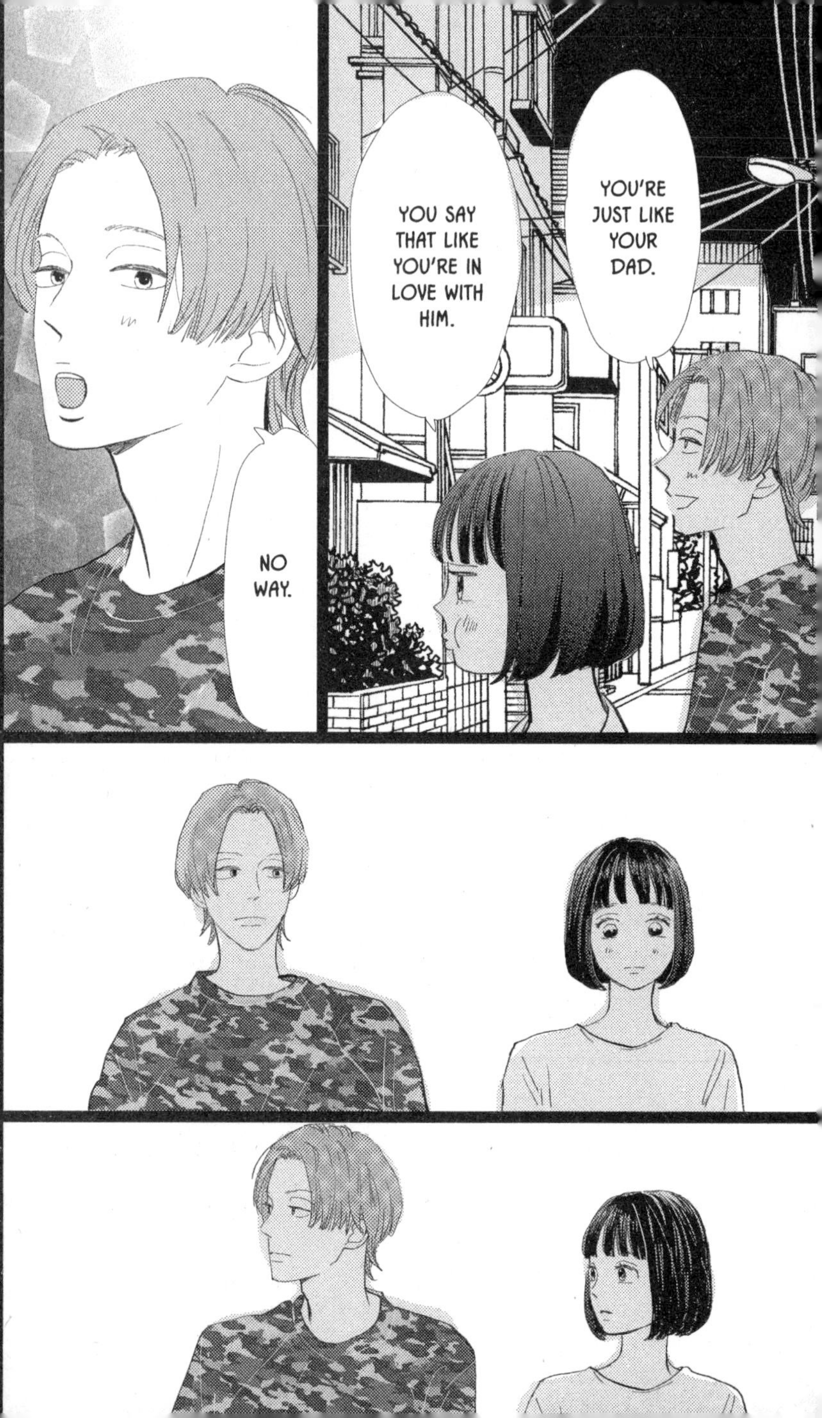
YOU'RE JUST LIKE YOUR DAD.
YOU SAY THAT LIKE YOU'RE IN LOVE WITH HIM.
NO WAY.

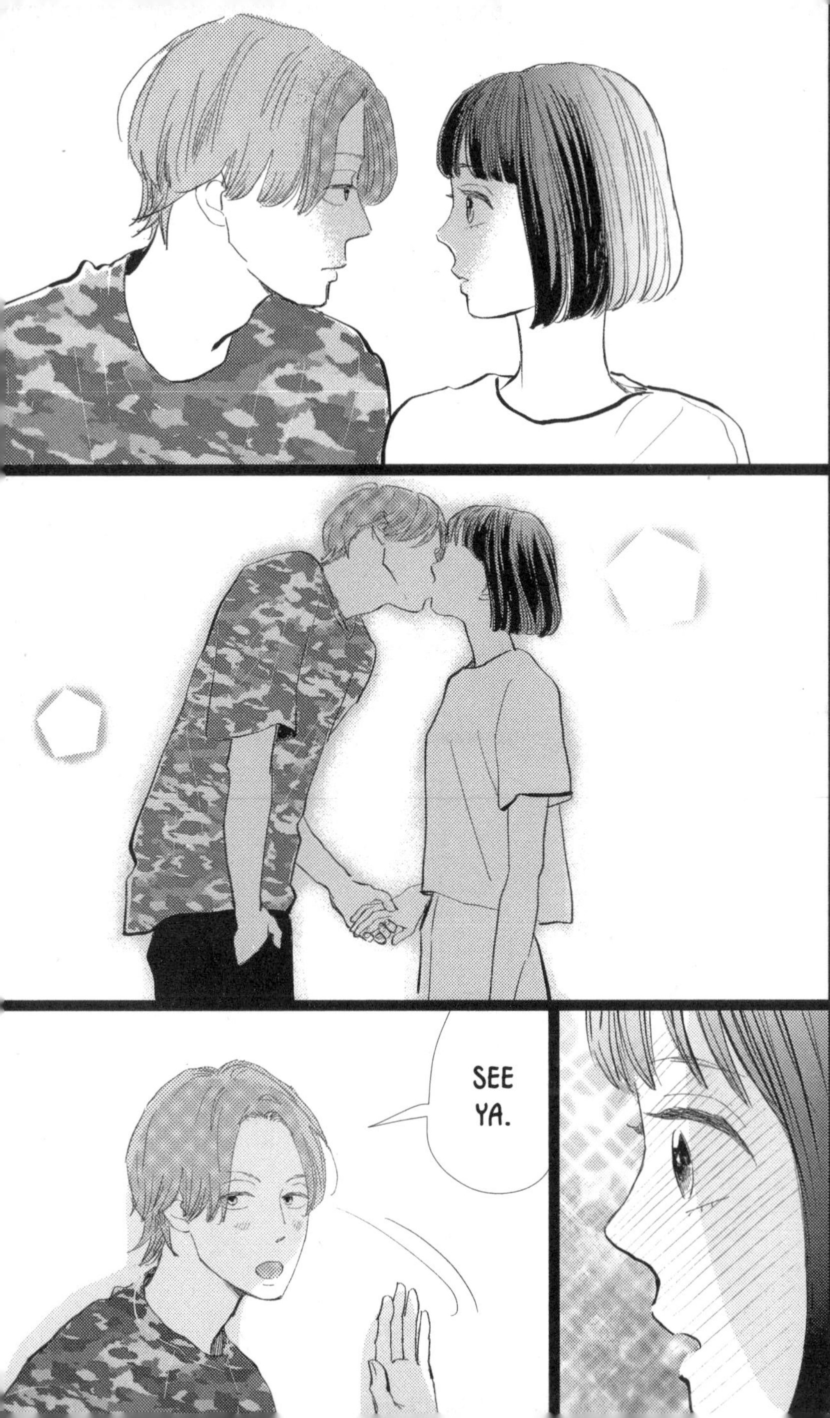
SEE YA.

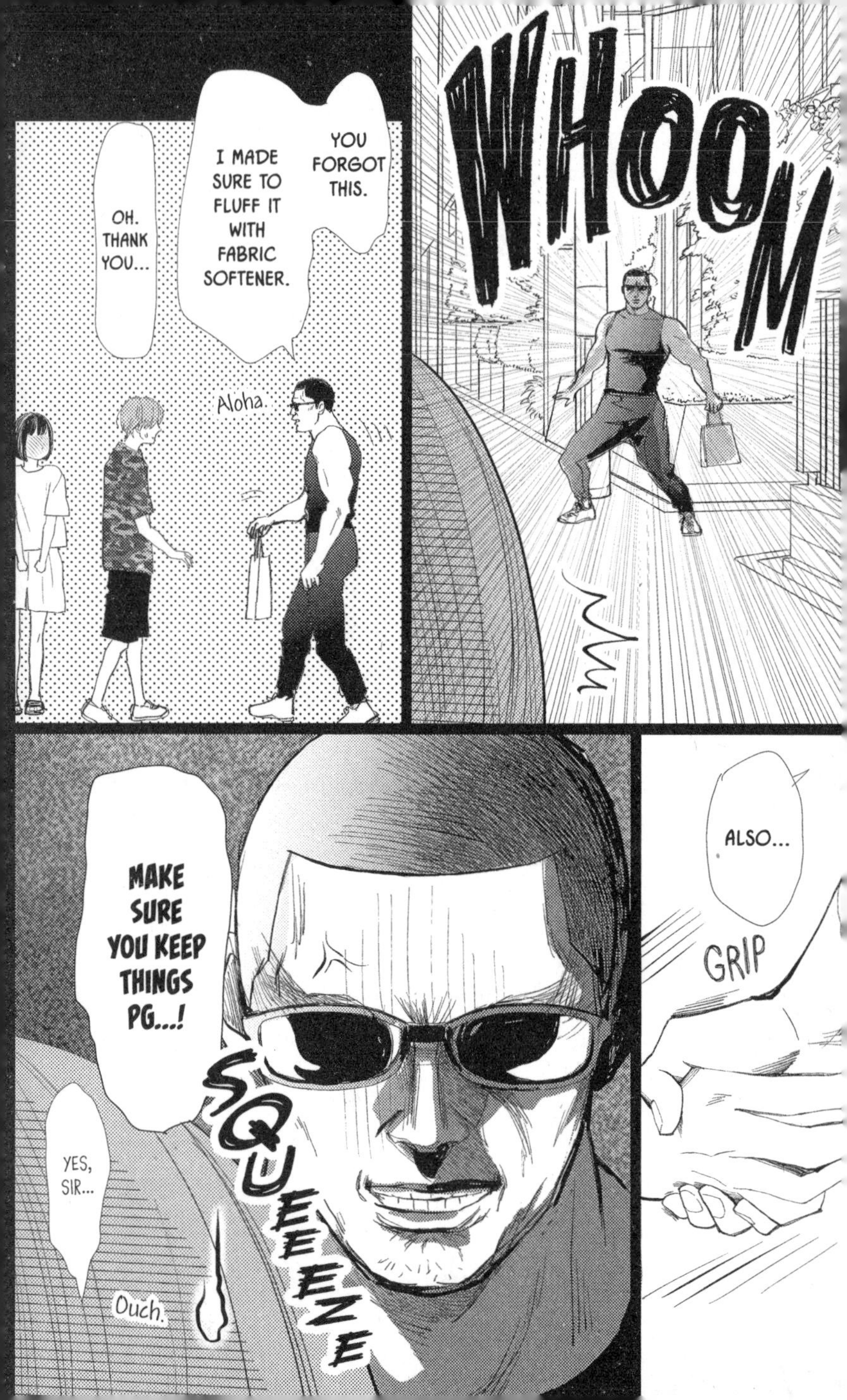
WHOOM
YOU FORGOT THIS.
I MADE SURE TO FLUFF IT WITH FABRIC SOFTENER.
OH. THANK YOU...
Aloha.
ALSO...
GRIP
MAKE SURE YOU KEEP THINGS PG...!
SQUEEEEZE
YES, SIR...
Ouch.

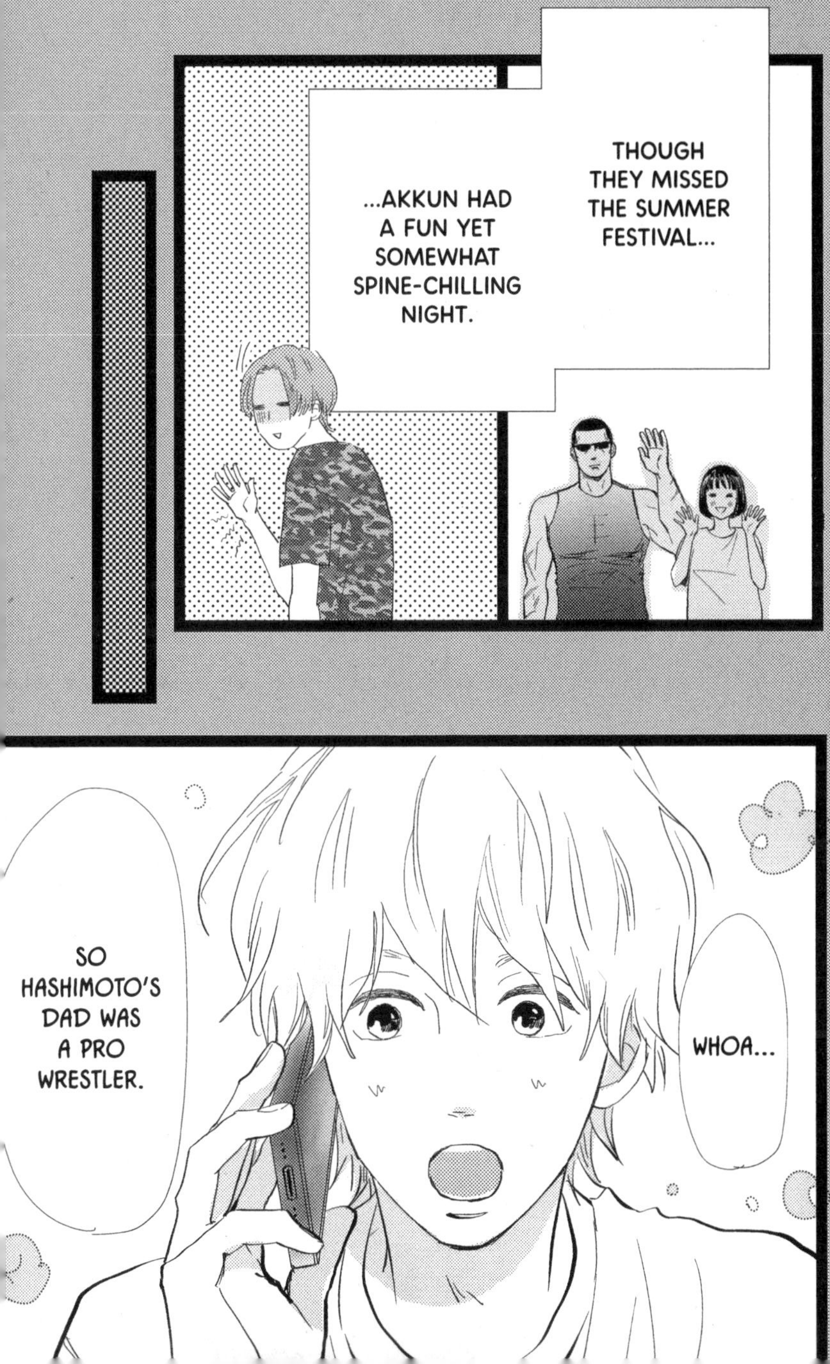
THOUGH THEY MISSED THE SUMMER FESTIVAL...
...AKKUN HAD A FUN YET SOMEWHAT SPINE-CHILLING NIGHT.
WHOA...
SO HASHIMOTO'S DAD WAS A PRO WRESTLER.

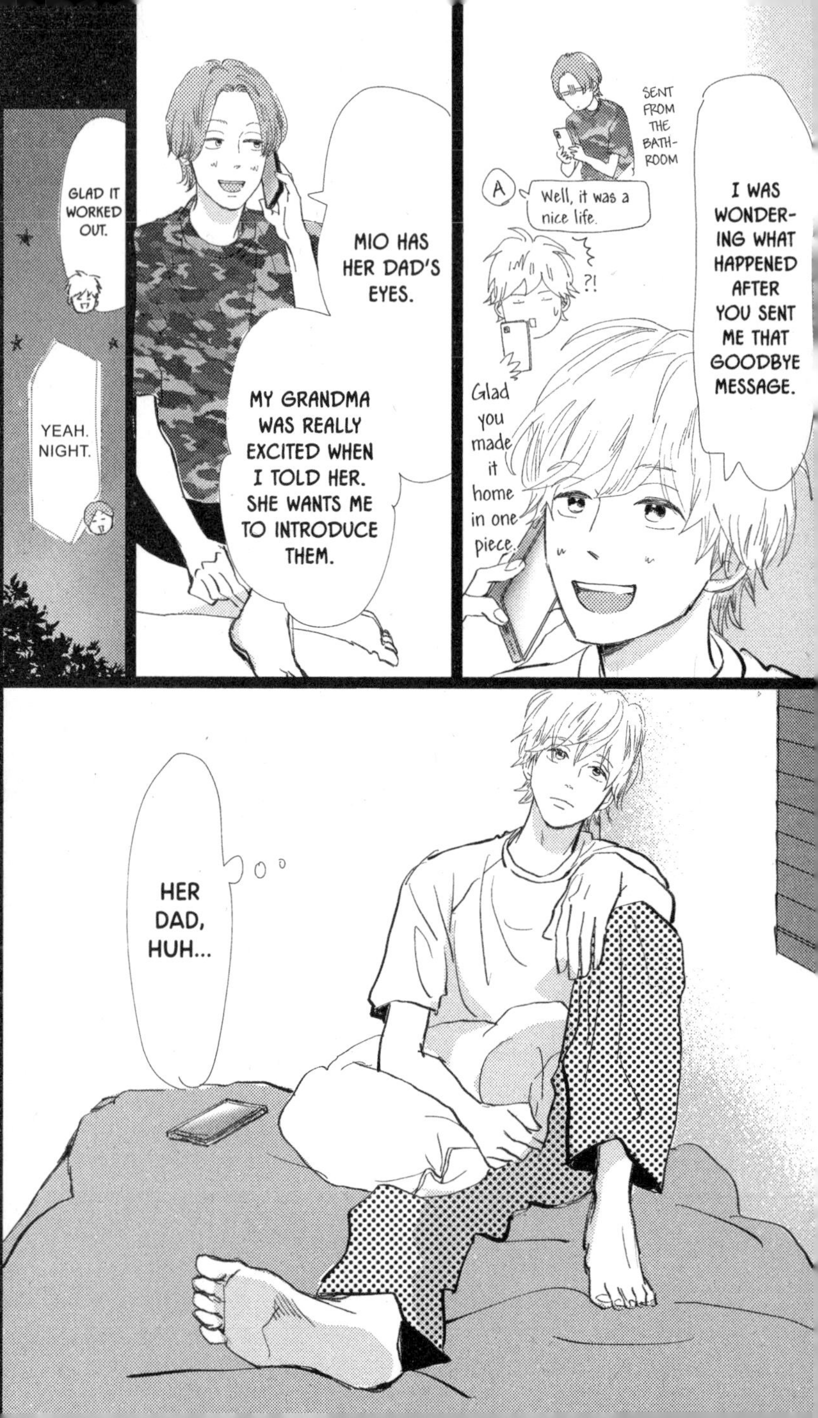
I WAS WONDERING WHAT HAPPENED AFTER YOU SENT ME THAT GOODBYE MESSAGE.
SENT FROM THE BATH-ROOM
A
Well, it was a nice life.
?!
Glad you made it home in one piece.
MIO HAS HER DAD'S EYES.
MY GRANDMA WAS REALLY EXCITED WHEN I TOLD HER. SHE WANTS ME TO INTRODUCE THEM.
GLAD IT WORKED OUT.
YEAH. NIGHT.
HER DAD, HUH...

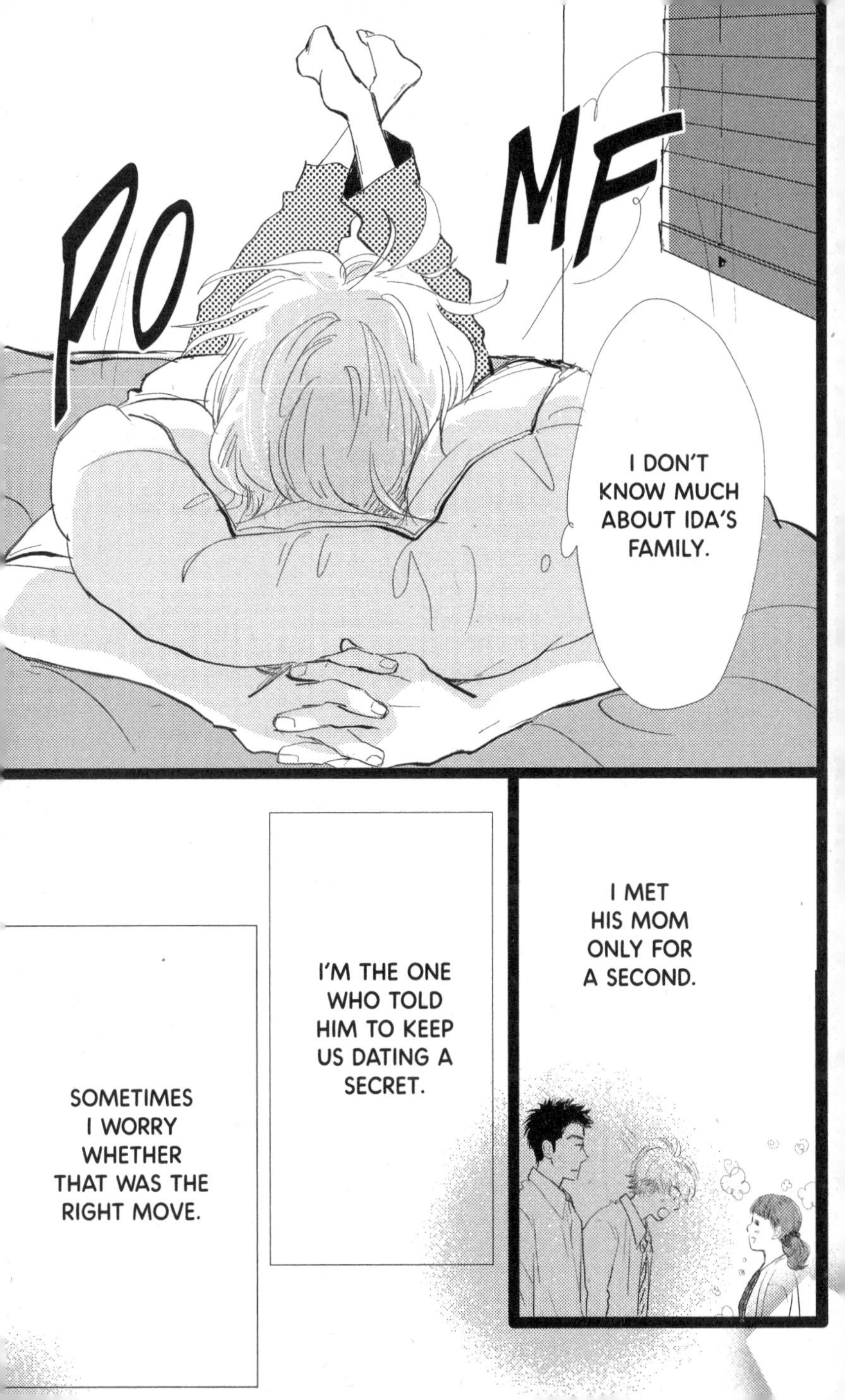
POMF
I DON'T KNOW MUCH ABOUT IDA'S FAMILY.
I MET HIS MOM ONLY FOR A SECOND.
I'M THE ONE WHO TOLD HIM TO KEEP US DATING A SECRET.
SOMETIMES I WORRY WHETHER THAT WAS THE RIGHT MOVE.

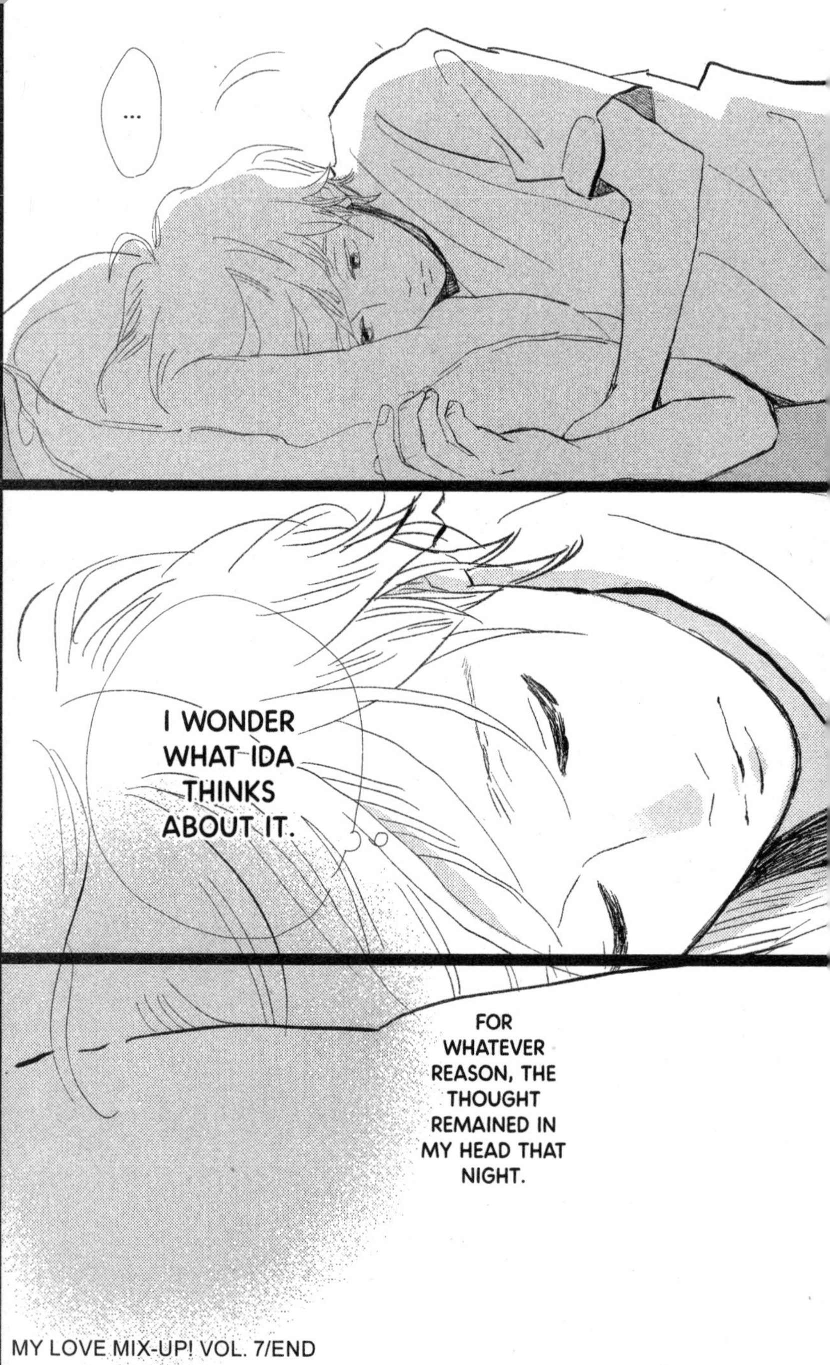
...
I WONDER WHAT IDA THINKS ABOUT IT.
FOR WHATEVER REASON, THE THOUGHT REMAINED IN MY HEAD THAT NIGHT.

MY LOVE MIX-UP! VOL. 7/END

←
We have included three limited-run Little
Theater shorts which were published in
Bessatsu Margaret in 2021, issues 8-10. ☆

Little Theater: Our Classmates' Popularity Reel

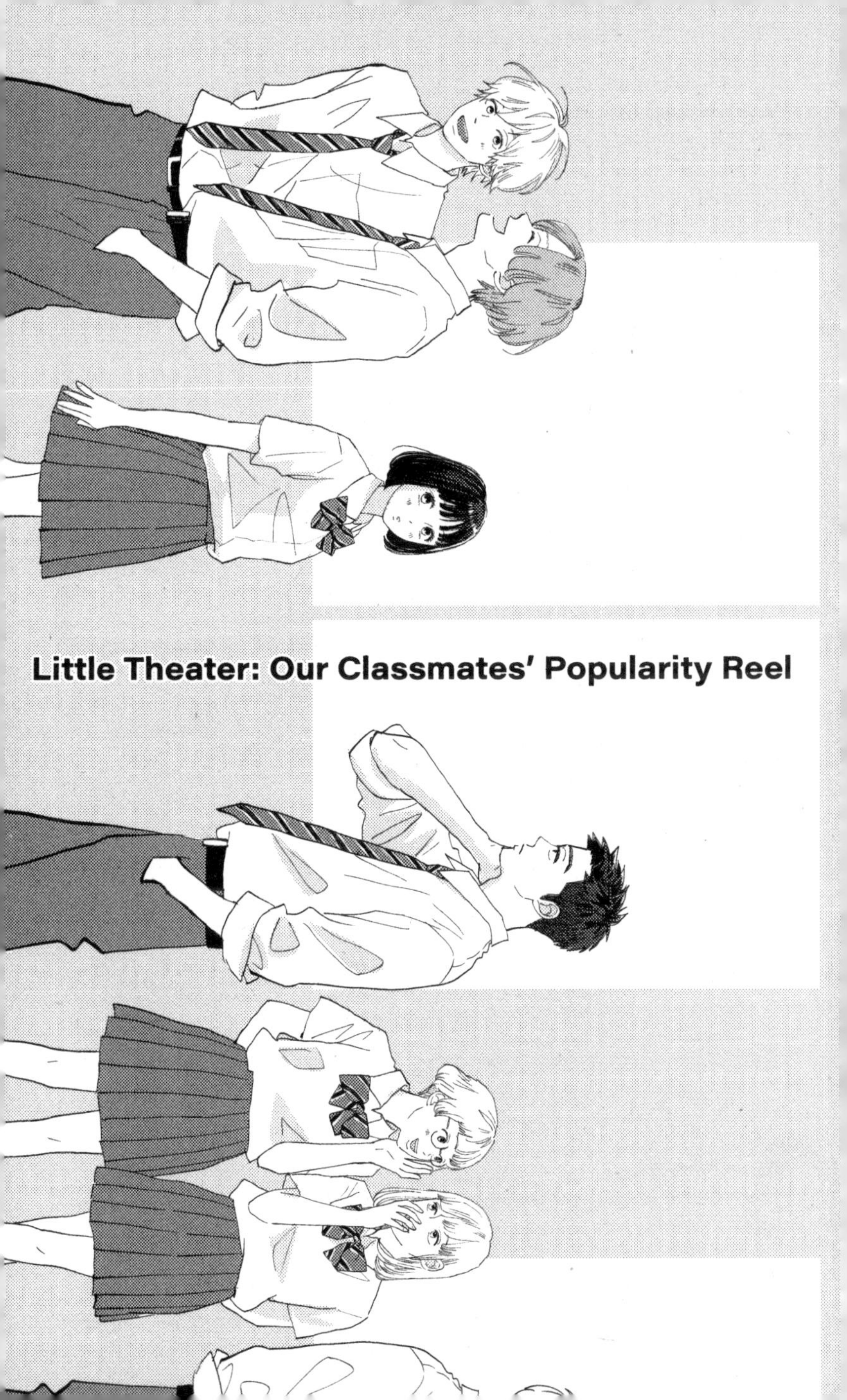

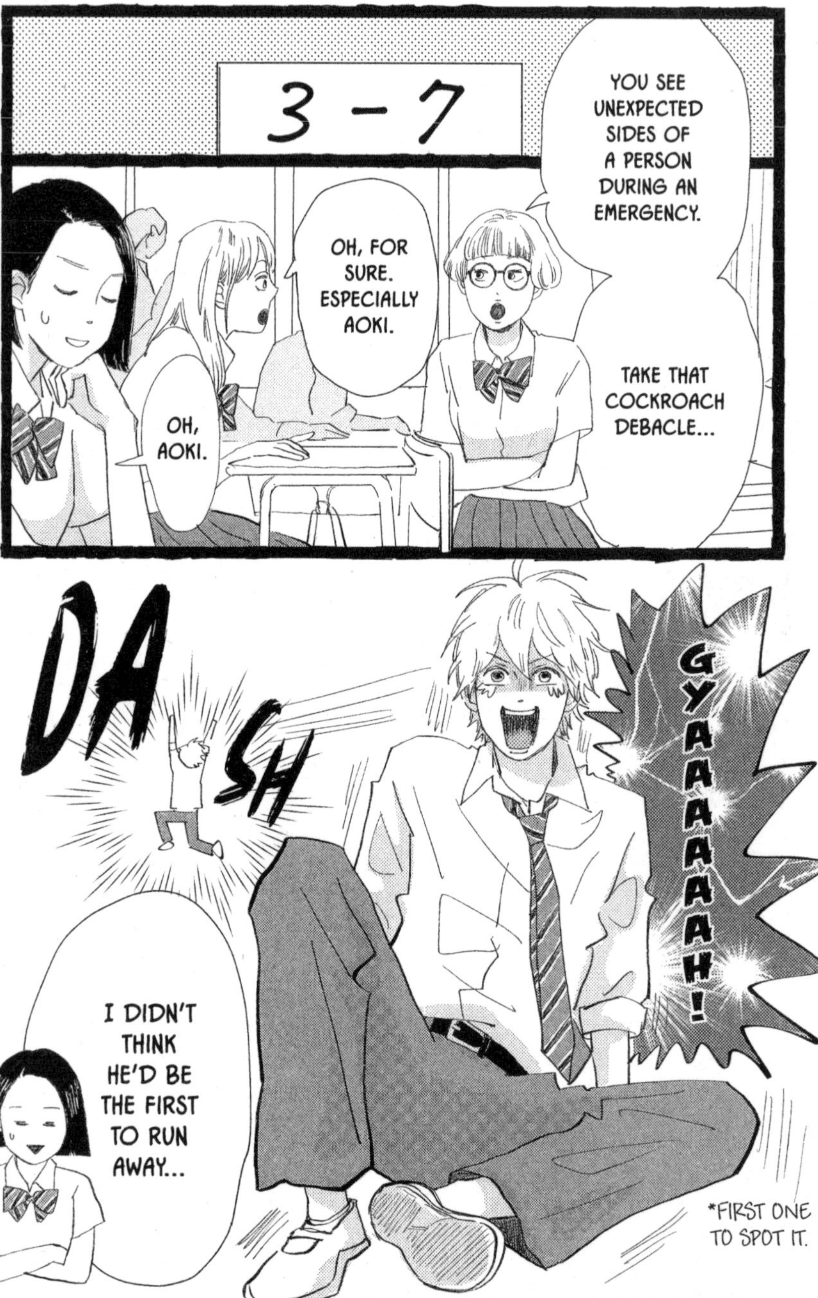
3-7
YOU SEE UNEXPECTED SIDES OF A PERSON DURING AN EMERGENCY.
TAKE THAT COCKROACH DEBACLE...
OH, FOR SURE. ESPECIALLY AOKI.
OH, AOKI.
GYAAAAAAAH!
DASH
I DIDN'T THINK HE'D BE THE FIRST TO RUN AWAY...
*FIRST ONE TO SPOT IT.

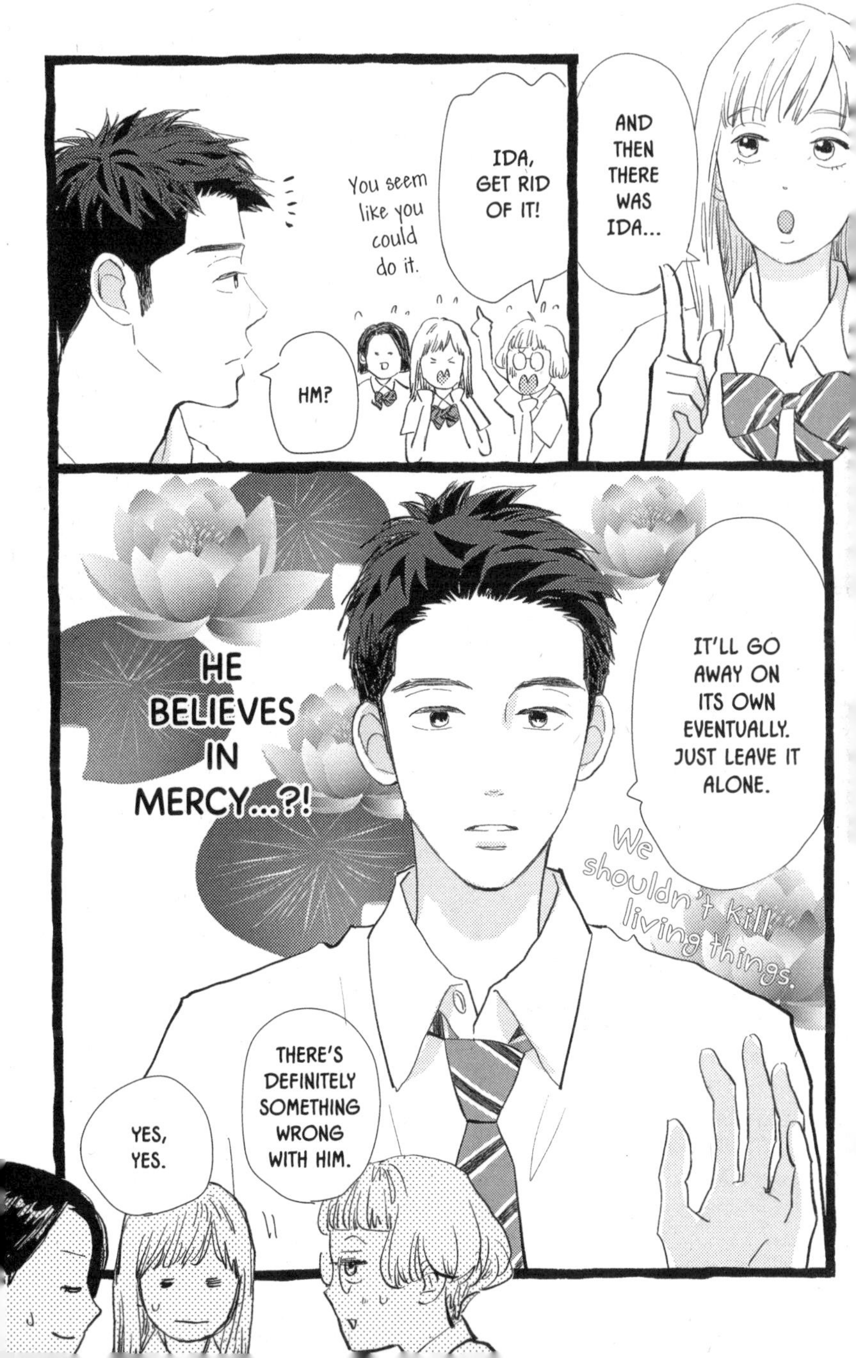
AND THEN THERE WAS IDA...
IDA, GET RID OF IT!
You seem like you could do it.
HM?
IT'LL GO AWAY ON ITS OWN EVENTUALLY. JUST LEAVE IT ALONE.
We shouldn't kill living things.
HE BELIEVES IN MERCY...?!
THERE'S DEFINITELY SOMETHING WRONG WITH HIM.
YES, YES.

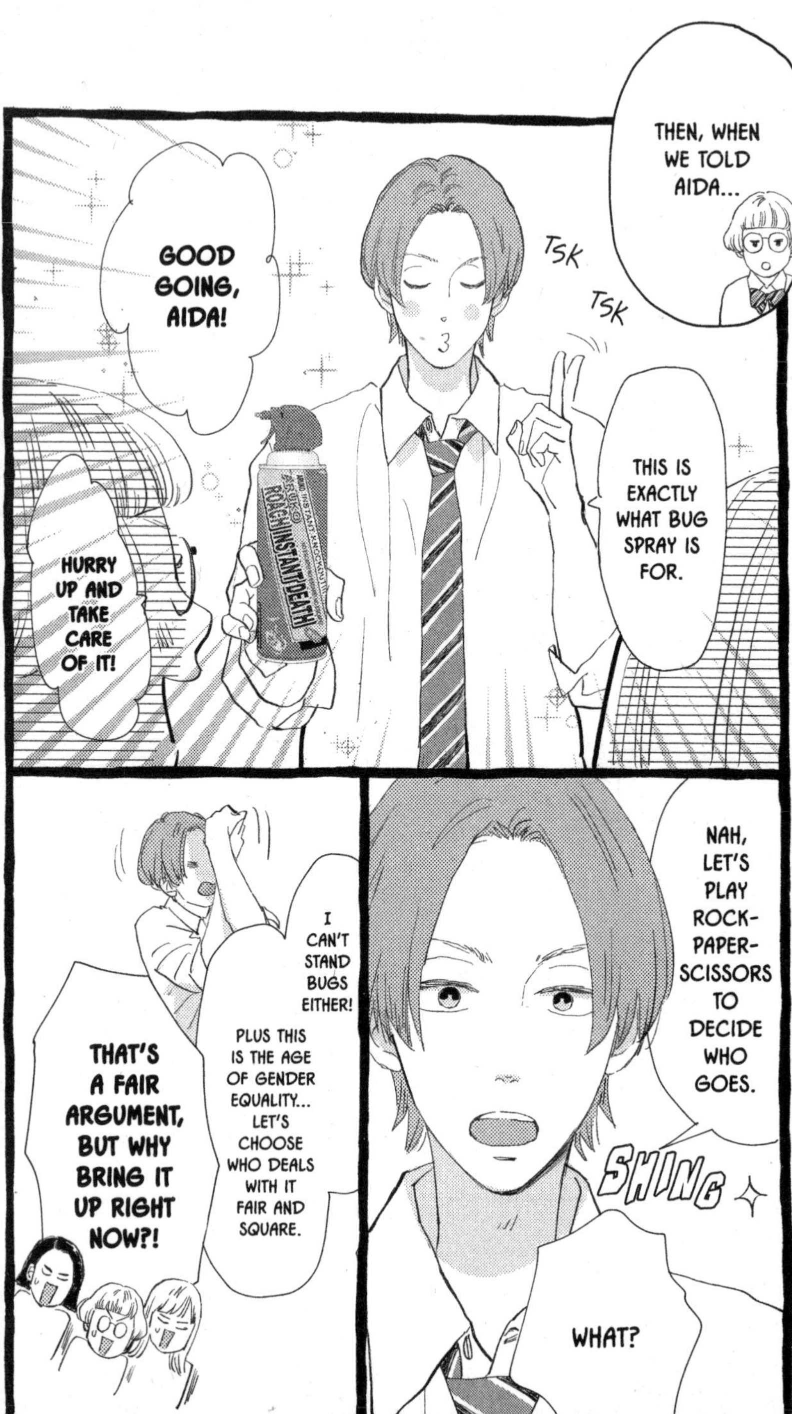
THEN, WHEN WE TOLD AIDA...
TSK
TSK
THIS IS EXACTLY WHAT BUG SPRAY IS FOR.
GOOD GOING, AIDA!
ROACH INSTANT DEATH
HURRY UP AND TAKE CARE OF IT!
NAH, LET'S PLAY ROCK-PAPER-SCISSORS TO DECIDE WHO GOES.
SHING
WHAT?
I CAN'T STAND BUGS EITHER!
PLUS THIS IS THE AGE OF GENDER EQUALITY... LET'S CHOOSE WHO DEALS WITH IT FAIR AND SQUARE.
THAT'S A FAIR ARGUMENT, BUT WHY BRING IT UP RIGHT NOW?!

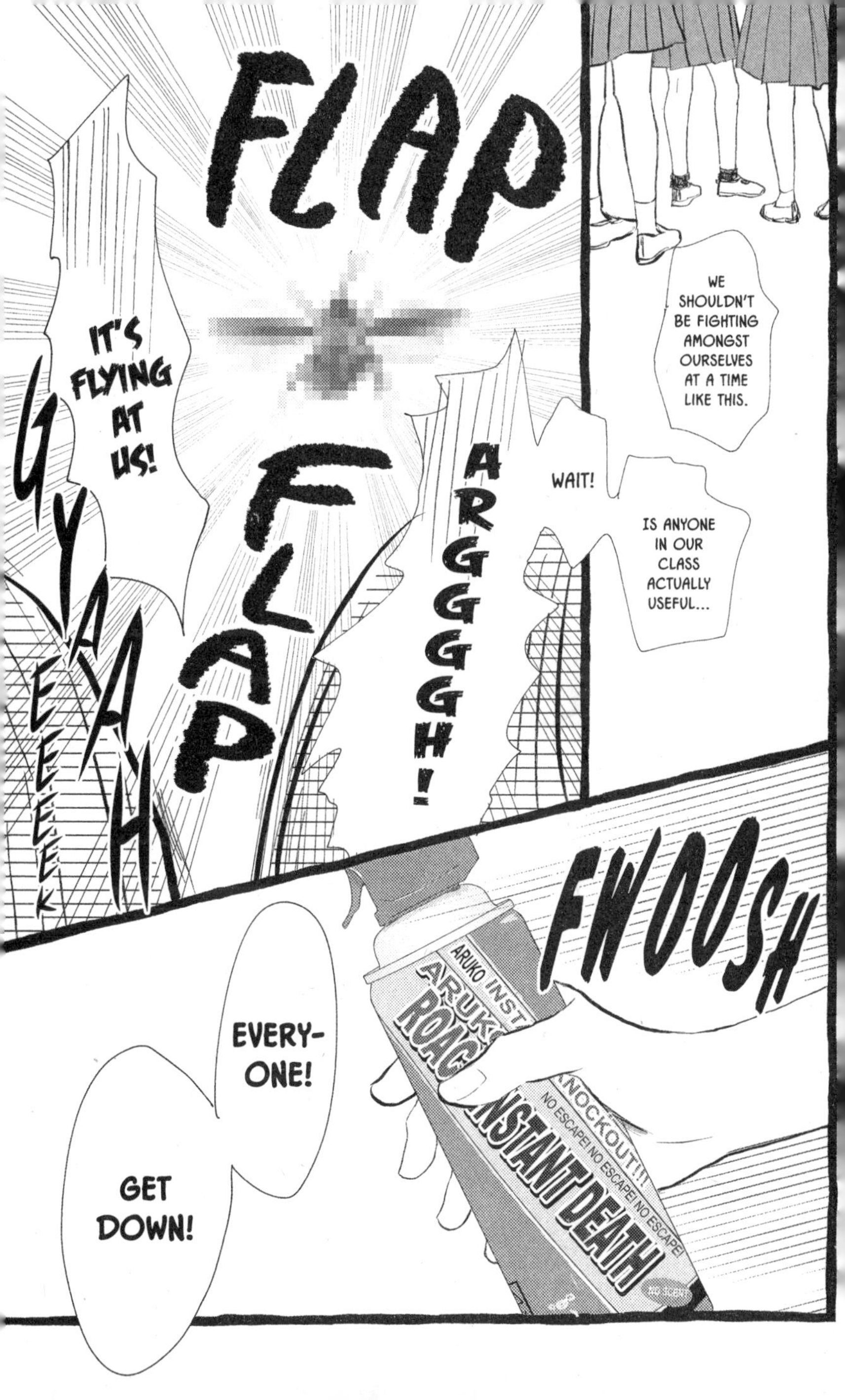
WE SHOULDN'T BE FIGHTING AMONGST OURSELVES AT A TIME LIKE THIS.
WAIT!
IS ANYONE IN OUR CLASS ACTUALLY USEFUL...
FLAP
ARGGGGH!
IT'S FLYING AT US!
GYAAAH
EEEEEK
FLAP
FWOOSH
EVERY-ONE!
GET DOWN!
KNOCKOUT!!!
NO ESCAPE! NO ESCAPE! NO ESCAPE!
INSTANT DEATH

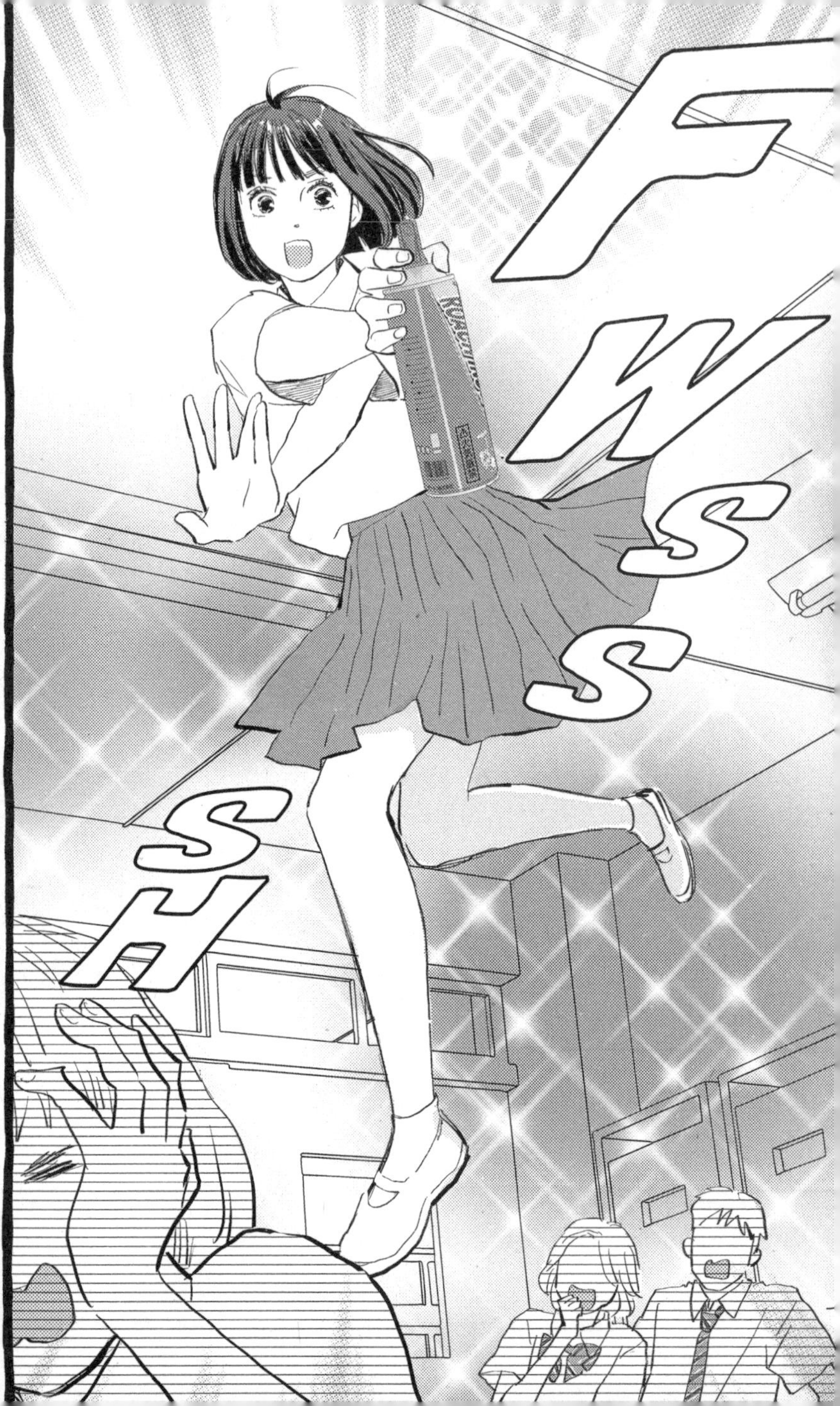
FWSSSH

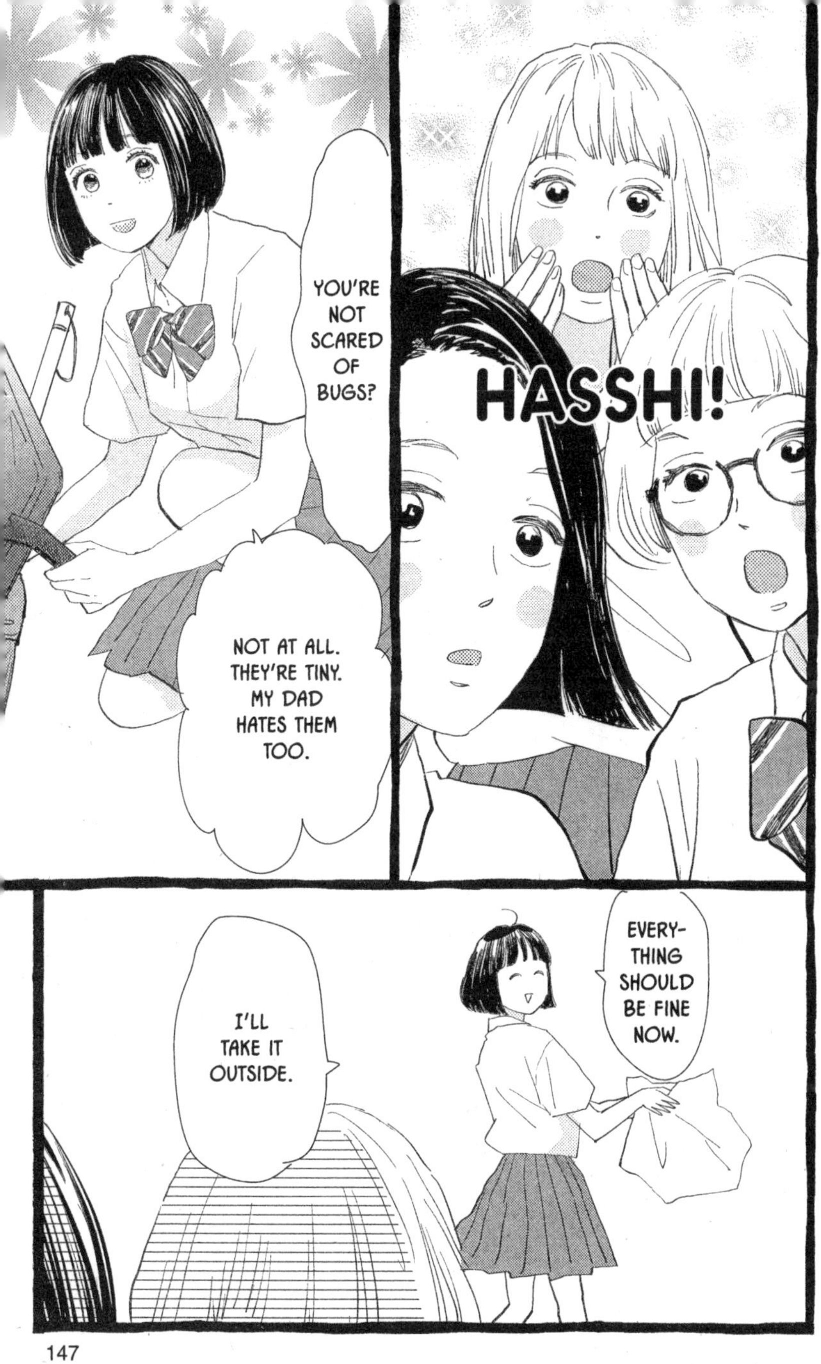
HASSHI!
YOU'RE NOT SCARED OF BUGS?
NOT AT ALL. THEY'RE TINY. MY DAD HATES THEM TOO.
EVERY-THING SHOULD BE FINE NOW.
I'LL TAKE IT OUTSIDE.

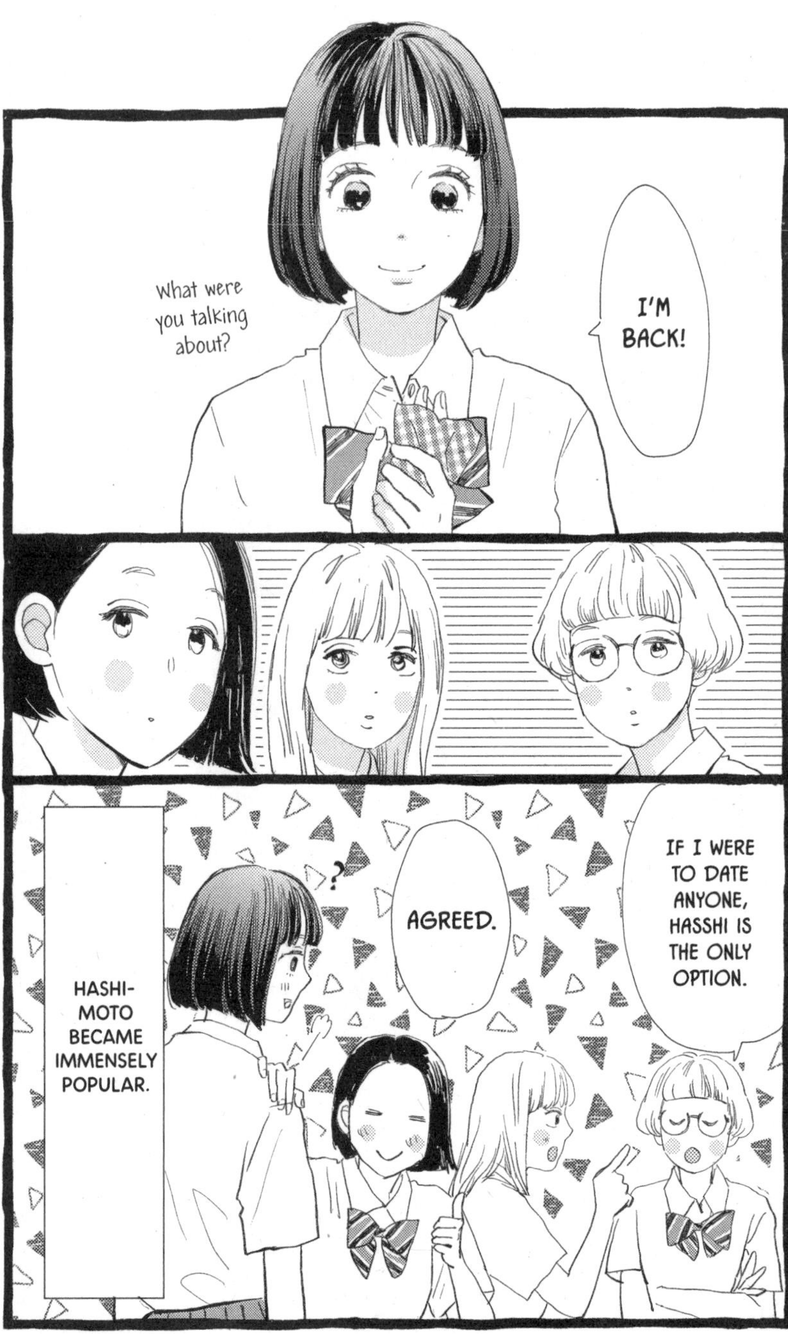
I'M BACK!
What were you talking about?
IF I WERE TO DATE ANYONE, HASSHI IS THE ONLY OPTION.
AGREED.
?
HASHI-MOTO BECAME IMMENSELY POPULAR.

Little Theater: Toyoda's First Love Reel

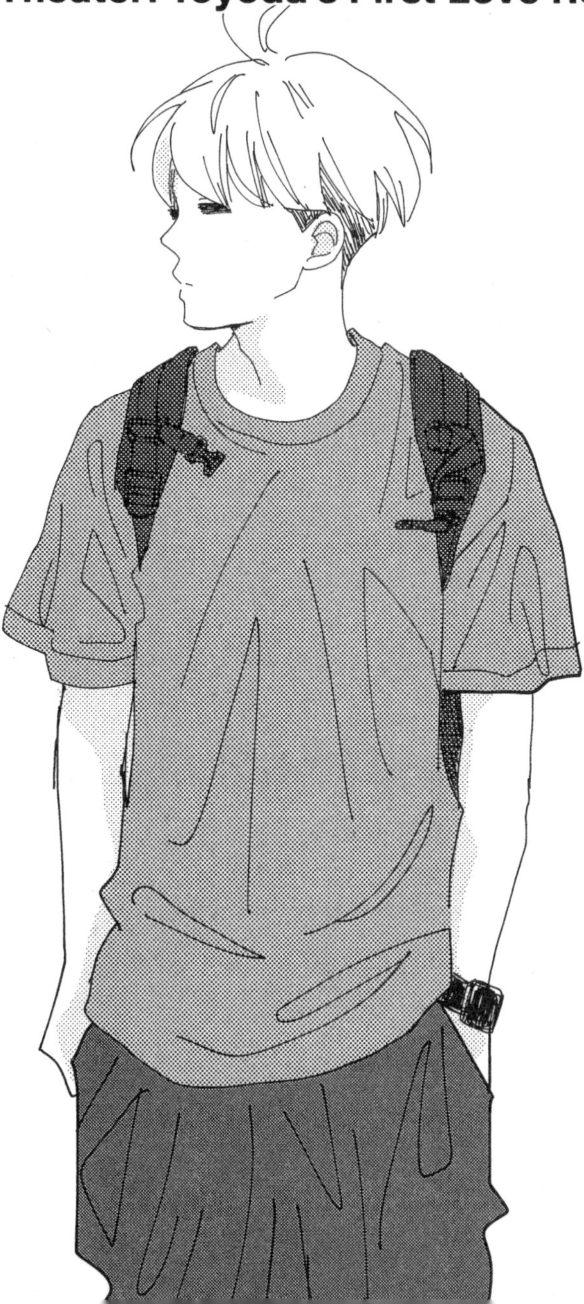

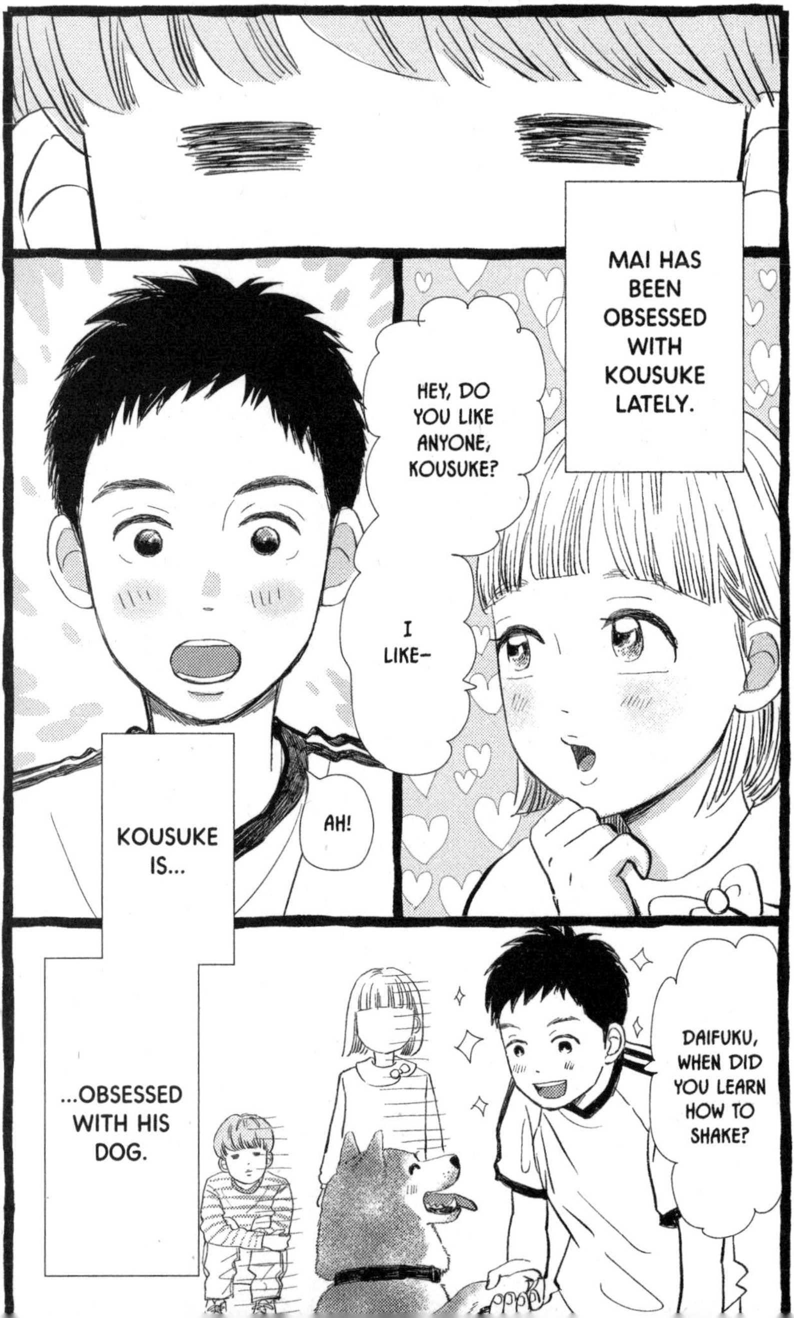
MAI HAS BEEN OBSESSED WITH KOUSUKE LATELY.
HEY, DO YOU LIKE ANYONE, KOUSUKE?
I LIKE-
AH!
KOUSUKE IS...
DAIFUKU, WHEN DID YOU LEARN HOW TO SHAKE?
...OBSESSED WITH HIS DOG.

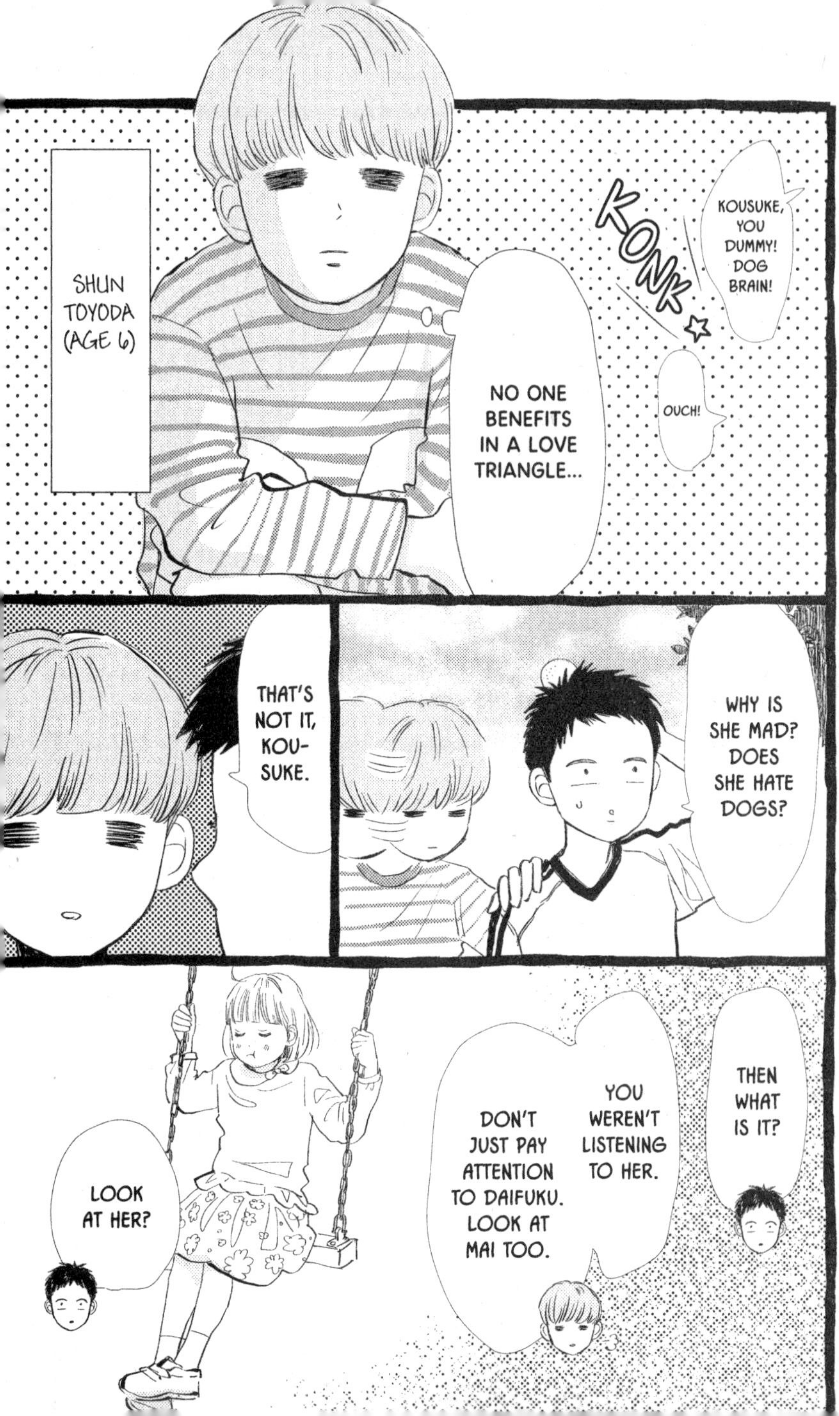
KOUSUKE, YOU DUMMY! DOG BRAIN!
KONK
OUCH!
NO ONE BENEFITS IN A LOVE TRIANGLE...
SHUN TOYODA (AGE 6)
WHY IS SHE MAD? DOES SHE HATE DOGS?
THAT'S NOT IT, KOUSUKE.
THEN WHAT IS IT?
YOU WEREN'T LISTENING TO HER.
DON'T JUST PAY ATTENTION TO DAIFUKU. LOOK AT MAI TOO.
LOOK AT HER?

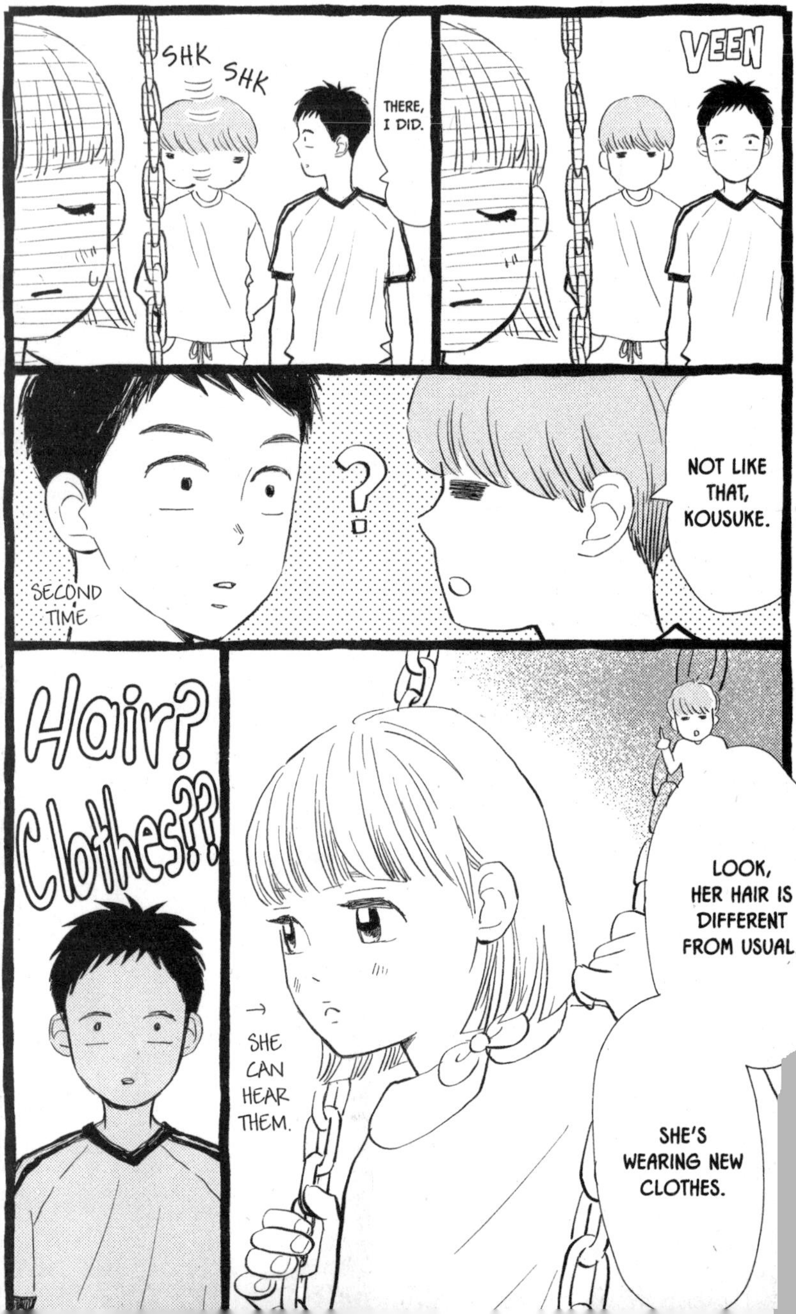
VEEN
SHK
SHK
THERE, I DID.
NOT LIKE THAT, KOUSUKE.
?
SECOND TIME
LOOK, HER HAIR IS DIFFERENT FROM USUAL.
SHE'S WEARING NEW CLOTHES.
→ SHE CAN HEAR THEM.
Hair? Clothes??

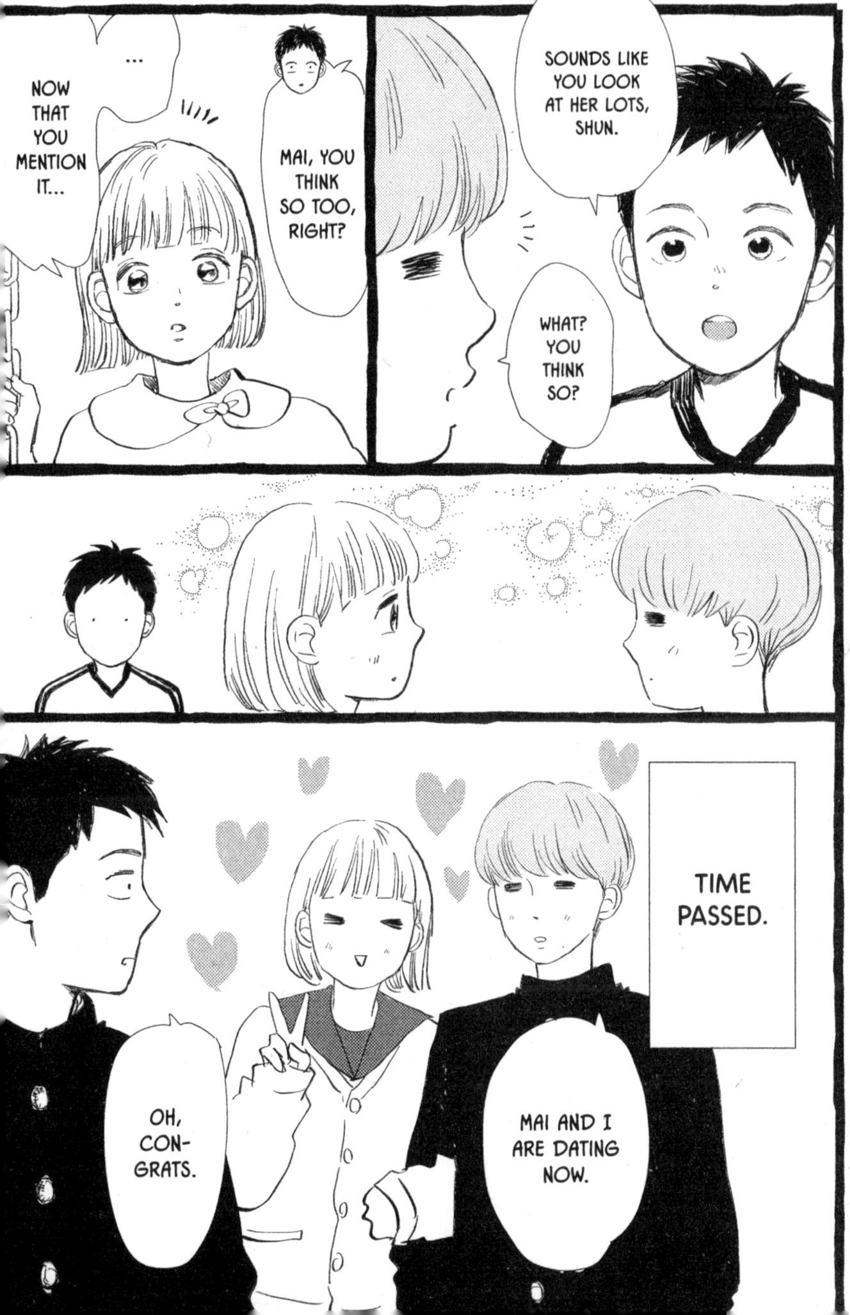
SOUNDS LIKE YOU LOOK AT HER LOTS, SHUN.
WHAT? YOU THINK SO?
MAI, YOU THINK SO TOO, RIGHT?
...
NOW THAT YOU MENTION IT...
TIME PASSED.
MAI AND I ARE DATING NOW.
OH, CON-GRATS.

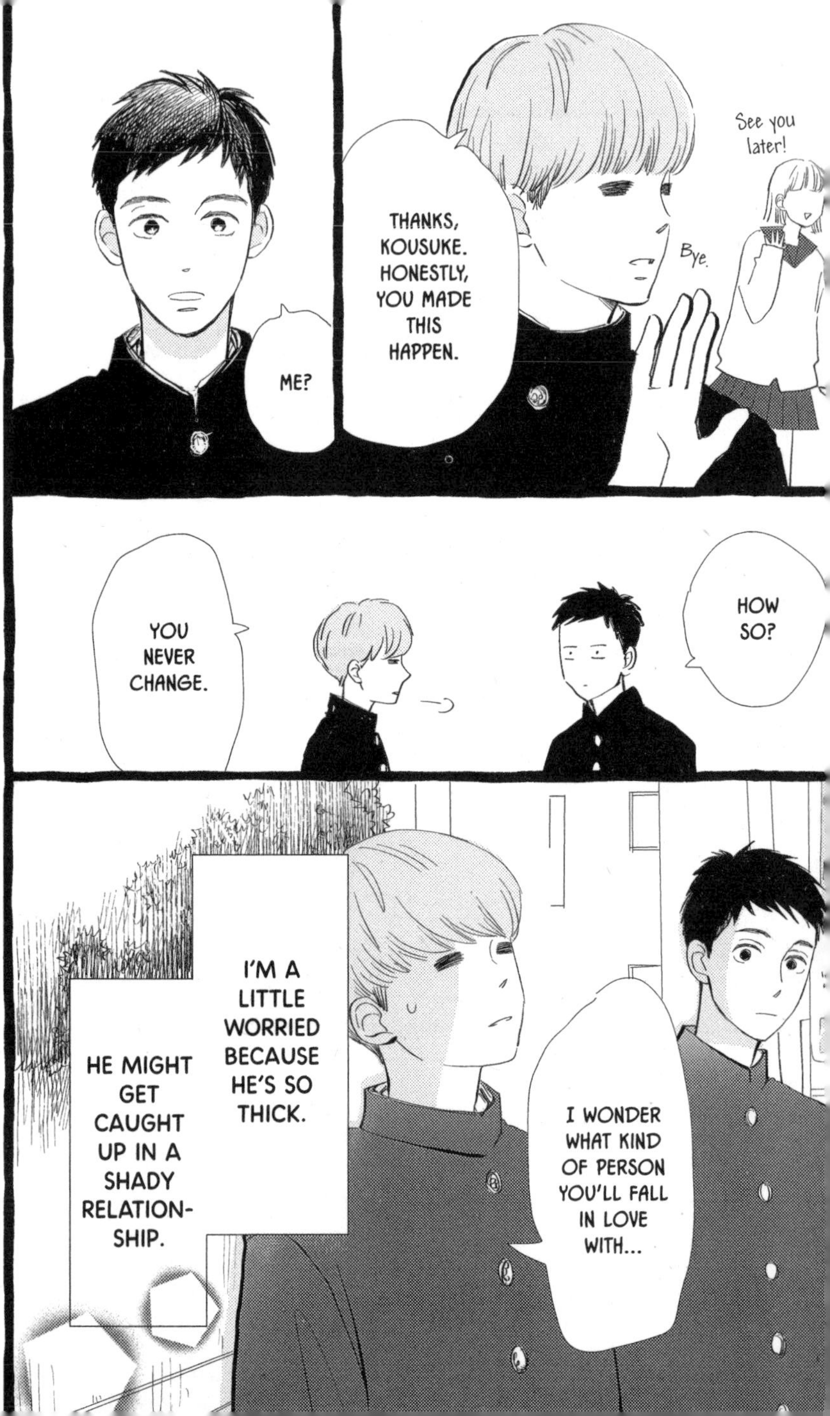
See you later!
Bye.
THANKS, KOUSUKE. HONESTLY, YOU MADE THIS HAPPEN.
ME?
HOW SO?
YOU NEVER CHANGE.
I WONDER WHAT KIND OF PERSON YOU'LL FALL IN LOVE WITH...
I'M A LITTLE WORRIED BECAUSE HE'S SO THICK.
HE MIGHT GET CAUGHT UP IN A SHADY RELATION-SHIP.

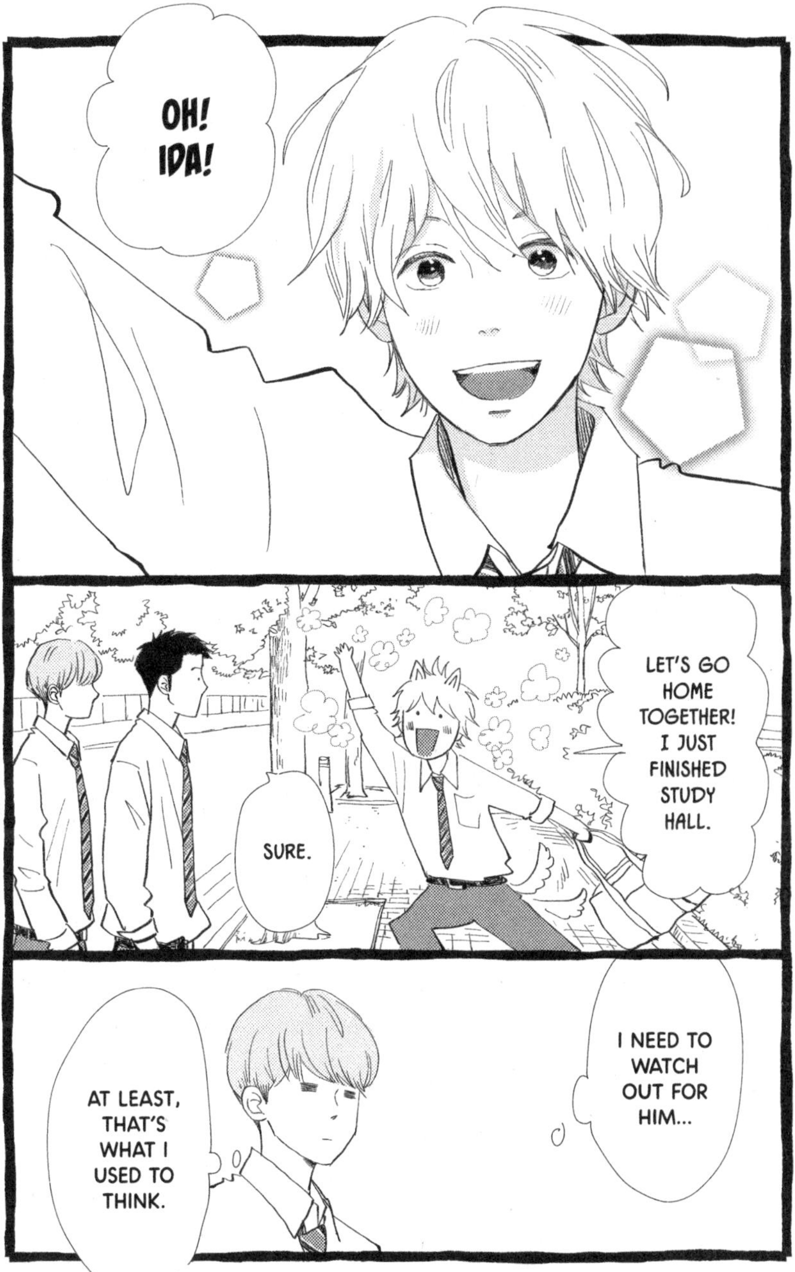
OH! IDA!
LET'S GO HOME TOGETHER! I JUST FINISHED STUDY HALL.
SURE.
I NEED TO WATCH OUT FOR HIM...
AT LEAST, THAT'S WHAT I USED TO THINK.

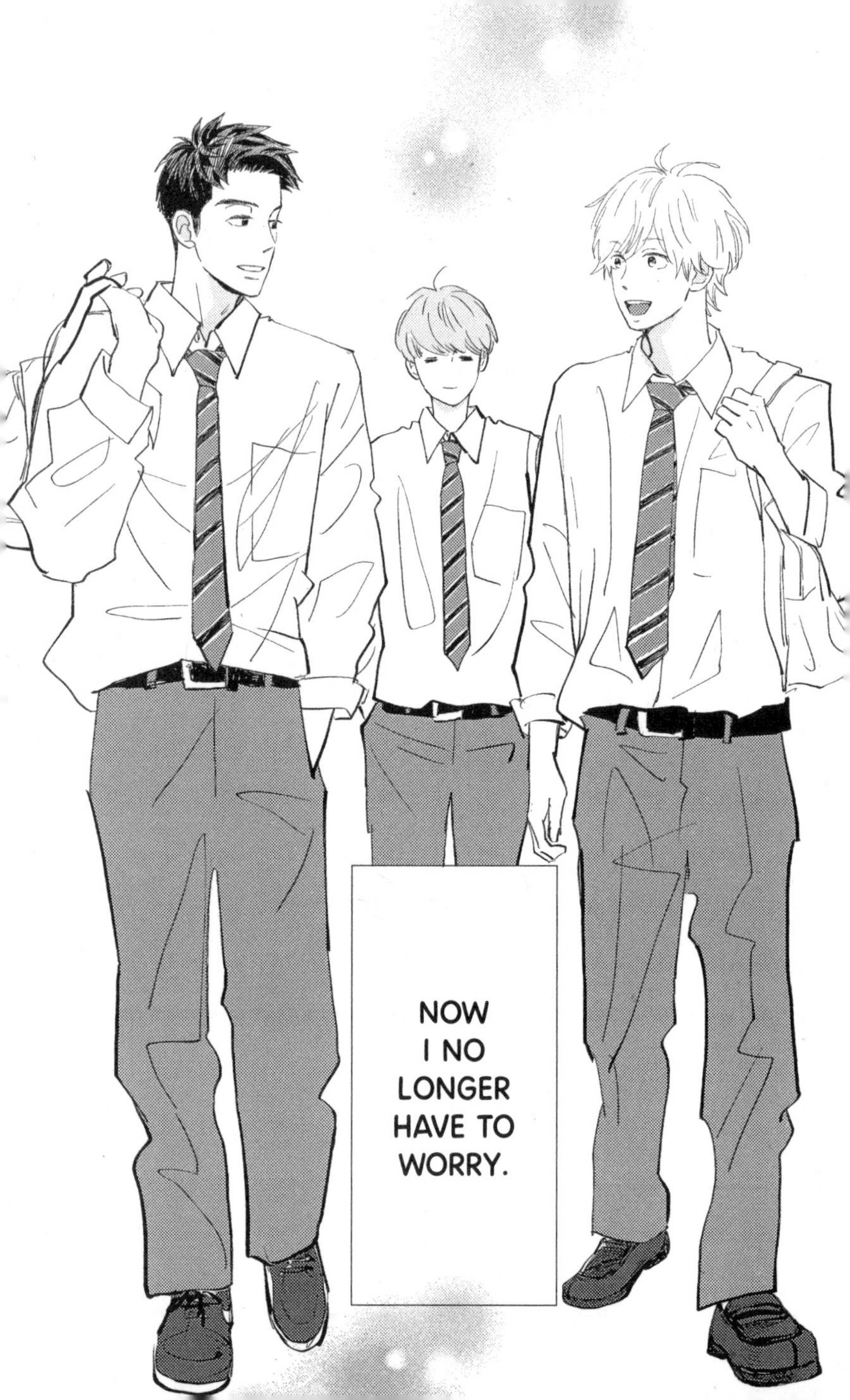
NOW I NO LONGER HAVE TO WORRY.

Little Theater: Congrats ☆ Made into a Live-Action Drama Adaptation Reel

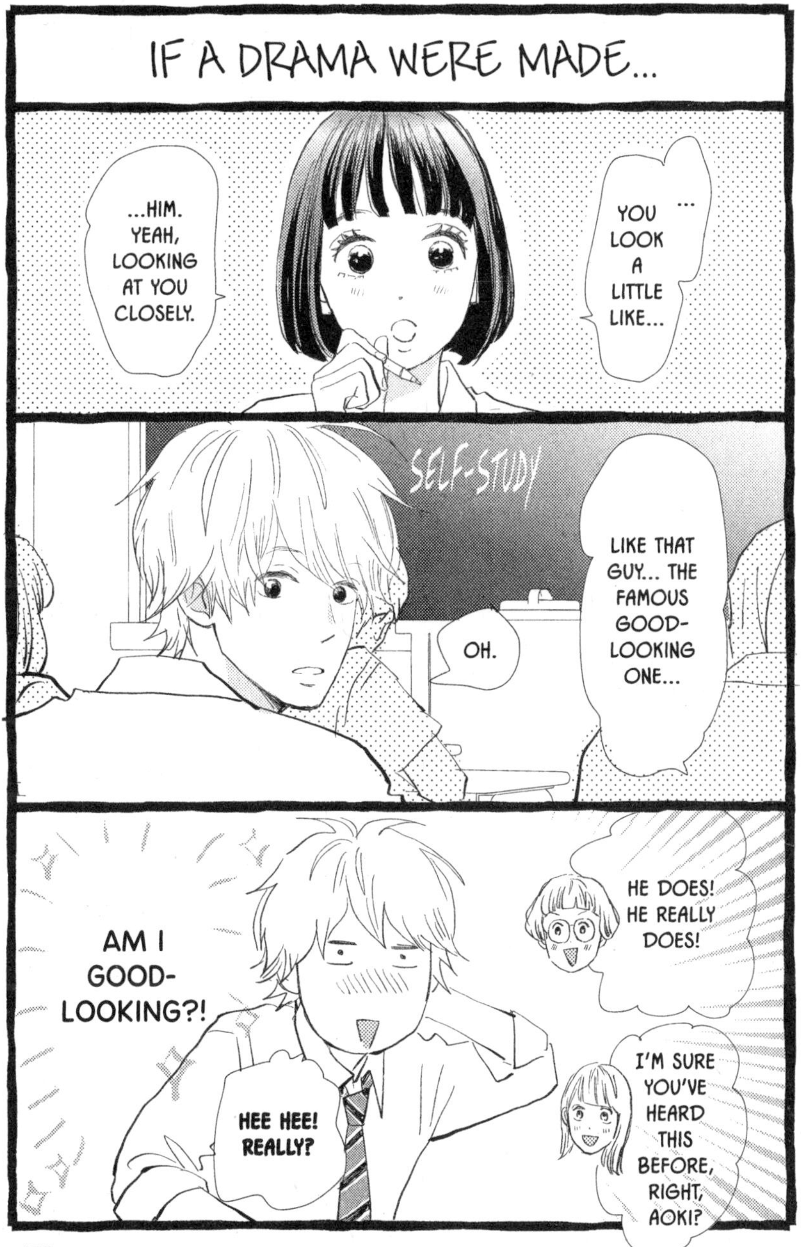
IF A DRAMA WERE MADE...
... YOU LOOK A LITTLE LIKE...
...HIM. YEAH, LOOKING AT YOU CLOSELY.
SELF-STUDY
LIKE THAT GUY... THE FAMOUS GOOD-LOOKING ONE...
OH.
HE DOES! HE REALLY DOES!
AM I GOOD-LOOKING?!
I'M SURE YOU'VE HEARD THIS BEFORE, RIGHT, AOKI?
HEE HEE! REALLY?

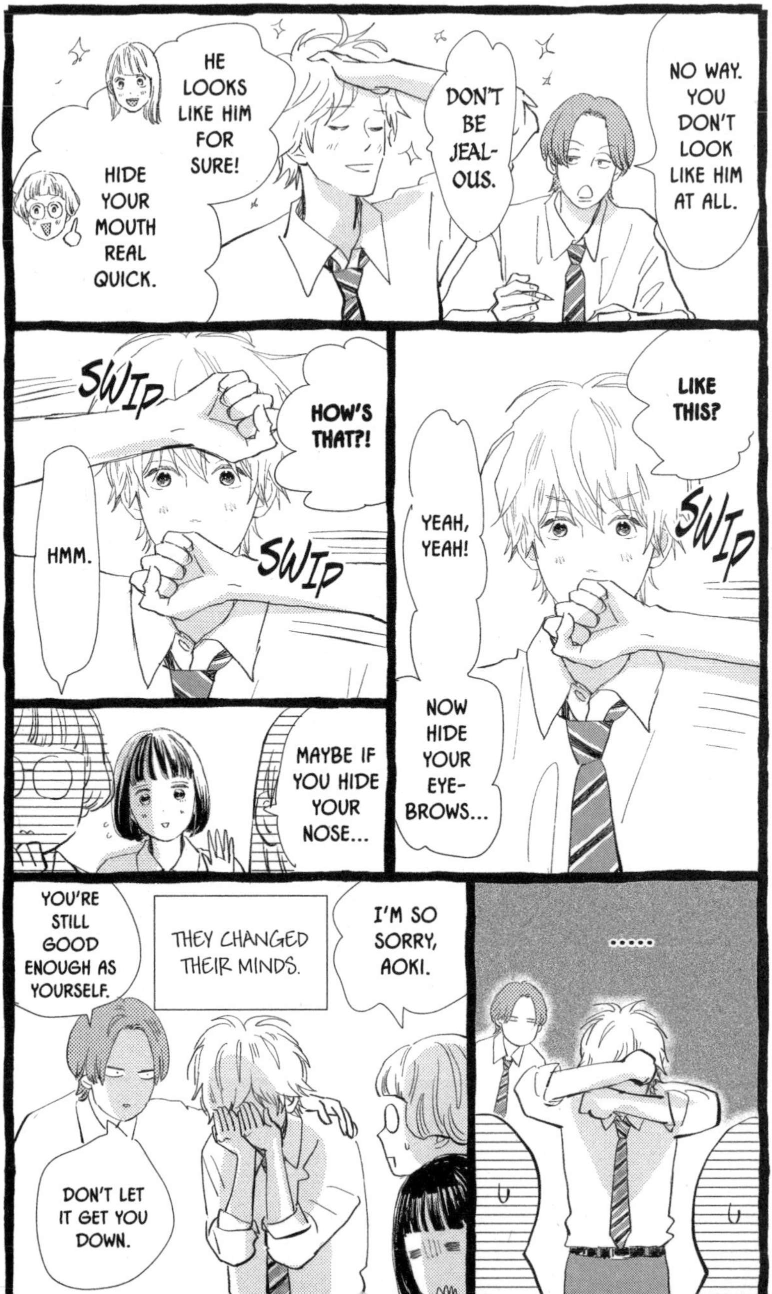
NO WAY. YOU DON'T LOOK LIKE HIM AT ALL.
DON'T BE JEAL-OUS.
HE LOOKS LIKE HIM FOR SURE!
HIDE YOUR MOUTH REAL QUICK.
LIKE THIS?
SWIP
YEAH, YEAH!
NOW HIDE YOUR EYE-BROWS...
SWIP
HOW'S THAT?!
HMM.
SWIP
MAYBE IF YOU HIDE YOUR NOSE...
......
I'M SO SORRY, AOKI.
THEY CHANGED THEIR MINDS.
YOU'RE STILL GOOD ENOUGH AS YOURSELF.
DON'T LET IT GET YOU DOWN.

TV DEBUT

HUH, SO THAT HAPPENED.
MAYBE I DON'T LOOK LIKE THAT FAMOUS GOOD-LOOKING GUY, BUT THERE HAVE GOT TO BE CELEBRITIES WHO ACT SIMILAR TO ME.
I DON'T WATCH MUCH TV.
I KNEW YOU'D SAY THAT.
OH, RIGHT.... ...I MIGHT BE ON TV TOO.
WHAT?!
MY PARENTS APPLIED WITHOUT ASKING ME. IT'LL SHOW AT 7 TONIGHT.

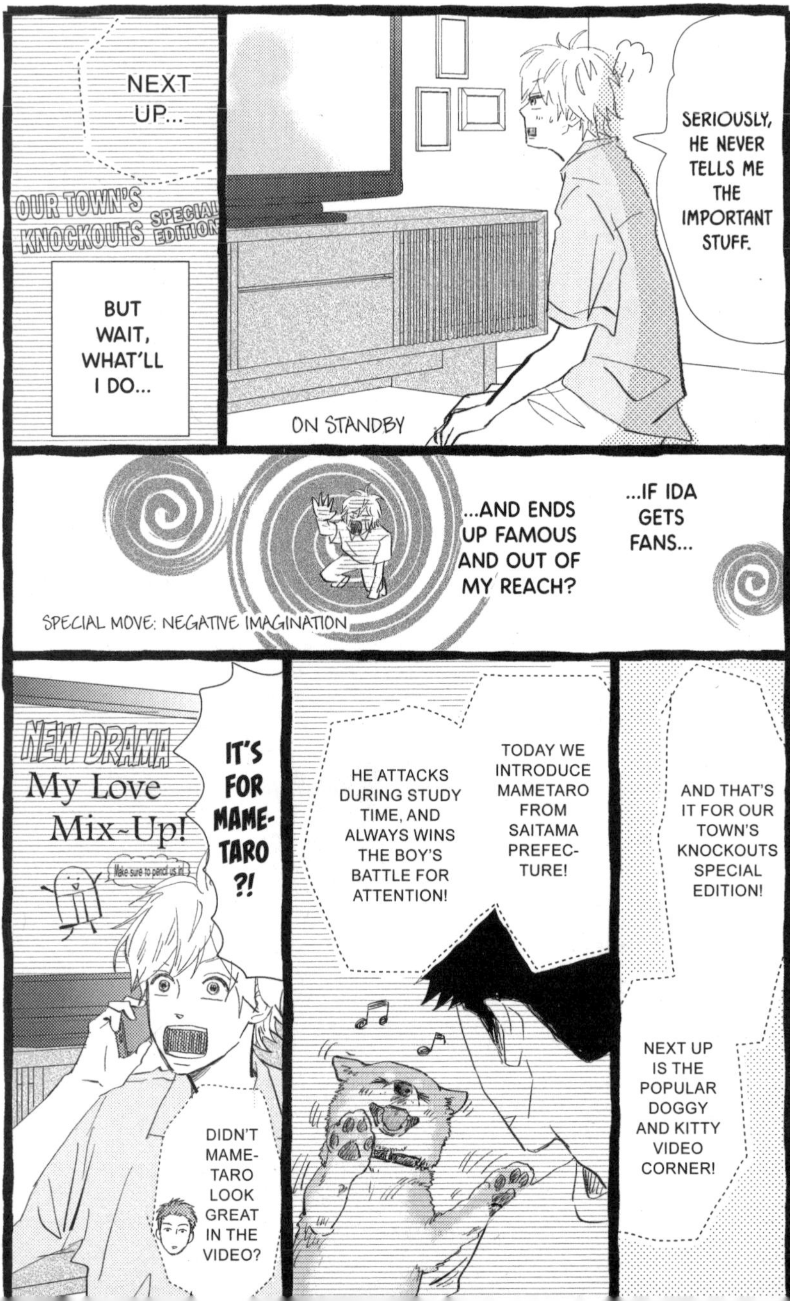
SERIOUSLY, HE NEVER TELLS ME THE IMPORTANT STUFF.
ON STANDBY
NEXT UP...
OUR TOWN'S KNOCKOUTS SPECIAL EDITION
BUT WAIT, WHAT'LL I DO...
...IF IDA GETS FANS...
...AND ENDS UP FAMOUS AND OUT OF MY REACH?
SPECIAL MOVE: NEGATIVE IMAGINATION
AND THAT'S IT FOR OUR TOWN'S KNOCKOUTS SPECIAL EDITION!
NEXT UP IS THE POPULAR DOGGY AND KITTY VIDEO CORNER!
TODAY WE INTRODUCE MAMETARO FROM SAITAMA PREFECTURE!
HE ATTACKS DURING STUDY TIME, AND ALWAYS WINS THE BOY'S BATTLE FOR ATTENTION!
IT'S FOR MAMETARO?!
NEW DRAMA
My Love Mix-Up!
Make sure to pencil us in!
DIDN'T MAMETARO LOOK GREAT IN THE VIDEO?

←

The next pages are end-of-the-volume extras!
They include "Aoki's End of Year" that ran in
Da Vinci magazine's first issue in 2021, and
early character designs (before serialization)
made public for the very first time. ♪

Side Story: Aoki's End of Year

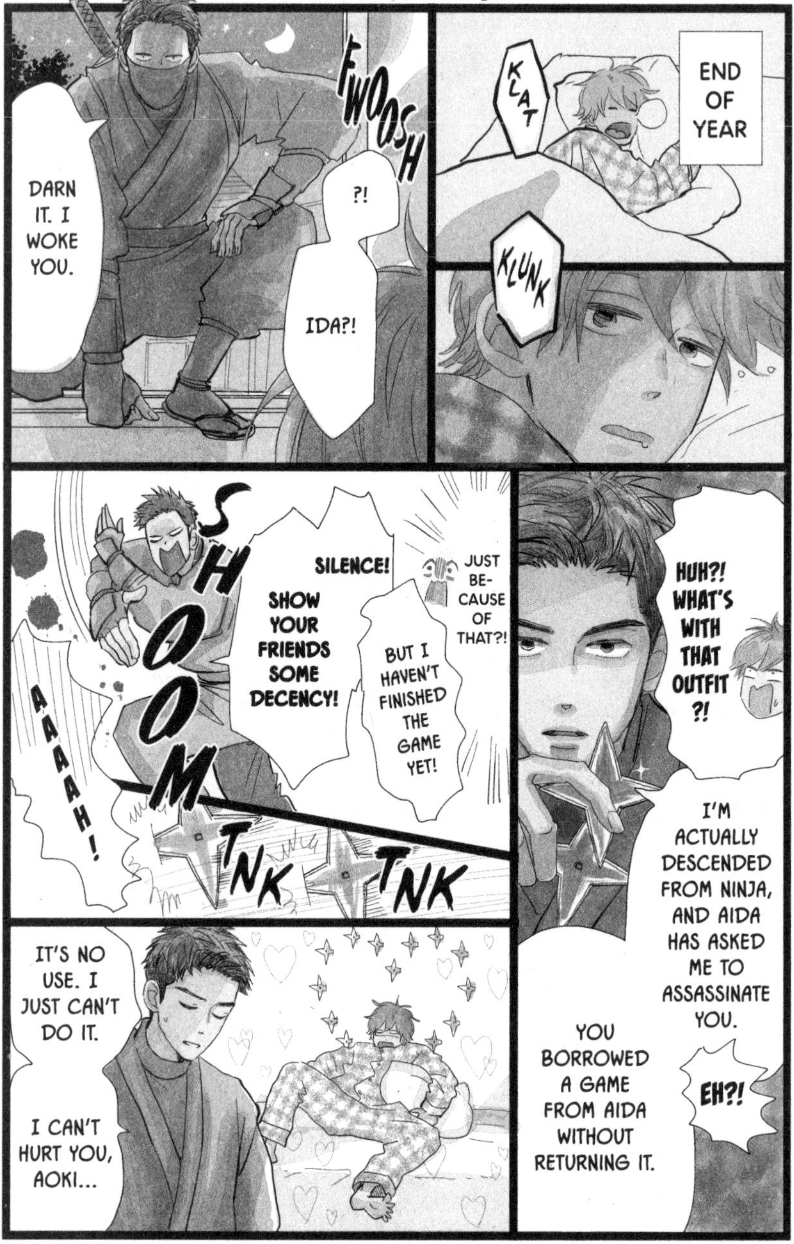
END OF YEAR
KLAT
KLUNK
FWOOSH
?!
IDA?!
DARN IT. I WOKE YOU.
HUH?! WHAT'S WITH THAT OUTFIT?!
I'M ACTUALLY DESCENDED FROM NINJA, AND AIDA HAS ASKED ME TO ASSASSINATE YOU.
EH?!
YOU BORROWED A GAME FROM AIDA WITHOUT RETURNING IT.
JUST BE-CAUSE OF THAT?!
BUT I HAVEN'T FINISHED THE GAME YET!
SILENCE!
SHOW YOUR FRIENDS SOME DECENCY!
SHOOOM
AAAAAH!
TNK
TNK
IT'S NO USE. I JUST CAN'T DO IT.
I CAN'T HURT YOU, AOKI...

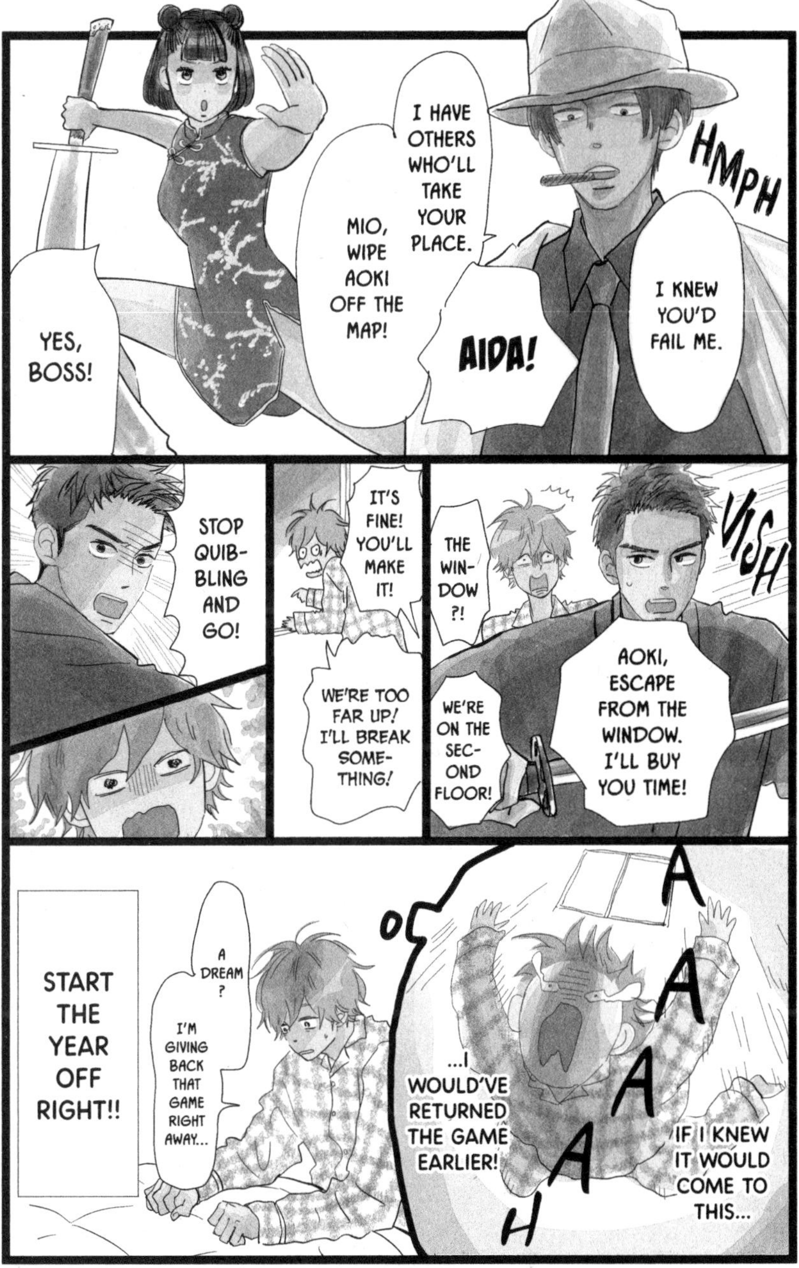
HMPH
I KNEW YOU'D FAIL ME.
AIDA!
I HAVE OTHERS WHO'LL TAKE YOUR PLACE.
MIO, WIPE AOKI OFF THE MAP!
YES, BOSS!
VISH
AOKI, ESCAPE FROM THE WINDOW. I'LL BUY YOU TIME!
THE WINDOW?!
WE'RE ON THE SECOND FLOOR!
IT'S FINE! YOU'LL MAKE IT!
WE'RE TOO FAR UP! I'LL BREAK SOMETHING!
STOP QUIBBLING AND GO!
OAAAAH
IF I KNEW IT WOULD COME TO THIS...
...I WOULD'VE RETURNED THE GAME EARLIER!
A DREAM?
I'M GIVING BACK THAT GAME RIGHT AWAY...
START THE YEAR OFF RIGHT!!

THE END

Early Character Designs

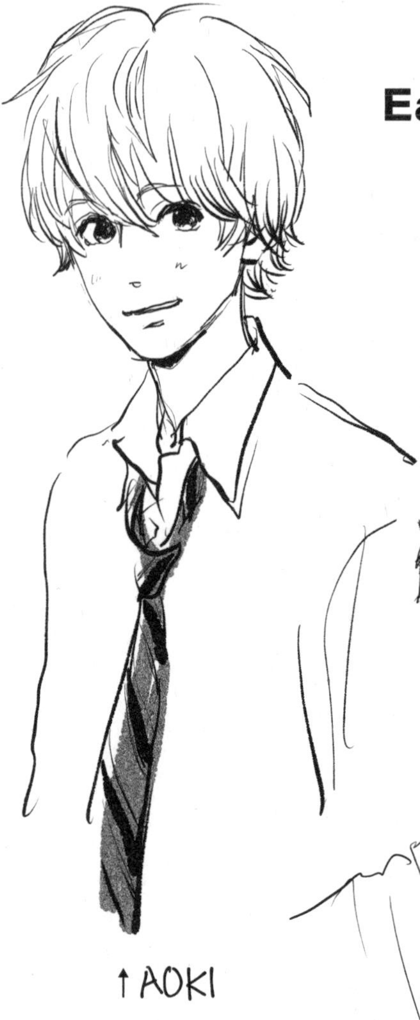
↑AOKI

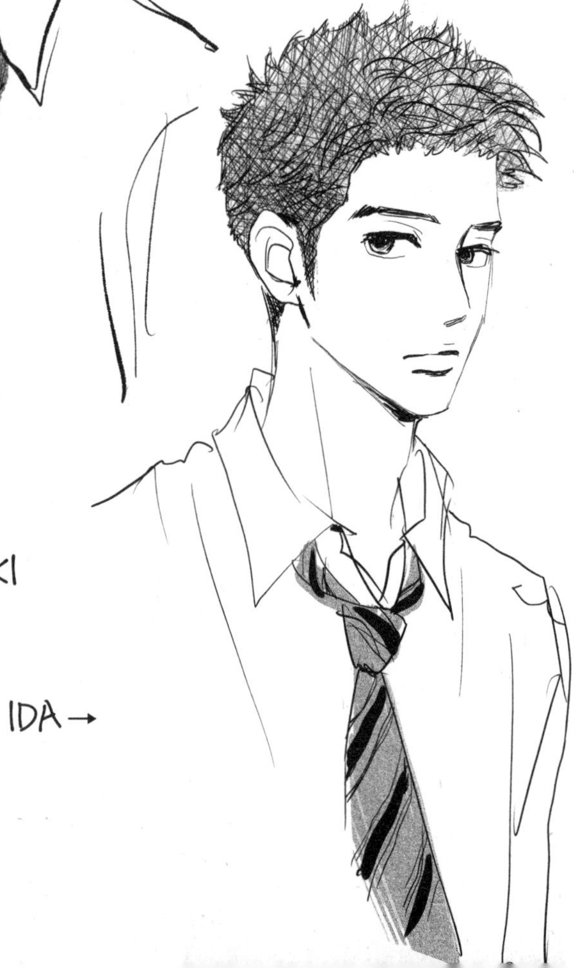
IDA→

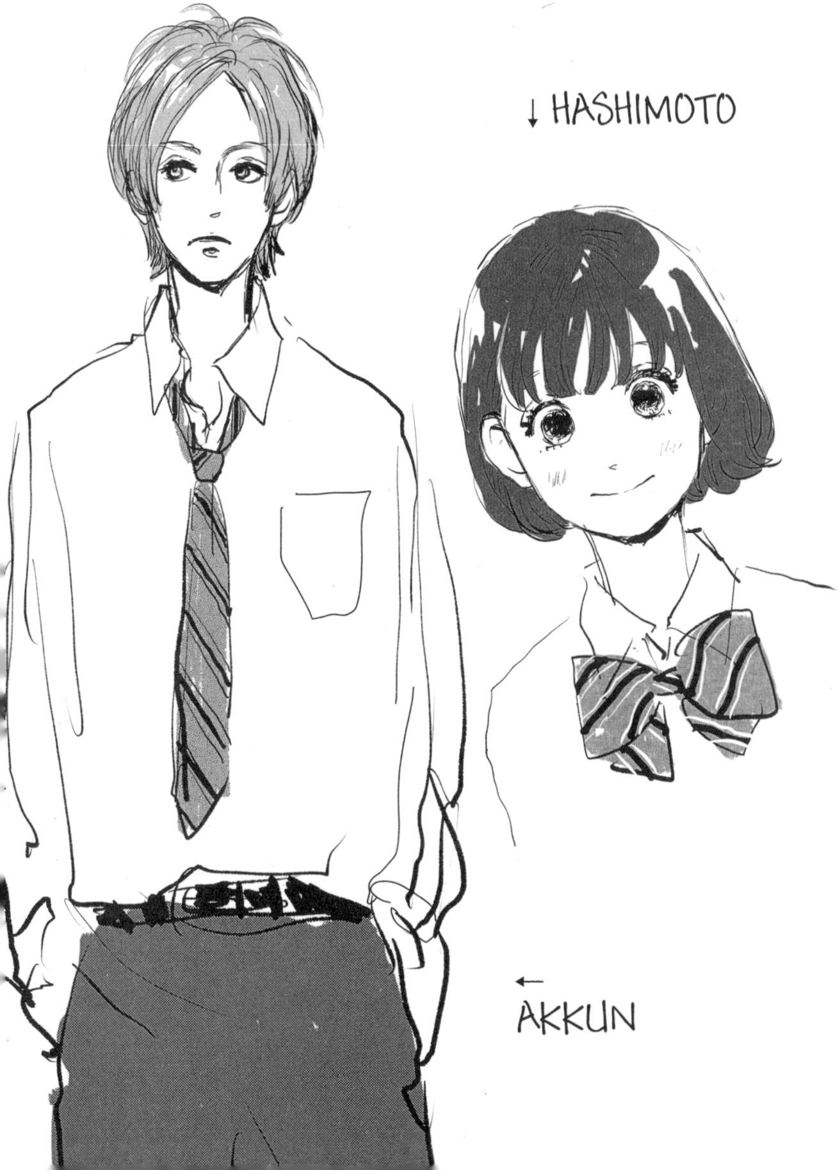
↓ HASHIMOTO
← AKKUN

Hello, I'm Aruko. 🐰

We've reached volume 7. Thank you so much. ♡ Yay! Ah!
We only made it here thanks to you readers. Thank you so very much.

Hinekure and I have met in person only a handful of times (especially considering this day and age), but I feel like we've met every day through this story. What I feel might be love because it was like you gave birth to the adorable characters. Maybe it is love.

Okay then, I'd like to tell you about the recent going-ons that happened while I was drawing this volume:

○ Ended up becoming dependent on medicine because of a random outbreak of hives.

○ Hit a car and had to send mine for repairs.

○ Invading geckos became my unintended houseguests.

○ Accidentally erased my work on chapter 28 close to the deadline and cried as I did it all over again.

○ A stranger said to me, "It's been forever!" and I was like, "Huh? Who is this?" I said "Hello! ☺" anyway. Then they made an "uh, now that I'm seeing you more closely, who are you?" face. Then I made an "I knew it" face, and they made a "sorry, I was mistaken" face. Then I made an "it's okay—this happens when you're masked up" face, which actually got through to them. In other news, I'm really looking forward to the drama!! Yeah! Yeah!! The cast is so wonderful! All I can say is thank you! To my editor, Sawada, thank you for the care you put in this work. Amane Koyama and Yuko Hishida, thank you for drawing cool backgrounds. Also, thank you to those who wrote me letters. I'm grateful to see the effort you put into writing physical letters in this day and age of social networks. Well, let's meet again in volume 8!!

Aruko,
Sept.
2021

Thank you for My Love Mix-Up! vol. 7 and...

...the little theaters and dramatization!!

In a past interview, I mentioned that *My Love Mix-Up!* was originally conceived as a short work of 80 pages. Then Aruko breathed life into that little short story to make it a wonderful manga, and my editor and the readers helped it develop so that many people have worked together to turn it into a drama... My heart is so full of gratitude. Thank you for everything!!

<Extra> My favorite part in vol. 7. ➡

Aruko Sensei drew it beautifully! Thank you!! Since they came across a zashiki-warashi, Aoki and Ida's luck has probably improved...

Let's play!

Let's play!

Whether you watch the drama or read the manga, I'd be so happy if you keep up as Aoki and his friends lead their delightful high school lives. I'll work hard on the next volume, so see you then!

Wataru Hinekure

Thank you for the seventh volume. Aoki, Ida, Hashimoto, and Akkun have all gradually been growing, which makes me happy and a little sad at times, but I'm still happy nonetheless.

Aruko

Thank you for the seventh volume. The little poltergeist on the back cover is so cute that I have her set as my phone wallpaper so I can look at her.

Wataru Hinekure

Aruko is from Ishikawa Prefecture in Japan and was born on July 26 (a Leo!). She made her manga debut with *Ame Nochi Hare* (Clear After the Rain). Her other works include *Yasuko to Kenji*, and her hobbies include laughing and getting lost.

Wataru Hinekure is a night owl. *My Love Mix-Up!* is Hinekure's first work.

My Love Mix-Up!

Vol. 7
Shojo Beat Edition

STORY BY
Wataru Hinekure
ART BY
Aruko

Translation & Adaptation/Jan Mitsuko Cash
Touch-Up Art & Lettering/Inori Fukuda Trant
Design/Yukiko Whitley
Editor/Nancy Thistlethwaite

Printed in the U.S.A.

Published by VIZ Media, LLC
P.O. Box 77010
San Francisco, CA 94107

10 9 8 7 6 5 4 3 2 1
First printing, April 2023

ratings.viz.com RATED T TEEN

PARENTAL ADVISORY
MY LOVE MIX-UP! is rated T for Teen and is recommended for ages 13 and up. No cinnamon rolls were harmed in the making of this manga.

VIZ MEDIA
viz.com

Shojo Beat
shojobeat.com

MY love STORY!!

KAZUNE KAWAHARA Story

ARUKO Art

Takeo Goda is a GIANT guy with a GIANT *heart*

Too bad the girls don't want him!
(They want his good-looking best friend, Sunakawa.)

Used to being on the sidelines, Takeo simply stands tall and accepts his fate. But one day when he saves a girl named Yamato from a harasser on the train, his (love!) life suddenly takes an incredible turn!

DAYTIME SHOOTING STAR

Story & Art by
Mika Yamamori

Small town girl Suzume moves to Tokyo and finds her heart caught between two men!

After arriving in Tokyo to live with her uncle, Suzume collapses in a nearby park when she remembers once seeing a shooting star during the day. A handsome stranger brings her to her new home and tells her they'll meet again. Suzume starts her first day at her new high school sitting next to a boy who blushes furiously at her touch. And her homeroom teacher is none other than the handsome stranger!

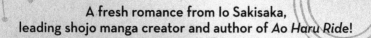

SHORTCAKE CAKE

STORY AND ART BY
suu Morishita

**An unflappable girl and a cast of
lovable roommates at a boardinghouse
create bonds of friendship and romance!**

When Ten moves out of her parents' home
in the mountains to live in a boardinghouse,
she finds herself becoming fast friends with
her male roommates. But can love and
romance be far behind?

VIZ

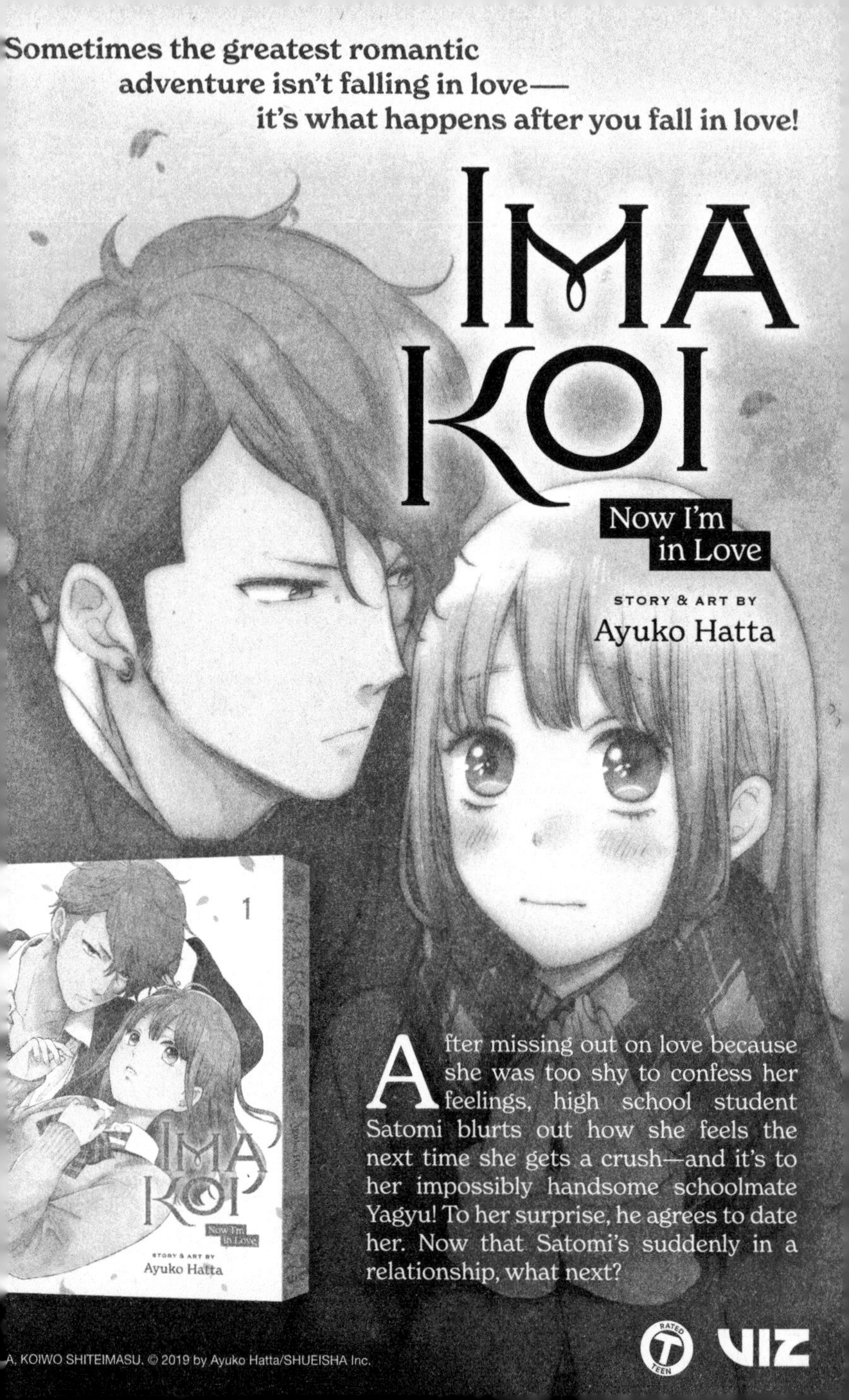
Sometimes the greatest romantic adventure isn't falling in love— it's what happens after you fall in love!
IMA KOI
Now I'm in Love
STORY & ART BY
Ayuko Hatta
1
IMA KOI
Now I'm in Love
STORY & ART BY
Ayuko Hatta
After missing out on love because she was too shy to confess her feelings, high school student Satomi blurts out how she feels the next time she gets a crush—and it's to her impossibly handsome schoolmate Yagyu! To her surprise, he agrees to date her. Now that Satomi's suddenly in a relationship, what next?
RATED T TEEN
VIZ
A, KOIWO SHITEIMASU. © 2019 by Ayuko Hatta/SHUEISHA Inc.